GLOBAL ECONOMICS IN EXTRAORDINARY TIMES
Essays in Honor of John Williamson

C. Fred Bergsten & C. Randall Henning, editors

GLOBAL ECONOMICS IN EXTRAORDINARY TIMES
Essays in Honor of John Williamson

C. Fred Bergsten & C. Randall Henning, editors

PETERSON INSTITUTE FOR INTERNATIONAL ECONOMICS
WASHINGTON, DC
NOVEMBER 2012

C. Fred Bergsten has been director of the Peterson Institute for International Economics since its creation in 1981. On January 1, 2013, he will step down as director and become president emeritus and senior fellow. He was assistant secretary for international affairs at the US Treasury (1977–81); assistant for international economic affairs to Henry Kissinger at the National Security Council (1969–71); and senior fellow at the Brookings Institution (1972–76), the Carnegie Endowment for International Peace (1981), and the Council on Foreign Relations (1967–68). Bergsten is a member of the President's Advisory Committee on Trade Policy and Negotiations (ACTPN) and the Advisory Committee to the Export Import Bank and co-chairman of the Private Sector Advisory Group to the United States–India Trade Policy Forum. He chaired the "Shadow G-7" during 2000–05 and was chairman of the Eminent Persons Group of the Asia Pacific Economic Cooperation (APEC) forum (1993–95) and the Competitiveness Policy Council created by Congress (1991–95). He was the most widely quoted think tank economist in the world during 1997–2005. Bergsten ranked 37 in the top 50 "Who Really Moves the Markets?" (*Fidelity Investment's Worth*) and was named "one of the 10 people who can change your life" (*USA Today*). He is the author, coauthor, or editor of 40 books on a wide range of international economic issues, including *The Long-Term International Economic Position of the United States* (2009), *China's Rise: Challenges and Opportunities* (2008), *China: The Balance Sheet—What the World Needs to Know Now about the Emerging Superpower* (2006), *The United States and the World Economy: Foreign Economic Policy for the Next Decade* (2005), and *Dollar Adjustment: How Far? Against What?* (2004).

C. Randall Henning, visiting fellow, has been associated with the Peterson Institute for International Economics since 1986. He is professor of international economic relations at American University's School of International Service and specializes in global economic governance, international and comparative political economy, and regional integration. His research focuses on the European debt crisis, regional cooperation in East Asia, relations between regional and multilateral financial institutions, exchange rate policy and macroeconomic policy coordination. Henning is the author or co-author of *Fiscal Federalism: US History for Architects of Europe's Fiscal Union* (2012), *Coordinating Regional and Multilateral Financial Institutions* (2011), *Accountability and Oversight of US Exchange Rate Policy* (2008), *East Asian Financial Cooperation* (2002), *Transatlantic Perspectives on the Euro* (2000), *Global Economic Leadership and the Group of Seven* (1996), *Currencies and Politics in the United States, Germany, and Japan* (1994), among other publications, and coeditor of *Governing the World's Money* (2002). Journals in which he has published articles include *International Organization*, *Review of International Political Economy*, *Journal of Common Market Studies*, and *The World Economy*. He has testified to several congressional committees and served as the European Community Studies Association Distinguished Scholar.

PETER G. PETERSON INSTITUTE FOR INTERNATIONAL ECONOMICS
1750 Massachusetts Avenue, NW
Washington, DC 20036-1903
(202) 328-9000   FAX: (202) 659-3225
www.piie.com

C. Fred Bergsten, *Director*
Edward A. Tureen, *Director of Publications, Marketing, and Web Development*

Typesetting/cover design: Susann Luetjen
Cover photo: Jeremey Tripp

Library of Congress Cataloging-in-Publication Data
Global economics in extraordinary times : essays in honor of John Williamson / C. Fred Bergsten & C. Randall Henning, editors.
   pages cm
 Includes bibliographical references and index.
 ISBN 978-0-88132-662-8
 1. Williamson, John, 1937–Political and social views. 2. International finance. 3. Economic policy. I. Williamson, John, 1937- II. Bergsten, C. Fred, 1941- III. Henning, C. Randall.
 HG3881.G57286 2012
 332'.042–dc23

                                2012036321

Contents

Acknowledgments

We are grateful to all those who came together to support this celebration of John Williamson's career and contributions. This community was easily mobilized and the contributors worked together in complete collegiality.

We owe Stanley Fischer special acknowledgment for originating the idea for this Festschrift several years ago. We thank him and the other authors of the chapters in this book for having rallied at relatively short notice to attend our organizational workshop at the Peterson Institute for International Economics in April 2012 and then to produce their contributions over the course of the summer. In addition to authoring a chapter, Marcus Miller took an early lead in helping to shape the volume.

We are also very grateful to the discussants of the chapter outlines and drafts, whose comments are not printed in this volume for reasons of timing and logistics. They are Nancy Birdsall, William Cline, Uri Dadush, Joseph Gagnon, Olivier Jeanne, Simon Johnson, Devesh Kapur, Pedro-Pablo Kuczynski, Paolo Mauro, and José Antonio Ocampo. We also benefited from Arminio Fraga's participation in the early stages.

The full group of senior fellows at the Institute and its junior research staff have been enthusiastic about this celebration and contributed in numerous ways not always fully acknowledged elsewhere in this book. Martin Kessler prepared the formidable list of publications that appears at the end of the volume and counted citations of Williamson's work in the scholarly literature. Ed Tureen's publications team prepared the book for publication with characteristic excellence and efficiency. Madona Devasahayam in particular managed the manuscript with a remarkable combination of speed, congeniality, and sensitivity to detail, and Susann Luetjen meticulously handled the production. We are especially grateful to them.

C. Fred Bergsten and C. Randall Henning
Washington, DC, September 2012

An Economist for All Seasons

C. FRED BERGSTEN AND C. RANDALL HENNING

Over the course of five decades, John Williamson has published an extraordinary number of books, articles, and other writings on topics ranging from international monetary economics to development policy. His work bridges the scholarly literature and policy debates in international economics. His publications on the Washington Consensus, exchange rate policy, and international monetary reform, for example, have profoundly influenced public discourse, government policy, and the evolution of the economics discipline. As John marked his 75th birthday, his friends and colleagues prepared this collection of essays to celebrate these many contributions and reflect on their relevance to the challenges that confront the world economy in the wake of the 2008–09 global financial crisis and that persist due to the ongoing European debt crisis.

Contributions

Williamson has written across an extraordinarily broad set of topics in international economics. The arc of his scholarship follows the main preoccupations of international economists during the second half of the 20th century and the first decade of the 21st. As a young scholar and policy practitioner in the 1960s and 1970s, he wrote mainly on the international monetary system and proposals for its reform. His purview subsequently broadened to the International Monetary Fund (IMF) and World Bank and their policies.

C. Fred Bergsten is the director of the Peterson Institute for International Economics. C. Randall Henning is professor of international economic relations at American University and visiting fellow at the Peterson Institute. They thank Morris Goldstein and Edwin M. Truman for comments on a previous draft of this chapter.

The rise of international capital mobility, which underlay the transition from fixed to flexible exchange rates in the early 1970s, became a particular focus of Williamson's work. That focus led in turn to examination of the capital account and then of financial crises—the third world debt crisis of the 1980s and then the crises in East Asia during the late 1990s and Argentina and Brazil early in the last decade.

Williamson's concern for the condition of humanity spawned his work on economic development and policies conducive to it as Latin America and other regions emerged from the crisis of the 1980s. At a conference in 1989, he coined the term "Washington Consensus" to identify a set of prescriptions for development inspired by the Latin American experience. It became the term for which he is undoubtedly best known (Williamson 1990a). Williamson responded to criticisms of the Washington Consensus and addressed capital markets and liberalization during the crises of the 1990s. He has said repeatedly that, had he known the term would become so widely used and especially so widely vilified, he would have chosen something other than "Washington" to label the consensus.

Having defined the Washington Consensus, Williamson was well positioned to address economic policy reform of countries in transition from command to market economies after the fall of communism and the Soviet Union. The volumes he edited, *Currency Convertibility in Eastern Europe* (1991) and *Economic Consequences of Soviet Disintegration* (1993), were particularly influential. At the turn of the century, the monetary union in Europe became a new focus as the euro came into being. In papers and commissions, Williamson examined the debate over the design of the euro area and the case for Britain's entry into the monetary union.

Williamson has authored 14 books, coauthored eight books, and authored or coauthored 56 journal articles. He has edited or coedited another 15 volumes and authored or coauthored 49 book chapters, among other types of publications. Google Scholar reports that his 1990 chapter on the Washington Consensus has been cited nearly 1,900 times in the literature, and the book in which it appeared, *Latin American Adjustment: How Much Has Happened?* (Williamson 1990b), is cited more than a thousand times. These results constitute a "grand slam home run" in scholarly economic circles. His next most widely cited piece is his 1983 Policy Analysis on target zones, *The Exchange Rate System*, with nearly 800 citations. His 22 top works have been cited more than 10,000 times, according to Google Scholar, and even that, as a standard catalog of such references, is not completely comprehensive.[1]

We believe that some of Williamson's less-heralded studies have been among his best. His *Financial Intermediation Beyond the Debt Crisis*, written with Donald Lessard in 1985, was ahead of its time because the Third World debt

---

1. For Williamson's own summary of his work for the Peterson Institute for International Economics, see www.piie.com/content/?ID=1#topic1 (accessed on September 1, 2012). We acknowledge Martin Kessler's assistance in researching these citations.

crisis continued for several more years, but it proposed some of the innovative types of capital flows that became prevalent in the following decade. His *The Political Economy of Policy Reform* (Williamson 1994a) became a go-to handbook for subsequent reform in numerous countries and is quite appropriately updated in his own contribution to this volume.

Williamson's body of work helped to set the research agenda for international economists with respect to international monetary reform, then with respect to debt and capital flows, and subsequently with respect to development policy and strategy. It influenced scholars well beyond economics and in the other social sciences. In particular, the Washington Consensus inspired follow-up research on the political economy of policy reform and the institutions of development.

Unlike many scholars, Williamson also sought to influence policy directly by working for his government and international institutions. He spent two years as an advisor to the British Treasury. While on the staff of the IMF, he participated actively in the work of the Committee of Twenty, the special group convened by the Fund in 1972–74 to construct a successor to the Bretton Woods system that dissolved during that period. He spent three years at the World Bank from 1996 to 1999 as its chief economist for South Asia. In 2001, he was project director of the United Nations' High-Level Panel on Financing for Development that was chaired by Ernesto Zedillo, the former president of Mexico.

Williamson also taught at some of the world's leading institutions on three different continents. In the United States, he taught at both Princeton (1962–63) and MIT (1967, 1980). In his native United Kingdom, he was an economist at the University of York (1963–68) and a professor at the University of Warwick (1970–77). In his wife Denise's native Brazil, he taught at Pontifícia Universidade Católica do Rio de Janeiro (1978–80).

Williamson spent most of his career, however, at the Institute for International Economics (which became the Peterson Institute for International Economics in 2006) in Washington. Fred Bergsten, who created the Institute in 1981, invited him to become its first senior fellow while he was still teaching in Brazil (during a meeting in a luxury apartment overlooking Copacabana Beach), and Williamson in fact joined the Institute even before it had formally begun operations. He played a central role in its success over the next 30 years and was explicitly cited by *The Economist* when it ranked the Institute as one of the top think tanks in the world. Williamson's facility in shifting his focus across research issues from exchange rates to debt to development and beyond—along with similar skills of other senior fellows such as William Cline and Gary Hufbauer—enabled the success of Bergsten's strategy as director to keep the Institute's thinking fresh.

Over a period of almost 50 years, both before and throughout his career at the Institute, Williamson probably has had more influence than anyone else in the world on academic and especially policy thinking on exchange rate systems for both high-income and developing nations. He provided a systematic case for managing exchange rates, a menu of options for doing so, and a framework for choosing among exchange rate policy options. Given that few countries preferred a free float, government and central bank officials around the world sought advice on how to operate their currency regimes. Williamson responded with a method for establishing policy objectives and a series of exchange rate proposals.

In the 1960s, Williamson (1965) coinvented the concept of "crawling pegs" which, along with the associated notion of wider currency bands, played a major role in facilitating the world's subsequent move away from fixed exchange rates (adjustable pegs) in the early 1970s by offering a moderate alternative to freely floating rates. During that period in the early 1970s, Williamson himself was directly involved in attempting to implement such ideas as part of the IMF's effort to devise comprehensive systemic reforms through the Committee of Twenty, as noted above.

The failure of such efforts, and the resultant "nonsystem" of unmanaged floating, led Bergsten and Williamson to invent the idea of "target zones" in 1983 (Bergsten and Williamson 1983). Williamson then developed the concept in great detail and soon complemented it with the associated concept of "fundamental equilibrium exchange rates" (FEERs) as the analytical foundation for such a regime (Williamson 1983, 1994b).

These ideas were probably the most influential of the many that Williamson designed and elaborated over the course of his distinguished career. They resonated in the policy world almost immediately. Williamson and several colleagues from the Institute described them extensively to Deputy Secretary of the Treasury Richard Darman in April 1985 and they played a central role in the Plaza Accord and, especially, the Louvre Agreement that the G-5 adopted at US insistence in September 1985 and February 1987. The Louvre Accord in fact adopted a comprehensive system of target zones, entitled "reference ranges" because Darman sheepishly admitted they could not use our own terminology. It marked a noteworthy implementation of a major policy idea less than five years after it was initially proposed.

The target zones/reference ranges of the Louvre did not last long—because of major errors in the way they were implemented, according to Williamson— and were eventually replaced by a widespread view in both policy and academic circles that the only viable exchange rate options were free floating or unalterable fixity: the "corner solutions." Williamson countered this new orthodoxy, however, by reviving the case for intermediate regimes and demonstrating how they had functioned successfully in a number of countries. Over the past 20 years he has steadily modified the original target zone idea with such variants as monitoring bands and reference rates in an effort to counter objections to the original blueprint and make it more palatable to the world's monetary authorities. Williamson and Henning (1994) specifically addressed the political and institutional questions associated with these proposals.

Williamson's concept of FEERs, which he has refined and applied to current global conditions throughout his career at the Institute, has had a lasting real-world impact. When the IMF was finally persuaded (including by Williamson and others at the Institute) to start analyzing exchange rates systematically, FEERs provided the basis for one of its three chosen methodologies, recently extended in the IMF's *Pilot External Sector Report*. The idea also was widely adopted in the private sector, for example in slightly modified form by Goldman Sachs when it began to estimate "Goldman Sachs desirable effective exchange rates" (GSDEERs) as it continues to do to this day. Williamson's own periodic assessments of the FEERs of the world's leading economies, coauthored in recent years with William Cline, have become a prime reference point for global discussion of exchange rates.

Williamson, like most policy-oriented economists, would of course prefer that his ideas be adopted more extensively and with greater fealty to his specific proposals. But he helped move the world from the demonstrably unviable fixed rates of the original Bretton Woods system to much greater flexibility, saw our target zones adopted quite explicitly for a time only a few years after they were developed, and witnessed the implementation of many variants of his intermediate system of managed flexibility. Along with the enormous impact of the Washington Consensus, as documented by Stanley Fischer in the next chapter of this book, the career of John Williamson has produced an impressive and indeed virtually unique set of policy triumphs as well as seminal intellectual contributions.

Philosophical Approach

Williamson's intellectual evolution is woven around four consistent philosophical convictions. First, model pluralism underpins his approach to economic analysis. Williamson has never subscribed to the one-model-fits-all-problems approach favored by some economists. He is always open-minded, drawing upon what he thinks is the best model for the circumstances faced by whichever government he is addressing at the time, as illustrated by his constant search for the most accurate and effective characterization of an exchange rate system for each country. His eclectic use of economic models derives from his practical approach to fixing problems. While some economists point out problems but fail to provide solutions, and others offer favored solutions that are not always appropriate to the problem, Williamson is a first-class problem solver.

Second, Williamson of course accepts the importance of markets but qualifies this acceptance by objective and factual analysis of their results. When markets fail to deliver, as he believes they have often done with respect to equilibrium exchange rates and capital flows, he has been ready to recommend institutional changes to them or governmental limitations upon them. His proposals for a menu approach to the resolution of the 1980s debt crisis and, more recently, growth bonds, are examples of the former. His refusal to endorse completely free movements of banking and portfolio capital is a leading example of the latter. Critics of the Washington Consensus often fail to understand that Williamson's 1989 conception did not provide for liberalization of international capital movements beyond foreign direct investment. His advocacy of target zones and subsequent mechanisms for limiting excessive exchange rate deviations from FEERs is another important qualification to his acceptance of markets.

Third, Williamson has shown a consistent concern for distributional equity, particularly with respect to policy reform in developing countries, emerging markets, and countries in transition. Examples include his advocacy of debt reduction as part of the menu approach to the Latin American debt crisis (Williamson 1988) and his working group report for the Center for Global Development (CGD 2010) on preventing odious debt. Distributional concerns were also expressed in public sector spending priorities in the Washington Consensus and in his proposals for tax fairness and tax collection, as well as for asset accumulation by the poor in response to critiques of the Consensus.

Fourth, Williamson has an unremitting faith in the strength of rational argument and scientific ideas in the policymaking process. In his conception, economic ideas are influential in the political economy of economic policy. Governments and the officials who lead them are ultimately susceptible to those ideas that are based on objective analysis, though perhaps after first having tried all or most of the alternatives. Such optimism underlies the complexity of his economic proposals, which require economic sophistication on the part of politically responsible officials, and thus his advocacy of "technopols," academic and professional economists who have assumed senior policymaking responsibilities in their countries.

Overview

We have brought together a first-rate team of authors to celebrate Williamson's contributions and their implications for contemporary analytical and policy problems. We begin with the Washington Consensus and then proceed to the sections on money, finance, and regions. We conclude with John's own chapter on economic policymaking during both normal times and crises.

Stanley Fischer addresses the Washington Consensus and its evolution over the course of the more than two decades since Williamson defined it. He also reviews the main critiques of the Consensus, such as Dani Rodrik's complaint that it simply described advanced countries without charting an actionable path for developing nations. Fischer observes that the original Consensus and its amended version, which John articulated in his overview chapter of the 2003 book he edited with Pedro-Pablo Kuczynski, were akin to the list of cooking ingredients for a meal. The full recipe also consists of instructions for combining the ingredients into the final dish, and the Consensus indeed lacked these. The lag between implementation of elements of the Consensus and realization of the benefits also proved to be much longer than was originally assumed and thus inconvenient for democratic policymakers. But the

Consensus-inspired reforms that emerging-market and developing countries introduced in the 1990s positioned them to weather the Great Recession relatively well.

John Williamson began his career writing on the international monetary system and exchange rates. These subjects are addressed in the first full section, comprising three chapters. The first, by Edwin M. Truman, traces the evolution of the international monetary system and John Williamson's academic and policy contributions along the way. Truman evaluates the extent to which John's concerns of 40 years ago with respect to international adjustment, liquidity, and exchange rates are still relevant today. He argues, among other things, that the adjustment process over the past 40 years has shown no improvement over that in the 1960s, including the contribution of exchange rates to that process. But followers of John's work can take comfort in the introduction into IMF analysis and (at least indirectly into) peer review within the G-20 of the concepts of FEERs, excessive current account imbalances, and multilateral consistency of external positions.

The second chapter in this section, by Paul De Grauwe and Yuemei Ji, examines Economic and Monetary Union in Europe in light of the European debt crisis. The authors focus on the problem that members of a monetary union borrow in a currency over which they have no individual control, and they show econometrically that these countries are more fragile financially than countries with their own central banks. They conclude that the European Central Bank (ECB) must use its unlimited capacity to create euros to stabilize sovereign finances and do so even if that commitment leads to losses. Given that governments back the ECB ultimately with their declaration that its currency is legal tender, and share the losses on its portfolio, there is no limit to the losses that it can sustain and no present threat to price stability. The authors also stress the importance of symmetrical adjustment and the creation of fiscal union to ensure the integrity and longevity of the euro area.

The third chapter, by Marcus Miller, reviews the intellectual history of proposals with respect to exchange rate regimes. Williamson's target zone and monitoring band proposals in his publications for the Peterson Institute are hallmark contributions that rank second only to the Washington Consensus in citations in the literature. Miller critiques the consensus that now favors exchange rate flexibility and models hypothetical bargaining between the United States and China over redesigning the international monetary system. His stylized game suggests that China and other emerging-market countries are likely to accept greater exchange rate flexibility and reliance on domestic demand if they are offered a stronger role in rewriting the rules of the system.

One of the hallmarks of Williamson's work is its selective acceptance of international capital flows and financial liberalization. The subject of international finance is addressed in the second full section of the book on finance, which again comprises three chapters—the first by Olivier Jeanne on capital mobility and regulation, the second by Avinash Persaud on financial regulation, and the third by Stephany Griffith-Jones and Dagmar Hertova on growth-linked securities. Proposals for curbing the "boom-bust cycle" in international capital markets, the focus of Williamson's 2005 Policy Analysis for the Peterson Institute, are the common theme among them.

In his chapter, Jeanne reviews the evolution of John's ideas for managing international capital movements, culminating in his proposal with Williamson and Arvind Subramanian for international rules for capital controls that would legitimize their use in appropriate circumstances and stigmatize their use in inappropriate ones (Jeanne, Williamson, and Subramanian 2012). Jeanne then sets out an agenda for further research, including strengthening the theoretical case for the Jeanne, Subramanian, and Williamson capital account regime and understanding the interaction between capital account policies within a Keynesian model of the global economy with insufficient demand.

In his chapter, Persaud prescribes a hybrid approach to financial regulation that combines internationally agreed-upon microprudential regulations administered by home-country regulators with nationally set macroprudential regulation administered by host-country authorities. He reiterates a proposal that he made with Charles Goodhart that regulators adjust capital adequacy requirements for banks depending on the overall rate of growth of bank assets and the size of liquidity buffers,[2] and he advocates "mark-to-funding" accounting, among other things.

Griffith-Jones and Hertova advocate expansion of the use of growth-linked bonds and other securities in order to lend stability to fiscal policy and stabilize international capital flows. The interest paid on some of the bonds issued as part of the restructuring of Argentine and Greek debt, for example, depends on the rate of economic growth. Griffith-Jones and Hertova discuss the potential for redesigning such securities and broadening their use for sovereign borrowing in international markets. Because the benefits of these bonds are partly systemic rather than fully private, international cooperation is probably needed for their adoption on a broad scale, and multilateral organizations should induce markets to introduce and develop them.

Williamson's work relating to the trajectories of economic development and the international position of developing and emerging-market countries is addressed in the two chapters in the book's third part. The first chapter, by Shankar Acharya, examines India and its experience before and after the global financial crisis. India's economic reforms of the 1990s and its policies during 2003–07 provided the foundation for resilience in the face of the crisis. Acharya argues that insistence on gradual and iterative liberalization of the capital account—which Williamson favored, in opposition to advocates of full liberalization—was an important ingredient of that success. The marked slowdown in the Indian economy since 2011, however, demonstrates the need for correction of macroeconomic imbalances, improvement in the investment climate, and advances in human-capital development and structural reforms.

---

2. Charles Goodhart and Avinash Persaud, "How to Avoid the Next Crash," *Financial Times*, January 30, 2008.

The second chapter, by José Antonio Ocampo, examines the experience of Latin America with the Washington Consensus and Williamson's prescriptions for external monetary policy. Latin American countries largely followed the macroeconomic elements of the Consensus, although they have also witnessed greater amplitudes in their business cycles and real exchange rate volatility. The trade and foreign direct investment liberalization components of the Consensus have been success stories, broadly speaking, but productivity growth has been very disappointing. Reflecting a "new structuralist" approach, Ocampo advocates policies to raise the technological content of production and exports. Notwithstanding some recent tilt in this direction, however, Ocampo writes that the principles of the Washington Consensus "still rule Latin America."

John Williamson's own chapter addresses the design of economic policy in both normal and abnormal times and the frameworks that are appropriate in each instance. Believing that demand shocks are important, he lays out rules for designing a neutral fiscal benchmark, built-in stabilizers, and monetary policy in normal times. Building on the 12-point scheme proposed by Anders Åslund (2011), Williamson presents the rules for countries in crisis or in transition to market economies. To extend periods of normality and to limit the severity of crises—the central challenge—Williamson argues that we need to "cultivate a general hostility to excessive expenditure and greed, and certainly not cultivate them." This is a philosophical position that pervades his work generally. Williamson advances two practical measures to extend normality: fiscal councils, such as those in the United Kingdom and the Netherlands, and "election watchdogs" to assess the economic policy positions of candidates in order to clear the fog of disinformation and uncertainty during national elections. This novel proposal reflects Williamson's enduring faith that, given the right institutions and sufficient time, reason can ultimately triumph over political expediency.

References

Åslund, Anders. 2011. The Failed Political Economy of the Euro Crisis. Realtime Economic Issues Watch, November 18. Washington: Peterson Institute for International Economics. Available at www.piie.com/blogs/realtime/?p=2515 (accessed on September 14, 2012).

Bergsten, C. Fred, and John Williamson. 1983 (revised in 1985). Exchange Rates and Trade Policy. In Trade Policy in the 1980s, ed. William R. Cline. Washington: Institute for International Economics.

CGD (Center for Global Development). 2010. Preventing Odious Obligations: A New Tool for Protecting Citizens from Illegitimate Regimes. Report of the Working Group on Odious Debt. Washington.

Jeanne, Olivier, Arvind Subramanian, and John Williamson. 2012. Who Needs to Open the Capital Account? Washington: Peterson Institute for International Economics.

Kuczynski, Pedro-Pablo, and John Williamson, ed. 2003. After the Washington Consensus: Restarting Growth and Reform in Latin America. Washington: Institute for International Economics.

Lessard, Donald, and John Williamson. 1985. Financial Intermediation beyond the Debt Crisis. Policy Analyses in International Economics 12. Washington: Institute for International Economics.

Williamson, John. 1965. *The Crawling Peg.* Princeton Essays in International Finance 50. Princeton, NJ: Princeton University.

Williamson, John. 1983 (revised in 1985). *The Exchange Rate System.* Policy Analyses in International Economics 5. Washington: Institute for International Economics.

Williamson, John. 1988 (revised in 1989). *Voluntary Approaches to Debt Relief.* Policy Analyses in International Economics 25. Washington: Institute for International Economics.

Williamson, John. 1990a. What Washington Means by Policy Reform. In *Latin American Adjustment: How Much Has Happened?* ed. John Williamson. Washington: Institute for International Economics.

Williamson, John, ed. 1990b. *Latin American Adjustment: How Much Has Happened?* Washington: Institute for International Economics.

Williamson, John, ed. 1991. *Currency Convertibility in Eastern Europe.* Washington: Institute for International Economics.

Williamson, John, ed. 1993. *Economic Consequences of Soviet Disintegration.* Washington: Institute for International Economics.

Williamson, John, ed. 1994a. *The Political Economy of Policy Reform.* Washington: Institute for International Economics.

Williamson, John, ed. 1994b. *Estimating Equilibrium Exchange Rates.* Washington: Institute for International Economics.

Williamson, John. 2005. *Curbing the Boom-Bust Cycle: Stabilizing Capital Flows to Emerging Markets.* Policy Analyses in International Economics 75. Washington: Institute for International Economics.

Williamson, John, and C. Randall Henning. 1994. Managing the Monetary System. In *Managing the World Economy: Fifty Years After Bretton Woods*, ed. Peter B. Kenen. Washington: Institute for International Economics.

2

The Washington Consensus

STANLEY FISCHER

Everyone who has had to think about economic development, or open econo-mies and exchange rates, or the (sometimes divergent) economic policies advo-cated by the "Nineteenth Street twins"—the International Monetary Fund and World Bank—is indebted to John Williamson. That is to say, everyone who has ever had to deal with the practical aspects of economic growth and develop-ment—especially with exchange rate issues—owes John Williamson a debt of gratitude, mostly for the content of what he has written but also for the calm, clear, and nonhistrionic style in which he writes.

The version of his curriculum vitae that I have lists 176 principal publi-cations during the 50 years from 1962 through 2011. Of those, 109 publica-tions, or 62 percent, are on exchange rates and closely related subjects, while only 17, or 10 percent, are on the Washington Consensus and closely related topics. Even adjusting for the shorter period during which Williamson has written on the Washington Consensus and development strategies, the annual rate strongly favors the exchange rate issue as having been his main topic of research.

Nonetheless, Williamson's work on the Washington Consensus is prob-ably his best-known contribution, and it is on this influential and remark-ably popular body of work that this chapter focuses. I start by describing the initial version of the Washington Consensus (Williamson 1990) and reactions

Stanley Fischer is governor of the Bank of Israel and has served in this position since 2005. He has also served as vice chairman of Citigroup (2002–05), first deputy managing director of the IMF (1994–2001), Killian Professor and head of the Department of Economics at MIT (1990–94), and vice president, development economics, and chief economist of the World Bank (1988–90). He is grateful to Nancy Birdsall for her insightful comments on the Washington Consensus at the pre-conference and to Noa Heymann and Sharona Cooperman of the Bank of Israel, and Randy Henning and John Williamson, for their assistance.

to it. I then discuss the evolution of Williamson's thinking about his most famous article and the changing reactions to it by the profession—including Williamson himself—and by practitioners. The chapter then briefly presents the views of three leading critics of the Washington Consensus before closing with concluding reflections and comments.

Washington Consensus I

The initial version of the Washington Consensus was focused explicitly on Latin America, which was at the time struggling toward the end of the lost decade of its debt crisis.[1] The 10 points were dedicated to topics on which Williamson argued that there was a consensus in the Washington of the second half of 1989.[2] Table 2.1 presents a list of the 10 areas that appeared in the initial formulation of the Washington Consensus, as summarized by Williamson (2008; originally published in 2004). The second column in table 2.1 presents my summary of Williamson's brief description of the main argument he was making—or in retrospect would have liked to have made—under each heading.

   In my then-role as chief economist of the World Bank, I was one of three discussants of the original paper. I started with "As usual, John Williamson has given us a good, sensible paper...." That meant that I basically agreed with what he had written. I noted that the consensus was far wider than only Washington, though not universal. I noted also that Williamson had omitted consideration of policies related to the environment, as well as to military spending. In addition, I said that Washington thought of financial liberalization as extending beyond real interest rates, "to the notion that the banking system and the financial sector in many developing countries need fundamental restructuring" (Fischer 2004). I also expressed doubt that Washington regarded the freeing up of capital flows as less urgent than the freeing up of goods flows, adding "I fear rather that much of Washington does believe strongly that financial capital flows should not be constrained...." (Fischer 2004, 26).[3]

---

1. Williamson presented the Washington Consensus at a conference on Latin American growth toward the end of 1989. The conference volume appeared in 1990, hence the classic article is dated 1990.

2. Williamson (1990) has emphasized the importance of a preceding conference and publication by Bela Balassa et al. (1986) on the same topic.

3. I have several times been characterized by Williamson, including in his 2004 paper, as being strongly in favor of rapid capital account liberalization by developing countries. I do not believe this is consistent with the two articles he quotes that I wrote in support of a capital account liberalization amendment to the IMF's Articles of Agreement. Although this is not the place to develop that argument fully, let me quote a sentence that was italicized in the 1997 article: "In a nutshell, *the prime goal of the amendment would be to enable the Fund to promote the orderly liberalization of capital movements*" (Fischer 2004, 131). This sentence reflects the view that several countries, including Korea, erred by opening the capital account to short- but not long-term flows, when the right approach would have been precisely the opposite.

Table 2.1 The 10 areas of John Williamson's Washington Consensus with comments on his 2008 description of each

Area	Comments on Williamson's 2008 description
1. Fiscal discipline	Budget deficits small enough to prevent high inflation and balance of payments crises.
2. Public expenditure priorities	Switching expenditures in a pro-growth and pro-poor way, particularly to basic health, education, and infrastructure.
3. Tax reform	Combining a broad tax base with moderate marginal tax rates.
4. Liberalizing interest rates (1989 heading)	More general financial liberalization, at an appropriate pace, combined with strengthened prudential supervision.
5. A competitive exchange rate	Meaning one that is not overvalued—not necessarily undervalued—which basically implies an intermediate regime.
6. Trade liberalization	This is the appropriate direction, though there may be arguments about speed.
7. Liberalization of inward foreign direct investment	But not comprehensive capital account liberalization.
8. Privatization	Properly done, this brings benefits.
9. Deregulation	To ease barriers to entry and exit but not to remove beneficial regulations (e.g., environmental or safety).
10. Property rights	As inspired by Hernando de Soto (2000).

Source: Williamson (2008, originally published in 2004).

In summarizing what I regarded as the then-consensus, I noted that "Emphasis on poverty reduction has increased in recent years and will continue to do so" (Fischer 2004).[4] I concluded with a discussion of proactive policies for growth, including industrial policy, where I argued that some countries may have the bureaucratic and political apparatus to make industrial policy work for some time, but most do not.

The other discussants were Allan Meltzer and Richard Feinberg, then of the Overseas Development Council. Williamson (2008) details their disagreements on some points, but concludes that by and large they agreed with his listing, even though Feinberg had started off asserting that there was not much consensus.

Williamson has written often about his creation of the Washington Consensus and aspects of the literature it engendered. One of his concerns has

---

4. My own education on this point was strongly reinforced by reading Cornia, Jolly, and Stewart's *Adjustment with a Human Face* (1987).

been over the name. In his words (Williamson 2000, 251), "While it is jolly to become famous for coining a term that reverberates around the world, I have long been doubtful about whether my phrase served to advance the cause of rational policymaking." His 2000 retrospective preference was for "universal convergence" or "one-world consensus."[5] These names would likely have led to a flood of articles explaining why the consensus was far from universal. Indeed, in thinking about the issue of the name, I suspect that one could apply to this issue the old saw, "It doesn't matter what they say about you as long as they spell your name right." And they certainly have spelled it right, multiple times.[6]

However, Williamson's main concern and main battle over the name have to do with "neoliberalism," which is the characterization that not a few critics have given to Washington Consensus I. This no doubt relates to the presence of privatization, deregulation, property rights, and various forms of liberalization that appear among the 10 commandments, as well as to the absence of a more positive role for government.[7]

In his writings between 1989 and 2004, Williamson often notes that the Washington Consensus does not provide a full policy agenda for development. The *World Development Report* (WDR) for 1991, subtitled *The Challenge of Development*, attempted to do that (World Bank 1991). The team for that report was led by Vinod Thomas, who reported to the recently appointed chief economist, Larry Summers.[8]

If the Washington Consensus was indeed the consensus in Washington, the WDR should have reflected that. In correspondence on the connection between the Washington Consensus and the 1991 WDR, Vinod Thomas wrote: "WDR 91 reported on a sea change in thinking on development and policy advice linked in part to the articulation of the Washington Consensus."[9] However, in another e-mail two days later, Thomas reported—to his evident surprise—that the 1990 Williamson paper was not included in the selected bibliography of the WDR, although Williamson was listed as an advisor on the WDR's first chapter. So the evidence of a close link between the Washington Consensus and what the leading development institution in Washington was advocating a little later is weak.

---

5. Moisés Naím (2000) includes a sympathetic discussion of the problem of the name of the consensus.

6. A Google search produces over 5 million references (which is a very high score for economics) to the Washington Consensus.

7. Williamson (2000, 251–52) contains a useful discussion of why the characterization of Washington Consensus I as neoliberal matters, namely because so describing it discredits the entire approach among some people and countries.

8. The 1991 WDR was started when I was chief economist, but the bulk of the work was done during Larry's period in office and under his guidance.

9. E-mail from Vinod Thomas to the author, August 12, 2012.

What was in the 1991 WDR? It focused on the relationships between governments and markets, and analyzed four main topics: (1) investing in people; (2) the business climate; (3) the integration of countries with the global economy, in terms of both trade and capital flows; and (4) the need for a stable macroeconomic foundation for sustained growth. Further, the words of the report summary could well be taken as adding two more topics: (5) "Above all, the future of developing countries is in their own hands;" and (6) "Domestic policies and institutions hold the key to successful development" (World Bank 1991).

This is a wider agenda than that presented in Washington Consensus I and is closer to the more comprehensive list of topics that Williamson presented in *The Washington Consensus as Policy Prescription for Development* (2004), which will briefly be called here "Washington Consensus II." Probably the difference arises because the 1991 WDR was indeed aiming to present a full development strategy, while the Washington Consensus is a list of what Williamson thought was generally accepted in Washington at the end of the 1980s.

In addition, one has the sense that Washington Consensus I was intended, inter alia, to suggest to Latin American policymakers that a variety of market-friendly policies made sense, even though they were associated with the policies of the governments of Margaret Thatcher and Ronald Reagan—governments whose basic positions were more criticized than admired by many Latin American governments and many development economists during the 1980s.

One last comment on Washington Consensus I. Many of the critics who wrote during the decade following publication of the 1990 paper noted that the consensus had not seemed to work—that the Latin American growth record in the period from 1980 to 2000 was on the whole poor, and that this reflected negatively on Washington Consensus I, or more generally on Washington's advice on growth strategies. Chile was clearly the most successful of the Latin American countries in the last decades of the 20th century, but as Williamson has emphasized, its success was due in part to its use of capital controls to keep out short-term capital flows.[10] Further, it took Chile a long time to become the poster child of market-friendly policies, for it suffered a severe overvalued exchange rate crisis in the 1970s and only began to grow relatively rapidly during the latter part of the 1980s. And since the 1990s were also the decade when the countries of the former Soviet bloc were trying to transform their economies—and receiving advice and policy conditionality toward this end from many in the West, including the Bretton Woods organizations—the Washington Consensus was often blamed for the difficulties of the transition countries, especially the output collapse at the start of the transformation process.[11]

---

10. In addition, Williamson several times (e.g., Williamson 2002, 2003, 2005) dismisses the argument that the failure of the Argentine economic strategy of the 1990s reflects negatively on the Washington Consensus, since Argentina neither prevented its exchange rate from becoming overvalued nor maintained fiscal discipline.

11. It would be interesting to revisit the history of the transformation strategies implemented in the former Soviet bloc now that enough time has passed to study the correlation between the speed

The Expanded "Washington Consensus II"

In response to both the large literature on Washington Consensus I[12] and the poor performance of developing economies in Latin America and the former Soviet bloc in the 1990s—as well as the impressive success of many East Asian economies during the same decade (except during the Asian crisis of 1997–98)—Pedro-Pablo Kuczynski and John Williamson called another conference on Latin American growth in 2003.[13] They then produced in that same year another important book on the subject for the Institute for International Economics, this one called *After the Washington Consensus: Restarting Growth and Reform in Latin America*.

Despite the title of the book, I shall refer to the expanded strategy presented by Williamson in *After the Washington Consensus* as Washington Consensus II. This section presents the strategy's additions to Washington Consensus I under four major headings. Table 2.2 shows Dani Rodrik's (2002) summary of the strategy.

New Agenda I: Crisis Proofing

This part of the agenda includes (1) running a countercyclical fiscal policy; (2) allowing the exchange rate to adjust somewhat in response to capital flows while using capital controls to prevent excessive appreciation resulting from potentially large inflows; (3) preventing dollarization; (4) maintaining a monetary policy close to inflation targeting; (5) strengthening the banking system; and (6) increasing domestic saving. Most of these items are part of the standard advice that would be offered today by the Bretton Woods institutions, and probably by much of the rest of Washington and the world, including the suggestion to use capital controls to moderate the impact of short-term capital flows on the exchange rate.

New Agenda II: Completing First-Generation Reforms

These reforms are presented as enabling faster growth. Here Williamson starts with (1) the need to make the labor market more flexible—an issue that he has from early on seen as the major omission from Washington Consensus I. His main concern is with union power that limits the ability of new workers to compete in the labor force, and he suggests a number of measures to increase labor market flexibility without jeopardizing the interests of organized labor.

---

of implementation of stabilization and reform strategies and subsequent growth. For instance, it is clear that Poland has done much better than the critics of its early rapid-reform strategy would have predicted.

12. The massive bibliography of Kuczynski and Williamson (2003) includes many of the articles that reacted to Washington Consensus I.

13. The East Asian experience was examined in a major World Bank project of the early 1990s, led by John Paige, that was entitled *The East Asian Miracle* (World Bank 1993).

Table 2.2   The Washington Consensus is dead: Long live the new Washington Consensus!

Original Washington Consensus	"Augmented" Washington Consensus: The previous 10 items, plus
1. Fiscal discipline	11. Corporate governance
2. Reorientation of public expenditures	12. Anti-corruption
3. Tax reform	13. Flexible labor markets
4. Financial liberalization	14. World Trade Organization agreements
5. Unified and competitive exchange rates	15. Financial codes and standards
6. Trade liberalization	16. "Prudent" capital account opening
7. Openness to foreign direct investment	17. Nonintermediate exchange rate regimes
8. Privatization	18. Independent central banks/inflation targeting
9. Deregulation	19. Social safety nets
10. Property rights	20. Targeted poverty reduction

Source: Rodrik (2002, table 1).

In addition, he notes three items: (2) that, although substantial progress has been made in domestic trade liberalization, there has been less success in opening up export markets and (3) that the privatization agenda has lagged, as has (4) prudential supervision of the financial sector.

New Agenda III: Second-Generation Reforms

In discussing second-generation reforms, Williamson emphasizes primarily the importance of institutional reforms.[14] He notes that "[s]econd-generation reforms have sometimes been pictured as politically boring esoterica.... [In] fact they are liable to involve political confrontation with some of society's most potent and heavily entrenched interest groups, such as the judiciary and public school teachers," as well as the civil service (Williamson 2003, 11–12).

He argues that the government has an important role in creating a business-friendly environment, which he defines broadly as including (1) the old-fashioned aspects, such as physical infrastructure, a stable and predictable macroeconomic, legal, and political environment, and a strong human resource base, as well as (2) the newer issues, including building a national innovation system. But he argues that (3) the government should not be making business decisions and therefore should not attempt to develop an industrial policy. He goes on to suggest that (4) governments need to modernize the institutional

---

14. He attributes to Naím (1994) the credit for both the name and for first raising the issue in the Latin American context.

infrastructure of a market economy,[15] not least in protecting property rights, and that (5) governments need to strengthen the financial system, including corporate governance. This agenda concludes with a brief discussion of political institutions.

It is clear that the material on second-generation reforms is both a central element in Washington Consensus II and not sufficiently developed in the overview chapter of *After the Washington Consensus*. However, the book as a whole certainly does contain a great deal of material on different aspects of these reforms.

New Agenda IV: Income Distribution and the Social Sector

This agenda includes a wealth of material. On income distribution, the goal is to suggest policies to reduce income inequality without affecting growth.[16] To partially redress the regressive shift from income to consumption taxation in Latin America in the 1990s, Williamson suggests (1) the development of property taxation as a major source of government revenue (particularly at the subnational level), the elimination of tax loopholes, and better tax collection. The latter two possibilities are often cited by finance ministers in trouble, but less often carried out successfully. Progress in these areas would certainly be welcome.

In addition, Williamson's subsequent items favor (2) improving education; (3) land titling, again with reference to Hernando de Soto (2000); (4) land reform; and (5) microcredit.

Three Critiques

The above description of Washington Consensus II makes it clear that by 2003 the original short list of 10 commandments had morphed into a more complete description of the elements of a development strategy. Williamson takes up the issue of whether the Washington Consensus succeeds as a policy prescription for development in his 2004 paper. In this regard, he suggests that while Washington Consensus I is not sufficiently detailed for that purpose, Washington Consensus II is. He also discusses critiques of the Washington Consensus by Joseph Stiglitz (1998) and Rodrik (2002, 2005). I shall also report here on more recent papers by Nancy Birdsall, Augusto de la Torre, and Felipe Valencia Caicedo (2010) and Birdsall and Francis Fukuyama (2011), and briefly discuss the relationship between Washington Consensus II and the approach to development strategy presented in the 1991 WDR.

---

15. Williamson (2003, 13) comments in passing that central banks "deserve autonomy even if not complete independence from the political process." This statement is sufficiently brief that it is not quite clear whether to agree or disagree with it.

16. This section draws on Birdsall and de la Torre (2001). Closely related work is presented in Birdsall and Szekely (2003).

Williamson notes that Stiglitz (1998) views the Washington Consensus as a neoliberal manifesto. Writing in 1998, Stiglitz was trying to move toward a new, broader consensus that included pursuing equitable, sustainable, and democratic development. Williamson's comment is that, in reviewing the list of extensions of Washington Consensus I, he is impressed that much of the economic content of Stiglitz's attempted consensus is included in Kuczynski and Williamson (2003)—that is, in Washington Consensus II. However, there are signs in his discussion of Stiglitz that Williamson (2004) does not believe that there is in fact a "consensus" on Washington Consensus II to the same extent that he believes there was one on Washington Consensus I. He argues that since Stiglitz wants the consensus to be owned by developing countries, it cannot be a "Washington" consensus. This last point is not self-evident—except if it was politically necessary for some developing countries not to appear to be close to Washington—since many had claimed that the original Washington Consensus was in fact widely shared, and could have been regarded as universal.

Rodrik's 2002 contribution is especially critical of Washington Consensus II, which he calls the "Augmented Washington Consensus." Table 2.2 reproduces Rodrik's table 1, entitled "The Washington Consensus Is Dead: Long Live the New Washington Consensus!" The table in fact provides a reasonably accurate description of the elements of Washington Consensus II.

But Rodrik does not come to praise the Washington Consensus, either I or II. Rather, he states: "The Augmented Washington Consensus is bound to disappoint.... It is an impossibly broad, undifferentiated agenda of institutional reform.... It does not correspond to the empirical reality of how development really takes place.... It describes what 'advanced' economies look like, rather than proscribing a practical, feasible path of getting there...." (Rodrik 2002).

He goes on to state: "The challenge for the critics of the Washington Consensus is this: they need to provide an alternative set of policy guidelines for promoting development, without falling into the trap of having to promote yet another impractical blueprint that is supposed to be right for all countries for all times" (Rodrik 2002). And he then proceeds to present an approach based on principles from mainstream economics that he says are universal, but that "do not map into unique institutional arrangements or policy prescriptions."

Rodrik concludes that the refurbished Washington Consensus II is not a useful guide to promoting development. He describes his alternative approach as "focusing on experimentation—both in the institutional and productive sphere—as an important driver of economic development. The key is to realize that neither technology nor good institutions can be acquired without significant domestic adaptations. These adaptations in turn require a pro-active role for the state and civil society...." (Rodrik 2002, 8–9). I return to these issues in my concluding comments.

Birdsall, de la Torre, and Caicedo (2010) assess the Washington Consensus and describe it as a damaged brand. They argue that it failed as a development strategy because of (1) shortfalls in implementation of reforms combined with impatience with regard to their effects; (2) fundamental flaws in the reform agenda, such as trying to operate with a fixed exchange rate, or prematurely opening the capital account; and (3) the omission from the framework of critical reforms, among them the need to deal with volatility, promote technological innovation, change institutions, and work to reduce inequality.

Birdsall and Fukuyama (2011) ask what the impact of the Great Recession will be on modern approaches to development. They start by noting that the crisis has not led to a rejection of capitalism, though in their view it has reduced the appeal of the American brand of capitalism. They suggest that countries will no longer be subject to the "foreign finance fetish," the view that developing countries could benefit substantially from greater inflows of capital. They foresee a greater role for the state and for increasing the efficiency of government. In addition, they believe we are moving to a more multipolar world, with the replacement of the G-7 by the G-20 in the international system as the visible symbol of this change.

Concluding Comments

In concluding, I present several comments and questions on the debate that started with John Williamson's 1990 paper.

- It is striking that the Washington Consensus came out of the Latin American experience, with relatively little reference to the development and growth problems that were afflicting much of the rest of the world at the same time in East Asia and the Indian subcontinent, Africa, the Middle East, and the countries of the former Soviet bloc. Surely Washington—in the sense of the word used by Williamson in 1990—had interests in the entire world. What made Latin America so central to development at that time? Was it that these were middle-income countries? Was it the geographical accident of their being so close to the United States? And did it matter that the Washington Consensus was based on Latin American experience, rather than that of East Asia?

- It is also notable that the developing world—and not least Latin America—has done much better so far in the 21st century than it did at the end of the 20th century. In the words of former Bank of Mexico Governor Guillermo Ortiz at an Aspen Conference in the summer of 2008: "This time it isn't us." What does the success of most of Latin America (as well as much of the rest of the non-West) in dealing with the Great Recession tell us about the Washington Consensus? For the record, I believe that the lessons learned in the 1990s, some of them in the context of IMF programs, have served these countries well during the Great Recession.[17]

---

17. For example, the acronym BRICS—invented by Jim O'Neill of Goldman Sachs for Brazil, Russia, India, China, and South Africa—has been accepted into the language at this point without

- It appears that the lag between deciding on and beginning to implement changes in structural policies and then their having an appreciable effect is much longer than was generally assumed in 1990. It is also much longer than is convenient for democratic policymakers.

- The development literature has not been comfortable with the relationship between political structure and economic performance. During the 1980s it was often asked whether Chile's success "proved" that authoritarian governments did better at economic reform—this at a time when almost all governments in Latin America were nondemocratic, and only one of them was doing well. The same question is sometimes raised in comparing India and China. It is clear that an effective state apparatus is needed, but it is less clear what makes a state effective with regard to development policy.[18]

- I still do not understand why the 1991 WDR, which included many elements of Washington Consensus II, received essentially no attention in the post-1990 literature on the Washington Consensus.

- In reading the Washington Consensus literature, I was struck by the prevalence of lists of policies and institutions that needed to be undertaken or dealt with. There is something slightly sterile about these lists, and it took me a while to figure out what the problem is. Essentially, authors are writing to promote development and to either directly or indirectly help those who have the responsibility for implementing policies. They are providing recipes for economic development. But a recipe starts with a list of ingredients, and then goes on to specify how to make the dish. *The difficult part of development is making the dish, not listing the ingredients.* It is this fact that leads Rodrik to emphasize the importance of local conditions, including political conditions, and to emphasize experimentation.

- Experimentation may be a good idea, of course, but it can be a disaster too. Rodrik quotes with approval China's experimental approach to development starting in 1978. But China experimented before that with the Great Leap Forward. That sort of experimentation is surely not a good idea.

- I have been struck in my work as a central banker with how extremely useful it is to have some knowledge of the history of central banks and how they—notably the Bank of England—have dealt with problems in the past. I suspect that the study of development would benefit greatly if students were to learn more about the history of decision making and policy execution in case studies of key episodes in economic development.

---

the need for explanation. O'Neill's most recent invention is the MIST—Mexico, Indonesia, South Korea, and Turkey. It is noteworthy that all four of the MIST countries had major programs with the IMF in the 1990s.

18. In the 1990s, I concluded—without doing the necessary empirical work—that it was typically easier to reach agreement on a program with an authoritarian government but that programs with democratic governments had a greater chance of being implemented.

- Whither the Washington Consensus? Washington Consensus I was extremely successful in providing a basis for a debate on development policies in the period from 1990 to nearly the present. Will there be a Washington Consensus III followed by a Washington Consensus IV, and so forth? It seems not, for the development literature has moved on, and there is far less controversy about Washington Consensus II than there was about Washington Consensus I.

- Nor does it seem that we will be moving on to a "Beijing Consensus." Williamson (2012) takes up the question of whether the Beijing Consensus is now dominant, and argues that the West should not take up this model of development. He makes a strong case for that viewpoint. But neither he nor anyone else would argue that we should not be studying the Chinese and other successes and failures of development policy, and trying to draw lessons from them, including lessons about the political and bureaucratic processes through which reforms were implemented.

- Are we in a world in which economic leadership has moved away from the G-7 or G-8 to the G-20? In two senses, yes. A group of countries more representative of the world's population sits around the table when global economic issues are discussed outside the context of the Bretton Woods institutions, including at the head-of-state level. Further, the "new" members of the group represent an increasing share of global GDP. But in one important sense, no. Aside from the London and Pittsburgh G-20 meetings, not much in the way of policy leadership has come out of the G-20. Serious work needs to be done to make the G-20 more effective, including by convergence between the membership of the G-20 and the IMF Board.

Which brings us back to John Williamson. His approach to economics is deceptively simple. He believes in economics, and he believes in applying it. As his replies to the critics of the Washington Consensus show, he stands his ground when challenged, for he has a firm and well-based belief in the benefits of a market economy. He does not try to impress by using fancy technique; rather he tries to be useful. In some ways he must be the prototype that John Maynard Keynes (1984) had in mind in writing about economics in 1930: "It should be a matter for specialists—like dentistry. If economists could manage to get themselves thought of as humble, competent people, on a level with dentists, that would be splendid!" Of course, we should also aspire, as modern dentists do, to be more efficient and to cause as little pain as possible as we go about our daily tasks.

Williamson believes in serious discussion and civilized dialogue as ways to advance understanding—and this is no small thing in a profession as important as ours.

Finally, looking back at Williamson's (2004) description of the Washington Consensus, its most striking characteristic—and one that Williamson emphasized—is that it incorporates a transition from a belief that there is a specialized economics for developing countries and another set of policies that work only or mostly in developed countries, to an understanding that marks, in Williamson's words (2004, 44), "[t]he end of the intellectual apartheid that used to divide the globe into the first, second, and third worlds, each with its own economic laws...." And he adds that this "is something to be celebrated rather than mourned."

We are indeed happy to be part of the celebration.

References

Balassa, Bela, Gerardo M. Bueno, Pedro-Pablo Kuczynski, and Mario Henrique Simonsen. 1986. *Toward Renewed Economic Growth in Latin America.* Washington: Institute for International Economics.

Birdsall, Nancy, and Augusto de la Torre. 2001. *Washington Contentious—Economic Policies for Social Equity in Latin America.* Washington: Carnegie Endowment for International Peace and Inter-American Dialogue.

Birdsall, Nancy, and Francis Fukuyama. 2011. The Post-Washington Consensus. *Foreign Affairs* 90, no. 2: 45-53.

Birdsall, Nancy, and Michael Szekely. 2003. Bootstraps, not Band-Aids: Poverty, Equity, and Social Policy. In *After the Washington Consensus: Restarting Growth and Reform in Latin America*, ed. Pedro-Pablo Kuczynski and John Williamson. Washington: Institute for International Economics.

Birdsall, Nancy, Augusto de la Torre, and Felipe Valencia Caicedo. 2010. *The Washington Consensus: Assessing a Damaged Brand.* CGD Working Paper 213. Washington: Center for Global Development.

Cornia, Giovanni Andrea, Richard Jolly, and Frances Stewart. 1987. *Adjustment with a Human Face: Protecting the Vulnerable and Promoting Growth.* Oxford: Clarendon Press for UNICEF.

de Soto, Hernando. 2000. *The Mystery of Capital: Why Capitalism Triumphs in the West and Fails Everywhere Else.* London: Black Swan.

Fischer, Stanley. 2004 (originally published in 1997). Capital Account Liberalization and the Role of the IMF. In *IMF Essays from a Time of Crisis: The International Financial System, Stabilization, and Development*, by Stanley Fischer. Cambridge, MA: MIT Press.

Keynes, John Maynard. 1984 (originally published in 1930). Economic Possibilities for Our Grandchildren. In *Essays in Persuasion.* Cambridge, UK: The Macmillan Press for the Royal Economic Society.

Kuczynski, Pedro-Pablo, and John Williamson, ed. 2003. *After the Washington Consensus: Restarting Growth and Reform in Latin America.* Washington: Institute for International Economics.

Naím, Moisés. 1994. Latin America: The Second Stage of Reform. *Journal of Democracy* 5, no. 4: 32-48.

Naím, Moisés. 2000. Washington Consensus or Washington Confusion? *Foreign Policy* (Spring): 87-103.

Rodrik, Dani. 2002. After Neoliberalism, What? Remarks at the Brazilian Development Bank (BNDES) seminar on New Paths of Development, Rio de Janeiro, September 12-13.

Rodrik, Dani. 2005. Growth Strategies. In *Handbook of Economic Growth*, Volume 1A, ed. Philippe Aghion and Steven Durlauf. Amsterdam: Elsevier.

Stiglitz, Joseph. 1998. *More Instruments and Broader Goals: Moving Towards the Post-Washington Consensus.* Helsinki: World Institute for Development Economics Research.

Williamson, John. 1990. What Washington Means by Policy Reform. In *Latin American Adjustment: How Much Has Happened?* ed. John Williamson. Washington: Institute for International Economics.

Williamson, John. 2000. What Should the World Bank Think about the Washington Consensus? *World Bank Research Observer* 15, no. 2: 51-64.

Williamson, John. 2002. Did the Washington Consensus Fail? Speech at the Center for Strategic and International Studies, Washington, November 6.

Williamson, John. 2003. Overview: An Agenda for Restarting Growth and Reform. In *After the Washington Consensus: Restarting Growth and Reform in Latin America*, ed. Pedro-Pablo Kuczynski and John Williamson. Washington: Institute for International Economics.

Williamson, John. 2004. The Washington Consensus as Policy Prescription for Development. In *Development Challenges in the 1990s: Leading Policymakers Speak from Experience*, ed. Timothy Besley and Roberto Zagha. Washington: World Bank and Oxford University Press.

Williamson, John. 2005. The Strange History of the Washington Consensus. *Journal of Post-Keynesian Economics* 27, no. 2: 195-206.

Williamson, John. 2008. A Short History of the Washington Consensus. In *The Washington Consensus Reconsidered: Towards a New Global Governance*, ed. Narcis Serra and Joseph E. Stiglitz. New York: Oxford University Press.

Williamson, John. 2012. Is the "Beijing Consensus" Now Dominant? *Asia Policy*, no. 13 (January): 1-16.

World Bank. 1991. *World Development Report*. Washington.

World Bank. 1993. *The East Asian Miracle: Economic Growth and Public Policy*. Oxford: Oxford University Press.

I

MONEY

3

The International Monetary System or "Nonsystem"?

EDWIN M. TRUMAN

Throughout his career John Williamson frequently has focused his considerable analytic skills and powers of persuasion on reform of the international monetary system (IMS). His second publication (Williamson 1963) examined international liquidity and the "multiple key currency proposal." His next publication was on the crawling peg (Williamson 1965). Exchange rates and international liquidity have been bookmarks of John's professional career. At least one-third of the entries on John's curriculum vitae address one aspect or another of the IMS and its reform.

John Williamson and the International Monetary System

As a consultant to Her Majesty's Treasury from 1968 to 1970, John Williamson was intimately involved in the policy process at the time of the collapse of the Bretton Woods system. Then, as advisor to the International Monetary Fund (IMF) Research Department from 1972 to 1974, he participated in efforts to rebuild the system during the operation of the Committee of Twenty (C-20). I first met John when he visited Yale University in the fall of 1971 to present a paper on customs unions (Bottrill and Williamson 1971), which was then a focus of my research as well. Our professional interactions multiplied after 1972, when I joined the staff of the Federal Reserve Board. We both worked on

Edwin M. Truman, senior fellow at the Peterson Institute for International Economics since 2001, served as assistant secretary of the US Treasury for International Affairs from December 1998 to January 2001 and returned as counselor to the secretary in March–May 2009. He thanks Allie E. Bagnall for her dedicated assistance in preparing this chapter and Randy Henning, Olivier Jeanne, Joseph E. Gagnon, Robert Kahn, and John Williamson himself for advice, comments, and suggestions. He alone is responsible for the views expressed and any errors of fact or interpretation.

C-20 issues, participating together on several C-20 technical groups. We were also both members of a rather subversive organization called the Second Row Dining Club that would meet over dinner at the time of various international meetings and criticize the lords and masters who sat in the first rows of the meetings we all attended.

John's experience with the C-20 left him with a very bad impression of prospects for reform of the IMS. Indeed, he wrote a book about the C-20 effort to reform the IMS, which he titled *The Failure of World Monetary Reform, 1971–1974* (Williamson 1977). John was one of the first to use the term "international monetary nonsystem" to characterize the IMS with which we have lived for the past 40-plus years (Williamson 1976). He elaborated on his views in his study of how the C-20 exercise failed to produce a set of well-defined rights and obligations.[1] As he put it: "There was no agreement on a set of rules for assigning adjustment responsibilities, no design of a viable adjustment mechanism, no introduction of an SDR standard [other than in empty words], no substitution account [to eliminate an overhang of reserve currencies in the system], and no curb on the asymmetries" (Williamson 1977, 73). Consequently, John's concise, 203-page account of the C-20 period provides a useful point of departure in considering his views on the IMS and its evolution.

John characterized the IMS as consisting of arrangements in five areas (Williamson 1977, 1): market convertibility (transactions in different currencies between private parties), the exchange rate regime, balance of payments adjustment, the supply of reserve assets, and the institution charged with managing the system. This last element brings in the IMF as the manager of the system. John favored then, as well as today, a system based as much as possible on rules and a major role of the IMF as the keeper and enforcer of those rules.

John considered the C-20 decision to try to perpetuate the adjustable-peg regime as "intellectual nihilism" (Williamson 1977, 125). He was, however, careful to note that two important components of the five elements of the Bretton Woods system—market convertibility and international management—remained even as arrangements governing the exchange rate regime, balance of payments adjustment, and the supply of reserves were swept away.

In John's view (Williamson 1977, 77), the participants in the C-20 reform negotiations shared a common interest in preserving the progress made under the Bretton Woods system in nine areas: (1) maintenance of a cooperative economic system, (2) incorporation of liberal trading policies, (3) maintenance of an international capital market, (4) minimization of global cyclical fluctuations, (5) provision of development finance, (6) absence of erratic exchange rate variations, (7) avoidance of competitive payments policies, (8) orderly methods

---

1. In John's view, circa 1977, the positive benefit of rules and automaticity (compared with indicators and discretion) was that they limit tensions and political maneuvering associated with attempts to link indicators to change in policies or behavior (Williamson 1977, 111).

of payments adjustment, and (9) provision of reserves through a fiduciary (fiat) reserve asset, that is, the then-nascent special drawing rights (SDR) system.[2]

Arguably, the post-C-20 system has been successful in the first four areas, which I would argue fall in the category of objectives achieved.[3] The fifth area (development finance) is not a feature of the IMS per se, though some may disagree. The remaining four areas are potentially desirable features of an IMS but have not been established. On the other hand, with the exception of the erratic exchange rate variations, which were constitutionally excluded under the Bretton Woods system, not much progress was made on them during the 25 years of the Bretton Woods system either. It is just that no progress has been made subsequently.

John attributes the failure of the C-20 negotiations to a lack of political will to cooperate on seeking common solutions, and to an intellectual failure, or technical inadequacy, when it came to devising a workable system, in particular with respect to the exchange rate regime (Williamson 1977, chapter 7).

The bulk of John's review of the C-20 negotiations (Williamson 1977) focused on the adjustment process, including the exchange rate regime (chapter 5) and reserve assets and liquidity (chapter 6). In his prescriptions for the future (chapter 8), John focused primarily on the exchange rate regime. He embraced the reference rate proposal of Wilfred Ethier and Arthur Bloomfield (1975) to establish foreign exchange market intervention rights but not impose intervention obligations.[4]

John was involved in the process that generated the IMF's guidelines for the management of floating exchange rates that were adopted by the IMF Executive Board in June 1974. The guidelines included some elements that were similar to those in the Ethier-Bloomfield approach—particularly the concept of an exchange rate target "within the range of reasonable estimates of the medium-term norm for the exchange rate in question"—but the guidelines went further in establishing the presumption that countries would "lean against the wind" in their intervention operations (IMF 1985, 487–91). When the IMF Articles of Agreement were formally amended in 1978 to legalize floating exchange rates—and when in anticipation of the approval of the second amendment, the IMF Executive Board in April 1977 adopted a decision governing the surveillance of members' exchange rate policies—the notion of a medium-term norm as well as the presumption that a member should lean against the wind in its exchange rate operations were not included (IMF 1985, 491–94). In John's view, these were steps backward that reinforced his sense that the C-20 process had created

---

2. The numbering and ordering are not those of John Williamson.

3. The first area relates to the role of the IMF. Whatever one thinks of the post–Bretton Woods IMS and the job that institution has done in that IMS, the IMF has retained its central role in international monetary cooperation, though it has been forced to share that role first with the G-7 and now with the G-20, just as before 1971 it shared its central role with the G-10.

4. The Ethier-Bloomfield approach had been presented at a conference in 1974.

a nonsystem. This setback has not deterred John from continuing to pursue the reference rate proposal, as documented by the contribution to this volume by Marcus Miller on target zones (see chapter 5 in this volume).

Although John's primary preoccupation with the IMS over the past 40 years has been the adjustment process and the role of exchange rates and exchange rate management in that process, he also has addressed the reserve asset system, and in particular the role of the SDR (Williamson 1977, chapter 8). In John's view at that time, the IMS should involve the collective management of international liquidity, preferably by providing reserve assets to participating countries in the form of fiduciary claims, in other words SDR. Although John was sympathetic to the European attachment to asset settlement as a means to discipline US economic and financial policies, and also to the SDR aid link as a mechanism for distributing SDR reserves to the system, his principal motivation appears to have been to redistribute the seigniorage associated with the provision of reserve assets that he saw accruing to the United States. He also held the view that controlling the volume of international liquidity was an important aspect of a healthy global economic, monetary, and (today some would emphasize even more) financial system. In recent years, as the topic of IMS reform has reemerged, some would say only marginally, on the international agenda John has returned to assessing the role of the SDR in the IMS (Williamson 2009a and 2009b).

In chapter 8 of Williamson (1977), he argued that, despite the failure of the C-20 negotiations and the modest adjustments to the IMS contained in the second amendment of the IMF Articles of Agreement, reform of the IMS was desirable. Based on the attention he has paid to IMS issues in his subsequent work, we can safely conclude that John still feels that way.

In Williamson (1977, 197–201), John presented five features of the post–Bretton Woods international monetary nonsystem as sources of economic concern: (1) the high volatility of exchange rates, (2) the lack of defenses against the pursuit of countercyclical exchange rate policies, (3) a lack of control over the volume of international liquidity, (4) the misdistribution or arbitrary distribution of seigniorage, and (5) the asymmetric position of the US dollar.[5] On each of these concerns, John offered arguments on both sides as to how serious these concerns might be in the future. In a later paper (Williamson 1985), John advanced a robust defense of the Bretton Woods system that rested on three rules: (1) exchange rates were normally to remain stable and not be subjected to short-run manipulation via monetary and fiscal policies; (2) monetary and fiscal policies were to be focused on the maintenance of internal stability in the form of full employment and price stability constrained by the first and

---

5. I have changed the order of the Williamson (1977) concerns somewhat to group the two concerns with respect to the adjustment process together; the other three relate to the reserve asset system. John did not include international capital movements in his list of concerns about the IMS in the mid-1970s. In the ensuing 40 years, as detailed by the contribution of Olivier Jeanne to this volume (chapter 8), John has directed considerable attention to global capital flows.

the third rules; and (3) countries were to restrict their deficits to what could be financed from available reserves, and drawing on the IMF and the United States would be constrained by the need to maintain confidence in the dollar. Although John's defense of the Bretton Woods system was vigorous and robust, he admitted that the system functioned as intended only from 1958 to 1967—less than a decade.

The balance of this chapter looks at John's five concerns about the post–Bretton Woods system in two groups: those about exchange rates and the adjustment process, and those about international liquidity, seigniorage, and the stability of the monetary system. I will to try to evaluate to what extent those concerns are or should be concerns today, as well as examine progress and prospects in these areas.

The Adjustment Process

This section examines two aspects of the IMS as it has evolved since the early 1970s: exchange rate variability and external imbalances. The two aspects are closely linked, although adjustment is not all about exchange rate movements, or nonmovements, and exchange rates are not all about maintaining external equilibrium.

Exchange Rate Variability

One frequently heard criticism of the IMS today is that there is excessive and unnecessary variability of exchange rates.[6] The argument is that exchange rate variability impedes trade and adversely affects growth and/or contributes to inflation. Joseph E. Gagnon (2011, chapters 4 and 5) exhaustively examines these arguments and finds little evidence to support them. Nevertheless, as Gagnon notes, lack of correlation does not establish a lack of causation.

It is difficult to believe that there are zero costs associated with the degree of exchange rate variability that has prevailed since the collapse of the Bretton Woods system. The question is, What is the appropriate comparison? As John Williamson in his many writings has stressed, the search for optimum exchange rate policies must start from the proposition that one can establish, in rough measure, equilibrium exchange rates for countries individually and collectively that are consistent with internal and external balance for each country and globally.

Exchange rate variability can be measured in several dimensions, including, for example, with respect to one or more time periods and with respect to one or more currencies. Concerns about the day-to-day variability in exchange rates distorting price signals in the short run differ from concerns about exchange rate variability over periods as long as a year or two, which are more relevant to the adjustment process and the costs of delaying adjustment. Those who advo-

---

6. Paul A. Volcker is a frequent critic. See Volcker (2012).

cate exchange rate stability, in general, focus on a particular bilateral exchange rate. It is more appropriate, in my view, to examine the behavior of effective, or average, exchange rates rather than bilateral exchange rates. In particular, the latter are more relevant for most economic questions. The economics profession over the past 40 years has failed to convince policymakers and the general public to focus not on a particular bilateral exchange rate but instead on an average exchange rate for the country.

Has exchange rate variability decreased in recent years? Table 3.1 examines this question in terms of month-to-month changes, 12-month changes, and 24-month changes for the G-20 countries and the euro area.[7] The summary results show that exchange rate variability has declined in all three time dimensions in a substantial majority of the 20 series, on average by 85 percent for the two tests, the two exchange rate series, and the three time periods.[8] Seventy-seven percent of the cases exhibited a significant reduction in variability, slightly more frequently for the nominal effective exchange rates, but the difference was not as pronounced as one might expect. This probably reflects the influence of nominal exchange rates on real exchange rates. On the other hand, the decline in variability has not been dramatic.[9] The mean 10-year effect ranges from 15 to 20 percent for most of the countries.

The apparent general decline in exchange rate variability suggests that markets today may be coping better with flexible exchange rates than several decades ago, but that does not necessarily mean that the external adjustment process has produced better results overall or that there has been a decline in the high volatility of exchange rates about which John was concerned (Williamson 1977, 197). On the other hand, from a medium-term perspective, adjustment of exchange rates may have been insufficient to contribute to an appropriate working of the adjustment process. The next subsection examines this issue.

External Imbalances

Turning to outcomes of the adjustment process, it is conventional to focus on external imbalances.[10] We worry about external imbalances for two reasons. First, for individual countries, external imbalances, and outsized deficits in particular, may trigger external payments crises that are disruptive to the

---

7. A companion working paper (Truman 2012) contains more detailed results.

8. Frequently, the exchange rates for the same countries exhibited an increase in variability. That was the case for India and Korea, which moved toward policies of greater exchange rate flexibility, but also for Canada and the United Kingdom.

9. Truman (2012) contains the background for this conclusion.

10. A case could be made that one should focus instead, or in addition, on broader indicators of macroeconomic performance such as growth, inflation, unemployment rates, and technical progress. However, such an examination is beyond the scope of this chapter.

Table 3.1 Summary of tests of trends in foreign exchange rate variability for G-20 countries (number of countries in each category)

Interval	Mean standard deviation test[a]	Regression standard deviation test[b]
Nominal effective exchange rate		
Month-to-month		
Less variability	18	18
Significant	18	15
Not significant	0	3
More variability	2	2
Significant	2	1
Not significant	0	1
12-month		
Less variability	18	17
Significant	16	16
Not significant	2	1
More variability	2	3
Significant	0	3
Not significant	2	0
24-month		
Less variability	18	16
Significant	17	16
Not significant	1	0
More variability	2	4
Significant	1	1
Not significant	1	3
Real effective exchange rate		
Month-to-month		
Less variability	13	17
Significant	11	17
Not significant	2	0
More variability	7	3
Significant	4	2
Not significant	3	1

(continues on next page)

Table 3.1   Summary of tests of trends in foreign exchange rate variability for G-20 countries (number of countries in each category) *(continued)*

Interval	Mean standard deviation test[a]	Regression standard deviation test[b]
Real effective exchange rate *(continued)*		
12-month		
Less variability	16	17
Significant	15	16
Not significant	1	1
More variability	4	3
Significant	1	2
Not significant	3	1
24-month		
Less variability	17	18
Significant	11	16
Not significant	6	2
More variability	3	2
Significant	1	1
Not significant	2	1

a. Test of whether the mean of the rolling five-year standard deviations of the series is higher or lower in the second half of the period.
b. Test of whether in a regression of the rolling five-year standard deviations against time the coefficient is positive or negative.

Source: Truman (2012).

economy in question and potentially to its neighbors and the global economy. Second, for the global system, external imbalances, and deficits in particular but also potentially surpluses, can trigger a global crisis as a consequence of a forced process of adjustment or an increase in protectionism.

Has the incidence of significant external imbalances increased or decreased since the collapse of the Bretton Woods system? To answer this question, we looked at a sample of important countries and, first, scaled their current account positions by national GDP.

Over the past five years, William Cline and John Williamson (2008, 2012) have teamed up to examine current account balances relative to national GDPs for 33 economies plus the euro area as projected by the IMF staff in its *World Economic Outlook* (WEO) report. They use the ratios to estimate the degree to which the effective exchange rate of the relevant economy is out of line with its fundamental equilibrium exchange rate; the rate that they estimate would produce a deficit or surplus less than their trigger, 3 percent of GDP.

In applying this approach to data and estimates for 1980 to 2017, I expanded the Cline-Williamson set of economies to 50 in order to cover the period before establishment of the euro area. Therefore, I added the 17 euro area countries individually.[11] I raised the cutoff for an imbalance to 4 percent of GDP because using the 3 percent cutoff generated an implausibly large number of imbalances.

As depicted in the top panel of figure 3.1, even applying the higher 4 percent cutoff, in 41 percent of the observations over the 32 years to 2012, the 50 economies recorded current account positions greater than that as an absolute value.[12] More than 40 percent of the countries had imbalances, by this measure, in the early 1980s. The incidence hit a low in 1990, but rose back above 50 percent in 2004, and hit a peak of 72 percent in 2007. The WEO projections are for the incidence to be in the 30 percent range over the next six years. For the historical period as a whole, the emerging-market economies accounted for a disproportionate share of total imbalances—44 percent of the observations for this group compared with 38 percent of the advanced economy group. The time series for the two groups are broadly similar, except that the incidence of imbalances was much larger for the emerging-market group in the 1980s. In 2007, however, both groups recorded rates of imbalance above 70 percent.

For the period as a whole, the average incidence of deficits and surplus was about the same, 21 and 20 percent, respectively. However, as shown in the lower two panels of figure 3.1, deficit imbalances were much more common in the early 1980s and surplus imbalances were more common in recent years. The IMF projects that this relative distribution will continue within a smaller overall total.[13]

To get a better handle on imbalances that are more likely to have global significance, an alternative approach is to use world GDP as the scale factor, as advocated in Truman (2010a). Figure 3.2 presents the results of this exercise using as the cutoff 0.05 percent of world GDP. We can see that, on average, the incidence of imbalances is smaller than when they are scaled by national GDP, and the incidence increases rather steadily over the period with only a small dip in the early 1990s. The contribution of emerging-market economies to the overall total of imbalances also increases over time. On this criterion, however, deficits for this group of countries disappeared between 2002 and

---

11. See Truman (2012) for more details. The 50 economies accounted for 92 percent of world GDP in 2011 at market prices and exchange rates and 89 percent on a purchasing power parity basis.

12. Using a 3 percent cutoff produces a figure of 54 percent of the observations, although the pattern in the time series is very similar.

13. See Truman (2012) for more details.

Figure 3.1 Current account imbalances relative to national GDP, 1980–2017

National imbalances

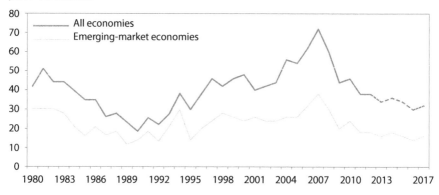

National deficits

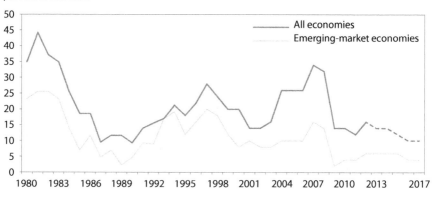

National surpluses

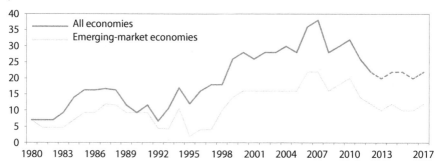

Note: Percent of countries with current account positions greater than or equal to 4 percent of national GDP.

Source: IMF, World Economic Outlook database, April 2012.

Figure 3.2   Current account imbalances relative to world GDP, 1980–2017

World imbalances

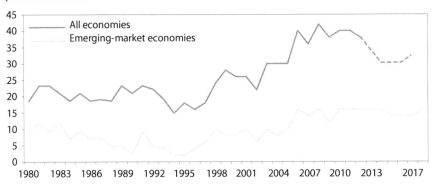

World deficits

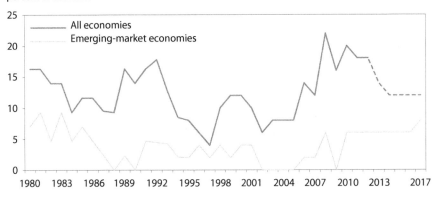

World surpluses

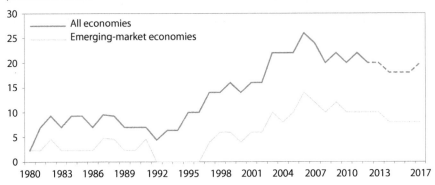

Note: Percent of countries with current account positions greater than or equal to 0.05 percent of world GDP.

Source: IMF, *World Economic Outlook* database, April 2012.

2005, and since 2003 the incidence of surplus imbalances for these countries has been high. Overall, when applying the world GDP criterion, emerging markets become relatively more prominent, reflecting the fact that the share of emerging-market economies in world GDP has increased substantially, in particular over the past decade.

Returning to what this evidence says about the working of the global adjustment process, has the incidence of significant external imbalances increased or decreased since the collapse of the Bretton Woods system? The clear answer is that the incidence of imbalances has increased. In 2011, the sum of the excess deficits and surpluses beyond the cutoff of 0.05 percent of world GDP was $1.36 trillion—$620 billion in deficits and $740 billion in surpluses.

The US contribution to the 2011 excess of deficits—$439 billion of its total deficit of $473 billion—accounted for 70 percent of the total excess of deficits. One might reasonably conclude that the external adjustment process definitely has not worked insofar as the United States is concerned. As under the Bretton Woods system, the United States has continued to have a more limited independent scope to manage its external position than other countries. For example, what would happen if the United States adopted, as some have advocated, an aggressive policy to depreciate the dollar and narrow its current account position? In other words, the present IMS, like its predecessor, has not facilitated a smooth and effective working of the international adjustment process, particularly for the United States.

Although there are imbalances among the advanced countries, particularly in Europe, the major development over the past decade has been the shift of the emerging-market and developing countries from aggregate positions in current account deficit to aggregate positions in current account surplus. This change in the pattern of deficits and surpluses might be taken as evidence supporting the view that capital is flowing uphill, contrary to view in the C-20 period that it is desirable to promote the transfer of real resources from "North" to "South." This is a mistaken interpretation of the evidence. As I have argued (Truman 2011a), the transfer of real resources from South to North has largely been facilitated by official sectors in the South accumulating reserves at a faster rate than their current account surpluses.[14] To the extent that policymakers in the South want to limit the overall net transfer from South to North, they have the means at their disposal: limit the accumulation of international reserves. This would tend to reduce their current account surpluses, increase their deficits, and encourage larger net private capital inflows to their countries and regions. The fact that they have not done so leads us to the next topic: international liquidity and its management.

---

14. See Truman (2012) for further demonstration of this point.

International Liquidity, Seigniorage, and the Stability of the Multicurrency System

This section examines three interrelated topics: international liquidity, foreign exchange reserves, and the role of the US dollar. In the wake of the final breakdown of the Bretton Woods system, John wrote a masterful, comprehensive review of the topic of international liquidity (Williamson 1973, 686).[15] He addressed three questions that had been debated since 1959: (1) Is there a need for additional liquidity? (2) What are the desirable characteristics of reserves? In particular, how should one design a fiduciary reserve asset, such as the SDR? and (3) In what quantity should reserves be provided? The updated counterparts of these three questions focus on (1) a lack of control over the volume of international liquidity, (2) the misdistribution or arbitrary distribution of seigniorage, and (3) the asymmetric position of the dollar in the IMS. We can examine these three issues today, but the difference is that they are embedded in a very different IMS than John envisaged in the early 1970s.

International Liquidity

In the 1960s and early 1970s, international liquidity was identified with international reserve assets. The analysis of international liquidity assumed that the IMS was based on at least heavily managed exchange rates. The focus was on the balance of payments as a whole and the need for most countries to settle their overall payments imbalances in reserve assets not on current account positions. In this context, the analysis presumed a rational demand on the part of each country for reserves, with the implication by many analysts that if a country held or accumulated more than its preferred optimum stock of reserves it would adjust, including via inflation, according to an international quantity theory of money.

One of the central controversies surrounding the collapse of Bretton Woods and the effort to reconstruct the IMS was whether the foreign currency component of international reserves, which was the only elastic element, was supply determined by an essentially capricious US overall balance of payments deficit that bore "no systematic relationship to the reserve-accumulation objectives of other countries...[but instead]...results from a complex of such factors as demand-management policies in the United States and the rest of the world and historically-determined relative cost structures" (Williamson 1973, 706). The alternative view was that the foreign currency component of reserves was demand-determined in that "the United States deficit is primarily a residual

---

15. John summarized the state of debate on international liquidity at the time, which was before the C-20 failed to agree on comprehensive reform of the international monetary system. In addition to clearly laying out the issues from a positive perspective (the optimal reserve holding for a single country) and from a normative perspective (the optimum supply of reserves to the system as a whole), John wrote with wit, clarity, and balance.

Table 3.2   Evolution of international reserves

Reserves and components	1970	1980	1990	2000	2011
			World		
Total reserves (billions of dollars)	95	997	1,293	2,282	12,103
Percent of world GDP	n.a.	9.3	5.8	7.1	17.4
Composition (percent)					
Foreign exchange	48	38	67	85	84
Gold	41	59	28	12	12
Special drawing rights	3	1	2	1	2
Reserve position in the IMF	8	2	3	3	1
			Advanced countries		
Total reserves (billions of dollars)	77	756	1,049	1,515	4,845
Percent of national GDP	n.a.	9.2	5.9	5.9	10.9
Percent of world GDP	n.a.	7.1	4.7	4.7	6.9
Composition (percent)					
Foreign exchange	43	30	65	80	70
Gold	44	66	30	15	23
Special drawing rights	3	2	2	1	4
Reserve position in the IMF	9	2	3	4	2
		Emerging-market and developing countries			
Total reserves (billions of dollars)	18	240	244	767	7,258
Percent of national GDP	n.a.	9.5	5.5	11.7	28.7
Percent of world GDP	n.a.	2.2	1.1	2.4	10.4
Composition (percent)					
Foreign exchange	67	61	76	94	94
Gold	25	35	20	5	4
Special drawing rights	3	1	1	1	1
Reserve position in the IMF	5	3	2	1	1

n.a. = not available

Source: IMF, *International Financial Statistics*, CD-ROM, June 2012 (accessed in June 2012).

which is determined by adjustment policies on the part of other countries designed to reestablish their desired rate of reserve growth" (Williamson 1973, 706).

Has this controversy been laid to rest? My answer is that it largely has been, and on the side of the demand-determined nature of the stock of international reserves. Table 3.2 provides a summary of the evolution of international reserves from 1970, before the United States closed its official gold window, to 2011. International reserves today are predominantly held in the form of foreign exchange, the most elastic component. That was not always the case; less than 50 percent of international reserves were in foreign exchange in 1970. However, today gold is clearly at the bottom of the pile of countries' international reserves. The concerns John expressed in 1977 that gold would become remonetized and once again distort the IMS have not been realized.[16] Even with a special allocation of SDR of $33.5 billion and a general allocation of SDR of $250 billion in August 2009, the share of SDR in international reserves remains trivial. The share of reserve positions in the IMF also is very small, but this component fluctuates with borrowing from the IMF by member countries. The share reached a low of 0.3 percent at the end of 2007.

No country is forced to accumulate foreign exchange, but countries do so with a range of both precautionary and nonprecautionary motives. The authorities in each country choose the level and currency composition of their foreign exchange holdings. Countries set the demand for international reserves, and the supply, as a first approximation, is perfectly elastic.

The need today is not to control international liquidity because not doing so threatens to increase global inflation or deflation; rather the need is to limit distortions to the adjustment process associated with policies that lead to excessive accumulations of international reserves. With a near-unlimited demand for international reserves on the part of many emerging-market and developing countries—along with their capacity to control their exchange rates to permit a continuing increase in those reserves, or more precisely the associated current account surpluses—the international adjustment process has become severely distorted, as was amply demonstrated in the previous section. The notion that lack of access to temporary financing or that the so-called precautionary motive for accumulating reserves is the primary reason for the outsized accumulation of reserves by some countries is simply not credible in the current environment.

Seigniorage

One critique of the post–Bretton Woods IMS focused on the presumptive financial gains to the country, the United States, whose currency was almost exclusively used in international transactions, importantly including assets that are held in countries' foreign exchange reserves. As John wrote, "In so far as the issuer of money enjoys monopoly power, it is able to extract the difference between the value of produced money and the cost of producing it as 'seigniorage'" (Williamson 1973, 723).

John focused on the social saving that could be captured by international liquidity (reserve) management at the international level, via the issuance of a fiduciary reserve asset, and how that saving should be distributed. In the

---

16. See Truman (2012) for more detail on this point as well as evidence on the lack of connection between the growth of international reserves and inflation.

context of an SDR-based system, he favored distribution of the associated seigniorage to poor countries through a link between SDR allocations and aid.

Against this backdrop, what can we say about the volume and distribution of international seigniorage today? Historically, seigniorage was associated with a difference between the cost of producing currency and the face value of that currency in circumstances where the issuer enjoyed a complete monopoly or was in a privileged position because of the convenience associated with the use of that currency.

Four questions are addressed here. How large a benefit does the United States accrue from the expanding stock of foreign exchange reserves in dollars? How are the benefits accruing to other countries or areas whose currencies are used to denominate reserve assets? How have these benefits to the United States and other countries evolved over the past dozen years? And is the size and distribution of seigniorage associated with the use of assets denominated in national or regional currencies a major flaw in the IMS?

In answering these questions with some back-of-the-envelope calculations, I make the simplifying assumption that the benefit accrues to the government in lowering the cost of its borrowing.[17] Based on an assumption that this benefit is 30 basis points on the total stock of US gross general government debt, the estimated seigniorage gain to the United States in 2011 was $47 billion. However, in my view, that figure might well be overstated. The figure is two to three times the estimated seigniorage from the use of the dollar as a physical currency. Is this a big number? Compared with what? It amounts to 0.3 percent of US GDP in 2011.

If the reduction in the cost of financing US government debt were 100 basis points, rather than 30 basis points, the associated estimated annual flow of seigniorage would be $155 billion or 1 percent of US GDP. Abstracting from the fact that interest rates on US treasury obligations were very low at the end of 2011, it is implausible that for the entire prior decade the average interest rate on US government debt had been reduced to 3.6 percent from 4.6 percent.

Setting aside for the moment the evolution of the seigniorage benefit to the United States, we can use the same framework to estimate the seigniorage gain to the euro area from the demand for euro-denominated assets as part of other countries' international reserves. On the assumption that the gain to the euro area is proportionate to the gain to the United States, the estimated gain to the euro area from the denomination of reserve assets in euros was $18.7 billion, or 0.14 percent of euro area GDP. Table 3.3 estimates total seigniorage in 2011 of $75 billion and the results of calculations for the other three currencies in which members of the IMF reported the currency composition of reserves at the end of 2011 (sterling, yen, and Swiss franc).

What about reserves issued in "other" currencies, which are not individually allocated in the IMF's Currency Composition of Official Foreign Exchange

---

17. See Truman (2012) for more details on these calculations as well as estimates of the seigniorage associated with the physical use of the dollar and the euro internationally.

Table 3.3 Estimates of seigniorage from foreign exchange holdings in 1999, 2006, and 2011 based on 2011 effect of 30 basis points on US interest cost

Country/region	Share of reserves/ seigniorage[a] (percent)	Reserves in currency (billions of dollars)	Gross general government debt (billions of dollars)	Reserves/debt (percent)	Reserves/debt relative to the United States	Seigniorage (billions of dollars)	Seigniorage/ GDP (percent)
2011							
United States	62.2	6,343	15,537	40.1	1.00	46.6	0.31
Euro area	25.0	2,552	11,555	22.1	0.54	18.8	0.14
United Kingdom	3.8	390	1,994	19.6	0.49	2.9	0.12
Japan	3.5	359	13,466	2.7	0.07	2.6	0.04
Switzerland	0.1	12	309	3.9	0.10	0.1	0.02
All other	5.3	539	n.a.	n.a.	n.a.	4.0	n.a.
Total	100.0	10,195	n.a.	n.a.	n.a.	74.9	n.a.
2006							
United States	65.5	3,440	8,913	38.6	1.00	25.7	0.19
Euro area	25.1	1,318	7,374	17.9	0.46	9.9	0.09
United Kingdom	4.4	230	1,056	21.8	0.56	1.7	0.07
Japan	3.1	162	8,103	2.0	0.05	1.2	0.03
Switzerland	0.2	9	253	3.6	0.09	0.1	0.02
All other	1.7	94	n.a.	n.a.	n.a.	0.7	n.a.
Total	100.0	5,253	n.a.	n.a.	n.a.	39.3	n.a.

(continues on next page)

43

Table 3.3 Estimates of seigniorage from foreign exchange holdings in 1999, 2006, and 2011 based on 2011 effect of 30 basis points on US interest cost *(continued)*

Country/region	Share of reserves/ seigniorage[a] (percent)	Reserves in currency (billions of dollars)	Gross general government debt (billions of dollars)	Reserves/debt (percent)	Reserves/debt relative to the United States	Seigniorage (billions of dollars)	Seigniorage/ GDP (percent)
1999							
United States	71.0	1,255	5,691	22.2	1.00	9.45	0.10
Euro area	17.9	319	4,938	6.5	0.29	2.38	0.03
United Kingdom	2.8	51	656	7.8	0.35	0.38	0.03
Japan	6.4	114	5,845	2.0	0.09	0.84	0.02
Switzerland	0.2	4	164	2.4	0.11	0.03	0.01
All other	1.6	28	n.a.	n.a.	n.a.	0.21	n.a.
Total	100.0	1,782	n.a.	n.a.	n.a.	13.31	n.a.

n.a. = not available.

a. As explained in Truman (2012), a country or region's share in foreign exchange assets held in its currency is the same as its estimated share of total seigniorage.

Note: Elements may not add to totals because of rounding.

Sources: IMF COFER database, June 29, 2012, www.imf.org/external/np/sta/cofer/eng/index.htm (accessed on July 26, 2012); IMF, *World Economic Outlook* database, April 2012, www.imf.org/external/pubs/ft/weo/2012/01/weodata/index.aspx (accessed on July 27, 2012).

Reserves (COFER) database?[18] Statistical and anecdotal reports indicate that some countries hold their foreign exchange reserves in the currencies of at least eight other advanced countries, using the IMF's WEO category of advanced countries: Australia, Canada, Korea, Singapore, Sweden, Denmark, New Zealand, and Norway. The $539 billion in estimated foreign exchange holdings in "other" currencies in 2011 would amount to 8.5 percent of the eight countries' combined GDP and 16.9 percent of their combined gross general government debt. This evidence suggests that the international financial and monetary system is evolving even more rapidly than thought toward a more extended multicurrency system.

What does the amount of seigniorage from foreign currency reserve holdings as of the end of 2011 tell us about trends in seigniorage? To make such comparisons, it is appropriate to make an adjustment to the rate of seigniorage gain for the United States in 2011, as described in Truman (2012). My estimate is that total seigniorage about doubled between the end of 2006 and 2011, from $39 billion to $75 billion and from 0.07 percent to 0.1 percent of global GDP (table 3.3). However, going back to the end of 1999, the first year of the euro, total seigniorage increased almost five times, from $13 billion, or 0.04 percent of global GDP.

This takes us back to the basic question of whether the size and distribution of seigniorage associated with the use of assets denominated in national or regional currencies is a major flaw in the IMS today. I am not convinced that this has been a significant issue affecting the system's performance, or even its fairness, as the system has evolved over the past 40 years.

First, even if one accepts an estimate that there is $250 billion in global seigniorage today associated with a benefit to the United States of 100 basis points on the cost of issuing its government debt (and I would argue that the true figure is less than $75 billion), this is a feature of the system that has manifested itself only over the past half a dozen years. For most of the past 40 years, the annual flow of seigniorage was trivial; at 100 basis points it would have been about $45 billion for the world in 1999 or 0.14 percent of world GDP.

Second, seigniorage has become increasingly widely distributed, in particular over the past dozen years. One can reasonably expect that the distribution of seigniorage will continue to widen as the international monetary and financial system evolves into even more of a multicurrency system.

Third, as a practical matter, it is difficult to envisage efficient mechanisms to capture and redistribute the seigniorage associated with the accumulation of reserve assets denominated in the currencies of other countries or areas. Of course, $250 billion or even $75 billion might be worth trying to capture, assuming that one is prepared to reject the view that seigniorage is payment for services rendered and risks taken. But it properly belongs way down the list of possible reforms of the IMS.

---

18. The IMF's COFER database is available at www.imf.org/external/np/sta/cofer/eng/index.htm (accessed on July 26, 2012).

Fourth, all this is not to say that there is not a strong case for limiting the accumulation of international reserves.[19] A case also can be made for regular allocations of SDR as part of such a reform, but that case rests on the distortion of the adjustment process introduced by that behavior.

Stability of the Multicurrency System

Over the past 15 years at least, the international monetary and financial system has evolved toward a multicurrency system. The concern raised by some observers is that a multicurrency system will be unstable, as private and official holders of assets denominated in the various currencies abruptly and in large volume change the currency composition of their portfolios. Not much could be done to affect the behavior of the private sector without returning to tight controls on all international financial transactions and portfolios. A case could be made that the official sector should be alert to abrupt changes in private sector asset preferences and be prepared to intervene to offset their effects, but there does not seem to be much appetite for doing so among the authorities issuing the major currencies, with the possible exception of the Japanese.

On the other hand, if changes in the asset preferences of the official sector were regarded as a problem, this would strengthen the case for creating a substitution account to take a large portion of reserve holdings in all currencies off the market in exchange for SDR-denominated assets. To be effective, the establishment of a substitution account would have to be accompanied by restrictions on the accumulation of additional sizable balances of foreign exchange reserves or by a code of conduct governing the composition of reserve portfolios and changes in that composition.

It would be preferable, first, to consider what evidence we have that there is a problem. Are changes in the currency composition of international reserves contributing to exchange rate volatility? To provide a partial answer to this question, we used estimates of exchange-rate-adjusted shares of international reserves from the IMF COFER database for 1999 to 2011, employing the method described in Truman and Wong (2006).[20] We estimated regressions of log changes in quarterly average exchange rates on log quarterly changes in exchange-rate-adjusted currency (quantity) shares of foreign exchange reserves. In general, we found no effect. The exception was in the case of changes in the share of the yen. The coefficient for the current quarter had the expected right sign, but it was only marginally significant. Moreover, the coefficient

19. See Gagnon (2011, 2012a, 2012b) for forceful presentations of this case.

20. If we did not adjust for the effect of exchange rate changes on shares of foreign exchange reserves, we would introduce a spurious positive correlation between changes in shares and changes in exchange rates even if the countries holding the reserves had not acted to adjust the currency composition of those reserves. If the dollar depreciates, the dollar's share in total reserves declines as the result of the devaluation of the existing stock of dollar-denominated assets relative to the dollar value of assets held in other currencies. See Truman (2012) for more details on these tests.

was small, and the change in the yen's quantity share over the period was a 55 percent decline, implying that the foreign exchange value of the dollar was boosted by the reduction in the yen's share.

How should these results be interpreted? The currency composition of international reserves at the aggregate level is influenced by many factors, including which countries are accumulating reserves, their asset preferences, and the factors affecting both their reserve accumulation and asset preferences. One cannot prove a negative: that the reallocation of official foreign exchange portfolios will never be a problem. But I conclude from this evidence that the evolving multicurrency international monetary and financial system is not at risk from this source. I further conclude that the substitution account proposal, whatever its merits may have been in a more structured IMS, today is a solution in search of a problem. The evidence presented earlier on the trend toward somewhat reduced exchange rate variability also suggests that the private sector portfolio reallocations have not been a source of instability in the global financial system. This is not to say that all private sector capital flows push exchange rates toward values consistent with external balance, but only that they are not a dominant source of instability.

Conclusion

This chapter has evaluated the extent to which the concerns that John Williamson had about the IMS 40 years ago are, or should be, concerns today. In this concluding section I also assess progress in reforming the IMS and prospects for future reforms.

Abiding Concerns?

Exchange rate variability appears to have been substantial over the past 40 years. However, because economists and policymakers lack a robust model of exchange rate determination, it is difficult to know how much variability is too much. The evidence provided in this chapter suggests that, in general, exchange rate variability has declined somewhat in recent years. However, John Williamson's concerns about exchange rate variability have been less about variability per se and more about countries' exchange rate policies or lack thereof and their consequences for the international external adjustment process. This process over the past 40 years has shown no improvement compared with the 1960s.

Turning to the management of international liquidity, the good news is that two of John's concerns 40 years ago have not materialized. Gold has not reemerged as a central reserve asset. International reserves, almost exclusively in the form of foreign exchange reserves, have expanded rapidly, in particular over the past 15 years. Moreover, the monetarists' link between rapid reserve growth and increased inflation has not been widely observed. Without a doubt, the expansion of international reserves has been demand-determined by the policies of individual countries accumulating those reserves rather than supply-determined by the policies of countries whose currencies are used to denominate reserve assets. The policies of the former group are an important distortion to the international external adjustment process.

Over the past decade or so, we have observed the evolution toward a multi-currency international monetary and financial system. In this context, any concerns about the maldistribution of seigniorage associated with countries' choices of currencies for the denomination of reserve assets are being defused. Moreover, seigniorage is not, and probably never was, substantial.

Private and official portfolio diversification in an increasingly multicur-rency international monetary and financial system has the potential to be destabilizing. But this chapter has provided indirect evidence that official reserve diversification has not magnified exchange rate movements.

Progress and Prospects for Reform

Although John Williamson's concerns about the IMS expressed 40 years ago have not materialized to the degree that the global economy and finan-cial system have been substantially adversely affected, the system could have worked better. The principal failings, as was the case with the Bretton Woods system that preceded the current arrangements, involve the working of the adjustment process, not the management of international liquidity. However, both could be improved.

The central challenge posed by the adjustment process is an unwillingness of participating countries to establish rules and procedures and to abide by them. In Truman (2010a), I proposed a comprehensive approach to strength-ening IMF surveillance that involves the establishment of norms, a procedure for reviewing compliance with those norms, and consequences in the form of escalating sanctions for countries that are found not to be in compliance.

It is unlikely that countries in the immediate future will agree to such an approach, although progress is always possible. An encouraging step is the *Pilot External Sector Report* recently released by the IMF (2012b). The report is a companion to the IMF Executive Board's approval, on July 18, 2012, of a new decision on bilateral and multilateral surveillance (IMF 2012a). The decision provides a formal framework for integrating the two types of IMF surveillance and establishing explicit procedures for multilateral surveillance, for example as part of annual Article IV consultations. Previously, only bilateral surveil-lance was covered by a formal decision and that surveillance was restricted to a limited set of policies. Multilateral surveillance and the stability of the global economic and financial system were in procedural limbo. Now, for the first time, the IMF Executive Board has recognized explicitly that a member's policies may affect other members and, consequently, the operation of the international monetary system as a whole. By agreeing to the decision, each member now implicitly accepts some responsibility in its own policies for global economic and financial stability. Operationally, the decision gives the

IMF staff and management the authority to discuss how a member's policies may affect the international monetary system and to report on those discussions to the Executive Board and to the public at large. In the past, members could, and did, decline to discuss such matters with IMF staff and management. For a number of years, some have been advocating addressing this loophole (Truman 2010a). More important, this type of framework would help to implement John's long-time recommendation, drawing on the reference rate proposal of Ethier and Bloomfield (1975), to establish norms for exchange rates, or, more formally, fundamental equilibrium exchange rates.

The *External Sector Report* itself provided for the first time a "multilaterally consistent analysis of the external positions of major world economies" (IMF 2012b, 1). The report defines an external imbalance for a country as the gap between its actual current account and the value of its current account that would be consistent with fundamental economic and financial conditions and desirable policies for the country (IMF 2012b, 4). For 28 major economies, the report provides estimates of differences between those countries' real effective exchange rates and the effective exchange rates that would be consistent with fundamentals and desirable policies (IMF 2012b, 11). The latter are exchange rate norms, fundamental equilibrium exchange rates, or reference rates even if the report did not use these precise terms that are associated with John's work.

One can quarrel with the estimates in the report, which are partly based on judgments and partly based on models, which are less normative than some would like because they include some variables that are merely a reflection of past behavior. Some of the results are far from intuitive, and the report itself is short on explanations. However, the report provides the basis for policy conversations between the IMF management and staff and the countries, between the particular country and its partners, and involving outside analysts.

Consequently, in my view, even if he has reservations about the *Pilot External Sector Report* itself, John Williamson should take some satisfaction and considerable pride that approaches to improving the international external adjustment process that he has advocated for 40 years are coming closer to fruition. These recent developments are evolutionary, not revolutionary. Moreover, the key to their success will be how the IMF staff and management implement the new integrated surveillance decision, including future External Sector Reports, and how responsive the general membership of the IMF is to that implementation. We are still a long way from a rules-based system of exchange rate norms that are supported by guidelines with respect to intervention and other policies influencing exchange rates and with sanctions for deviations (Williamson 2006, 158), but we are closer to that objective.

With respect to the management of international liquidity, the first requirement is to recognize that the global economic and financial system remains underprepared financially to deal with crises. I favor a doubling of IMF quotas to $1 trillion in effective available financing and a doubling of the IMF New Arrangements to Borrow to $500 billion, making a total potential IMF financing capacity of $1.5 trillion.

Turning to the SDR, I do not see it becoming the principal reserve asset in the IMS. Nor do I foresee the development of a private market in SDR-denominated assets; the demand is not there and a convincing case has not been made for official sponsorship. However, the SDR has a useful role to play in the IMS. In Truman (2010b), I advocated giving the IMF temporary expedited authority to allocate SDR in a crisis. I have also advocated an experiment under which $200 billion in SDR would be allocated per year for five years for a total of $1 trillion, with the authorities tracking whether such substantial cumulative allocation affects the propensity of countries to accumulate foreign exchange reserves (Truman 2011b). Absent such evidence, or a commitment on the part of IMF members to limit their reserve accumulations, I would not join John in support of a resumption of regular SDR allocations, and I doubt it will happen.

All of these steps would not turn the IMF into an international lender of last resort. For that reason, I favor an addition to the global financial safety net that would institutionalize a global network of swaps centered on the central banks that issue the principal international currencies: the US dollar, euro, sterling, yen, and Swiss franc.

The principal benefits of the Bretton Woods international monetary system remain today: an open and cooperative international trade and financial system, a generally prosperous global economy, and an IMF essentially in the center of the system. A more controversial issue is whether the international economic and financial system is more crisis-prone today than it was prior to 1971, and, if so, whether the post–Bretton Woods system can be held responsible. I would be inclined to argue no on both points. In the 1960s, the advanced countries of the day had their share of crises. Their global ramifications were smaller, but that is primarily because the global economic and financial system was not as integrated. Not everyone in the mid-1970s would have predicted that the international monetary nonsystem would have performed as well as it has.

This conclusion, to the extent that one accepts it, does not mean that, with a reformed or more coherent international monetary system, global economic and financial performance might not have been better in the past and be better in the future. Therefore, consideration should continue to be given to international monetary reform and the role of the IMF in this process, drawing on an impressive body of work by John Williamson. The most promising initiatives are enhancing the role of the IMF with respect to the international adjustment process and as the international lender of last resort. But any reforms will be evolutionary, rather than revolutionary.

References

Bottrill, Anthony, and John Williamson. 1971. The Impact of Customs Unions on Trade in Manufactures. *Oxford Economic Papers* 23, no. 3: 323–51.

Cline, William R., and John Williamson. 2008. *New Estimates of Fundamental Equilibrium Exchange Rates*. Policy Briefs in International Economics 08-7. Washington: Peterson Institute for International Economics.

Cline, William R., and John Williamson. 2012. *Estimates of Fundamental Equilibrium Exchange Rates, May 2012*. Policy Briefs in International Economics 12-14. Washington: Peterson Institute for International Economics.

Ethier, Wilfred, and Arthur Bloomfield. 1975. *Managing the Managed Float*. Princeton Essays in International Finance 112. Princeton, NJ: Princeton University Press.

Gagnon, Joseph E. (with Marc Hinterschweiger). 2011. *Flexible Exchange Rates for a Stable World Economy*. Washington: Peterson Institute for International Economics.

Gagnon, Joseph E. 2012a. *Global Imbalances and Foreign Asset Expansion by Developing-Economy Central Banks*. Working Paper 12-5. Washington: Peterson Institute for International Economics.

Gagnon, Joseph E. 2012b. *Combating Widespread Currency Manipulation*. Policy Briefs in International Economics 12-19. Washington: Peterson Institute for International Economics.

IMF (International Monetary Fund). 1985. *The International Monetary Fund 1972–1978: Cooperation on Trial: Documents,* Volume III, ed. Margaret Garritsen de Vries. Washington.

IMF (International Monetary Fund). 2012a. *Bilateral and Multilateral Surveillance: Executive Board Decision—July 18*. Washington.

IMF (International Monetary Fund). 2012b. *Pilot External Sector Report*. Washington.

Truman, Edwin M. 2010a. *Strengthening IMF Surveillance: A Comprehensive Proposal*. Policy Briefs in International Economics 10-29. Washington: Peterson Institute for International Economics.

Truman, Edwin M. 2010b. *The G-20 and International Financial Institution Governance*. Working Paper 10-13. Washington: Peterson Institute for International Economics.

Truman, Edwin M. 2011a. *Asian Regional Policy Coordination*. Working Paper 11-21. Washington: Peterson Institute for International Economics.

Truman, Edwin M. 2011b. Three Evolutionary Proposals for Reform of the International Monetary System. Extension of prepared remarks delivered at the Bank of Italy's Conference in Memory of Tommaso Padoa-Schioppa, Rome, December 16.

Truman, Edwin M. 2012. *John Williamson and the Evolution of the International Monetary System*. Working Paper 12-13. Washington: Peterson Institute for International Economics.

Truman, Edwin M., and Anna Wong. 2006. *The Case for an International Reserve Diversification Standard*. Working Paper 06-2. Washington: Peterson Institute for International Economics.

Volcker, Paul A. 2012. Toward a New World of Finance. Keynote address at the Asia-Global Dialogue 2012, Hong Kong, May 31.

Williamson, John. 1963. Liquidity and the Multiple Key Currency Proposal. *American Economic Review* 3, no. 2: 427–43.

Williamson, John. 1965. *The Crawling Peg*. Princeton Essays in International Finance 50. Princeton, NJ: Princeton University Press.

Williamson, John. 1973. Surveys in Applied Economics: International Liquidity. *Economic Journal* 83, no. 331: 685–746.

Williamson, John. 1976. The Benefits and Costs of an International Monetary Nonsystem. In *Reflections on Jamaica*, ed. Edward M. Bernstein et al. Princeton Essays in International Finance 115. Princeton, NJ: Princeton University Press.

Williamson, John. 1977. *The Failure of World Monetary Reform, 1971–1974*. Sunbury-on-Thames, Middlesex: Nelson & Sons.

Williamson, John. 1985. On the System in Bretton Woods. *American Economic Review* 75, no. 2: 74–79.

Williamson, John. 2006. Revamping the International Monetary System. In *Reforming the IMF for the 21st Century*, ed. Edwin M. Truman. Special Report 19. Washington: Institute for International Economics.

Williamson, John. 2009a. *Understanding Special Drawing Rights (SDRs)*. Policy Briefs in International Economics 09-11. Washington: Peterson Institute for International Economics.

Williamson, John. 2009b. *Why SDRs Could Rival the Dollar*. Policy Briefs in International Economics 09-20. Washington: Peterson Institute for International Economics.

4

Economic and Monetary Union in Europe

PAUL DE GRAUWE AND YUEMEI JI

The traditional theory of optimum currency areas has stressed that when countries are hit by asymmetric shocks, they need a combination of flexibility (including mobility) in labor markets and some budgetary union that allows for transfers (Mundell 1961, McKinnon 1963, Kenen 1969). The euro area has experienced large asymmetric developments in competitiveness since 2000, with little flexibility and nonexistent budgetary union. It is little wonder that the euro area got into trouble, and it was all predicted by the optimal currency area theory. Many skeptics on both sides of the Atlantic now feel vindicated; some are even gloating.

However, while this optimum currency area analysis is certainly true, it is incomplete. What traditional optimum currency area analysis has overlooked is that there is another deep source of fragility in the euro area that, when it interacts with the asymmetry problem, can have lethal effects. This is the theme that will be developed in this chapter. It is a theme that has played an important role in John Williamson's research.

The Fragility of the Euro Area

Members of a monetary union issue debt in a currency over which they have no control. As a result, the governments of these countries cannot give a guarantee that the cash will always be available to pay out bondholders at maturity.

Paul De Grauwe is the John Paulson Professor at the London School of Economics. He was a member of the Belgian parliament from 1991 to 2003. Yuemei Ji is a researcher at LICOS, University of Leuven, and a visiting fellow at the Center for European Policy Studies, Brussels. The authors thank Uri Dadush and John Williamson for comments on a previous draft at the organizational workshop for this volume held at the Peterson Institute for International Economics on April 20, 2012.

It is altogether possible these governments might find that when a given bond comes due, the liquidity is lacking to pay out bondholders.

This is not the case in "standalone countries," which are countries that issue debt in their own currency. These countries can give a guarantee to the bondholders that the cash will always be available to pay them out. If the government were to experience a shortage of liquidity it would call upon the central bank to provide that liquidity. And there is no limit to the capacity of a central bank to do so.

The absence of a guarantee that the cash will always be available creates fragility in a monetary union. Member countries are susceptible to distrusting one another. When investors fear some payment difficulty—triggered by a recession, for example—they sell that particular country's government bonds. This has two effects. It leads to a liquidity outflow, and it raises the interest rate as the investors who have sold the government bonds look for safer places to invest. This "sudden stop" can lead to a situation in which the government cannot roll over its debt except at prohibitive interest rates.

The ensuing liquidity crisis can easily degenerate into a solvency crisis. As the interest rate shoots up, the country is likely to be pushed into recession. This tends to reduce government revenues and increase the deficit and debt levels. The combination of increasing interest rates and debt levels can push the government into default. There is a self-fulfilling element in this dynamic. When investors fear default, they act in such a way that default becomes more likely. In other words, a country can become insolvent because investors fear default.[1]

The liquidity crises in a monetary union also make possible the emergence of multiple equilibria. Countries that are distrusted by the market are forced into a bad equilibrium characterized by high interest rates and the need to impose strong budgetary austerity programs that push these countries into a deep recession. Conversely, countries that are trusted become the recipients of liquidity inflows that lower the interest rate and boost the economy. They are pushed into a good equilibrium.

The problem for member countries of a monetary union is similar to the problems faced by emerging countries that issue debt in a foreign currency, usually the dollar. These countries can be confronted with a sudden stop when capital inflows come to an immediate halt, leading to a liquidity crisis. This problem has been analyzed intensively by economists—particularly John Williamson—who have concluded that financial markets acquire great power in these countries and can force them into default (Eichengreen, Hausmann, and Panizza 2005). This has led John to criticize the movement to liberalize capital flows that produced significant macroeconomic dislocations and ultimately led to large speculative crises with huge costs for the countries involved (Williamson 1990, 1999).

---

1. See De Grauwe (2011a) for a more detailed analysis.

It is useful to go through the analysis that John has developed in this context. Emerging countries that are forced to open up their capital markets become recipients of large capital inflows. These inflows lead to a boom mainly in the nontraded goods sector, including the real estate sector. The boom is transformed into a bubble leading to excessive debt accumulation. After the bubble comes the crash and a sudden stop in capital flows, leading large sectors of the economy into default. A deep recession follows.

For many southern European countries, the euro area was the equivalent of a sudden opening of capital markets. It induced large capital inflows in countries such as Ireland, Spain, and Greece, which in turn led to booms and bubbles in these countries. When the crash occurred, liquidity was squeezed out of these countries. The liquidity crises degenerated into solvency crises and deep recessions. The countries were pushed into a bad equilibrium. Had policymakers read some of John's work of the 1980s and 1990s, they may not have been as unprepared as they turned out to be when the sovereign debt crises erupted in the euro area in 2010.

This paper elaborates on the theme of multiple equilibria that can arise in a monetary union without a lender of last resort. We first develop a simple model showing how such multiple equilibria can arise. The model is essentially an extension of Obstfeld (1986).[2] We then test the hypothesis on the euro area countries, compare it against standalone countries, and derive policy implications.

A Simple Model of Good and Bad Equilibria

This section presents a simple model illustrating how multiple equilibria can arise. The starting point is that there is a cost and a benefit of defaulting on government debt, and investors take this calculus of the sovereign into account. We will assume that the country involved is subject to a shock, which takes the form of a decline in government revenues. Such a decline may be caused by a recession or a loss of competitiveness. We will call this a "solvency shock." The greater this shock, the greater the loss of solvency. We concentrate first on the benefit side, which is represented in figure 4.1. The horizontal axis shows the solvency shock, and the vertical axis represents the benefit of defaulting. Since there are many ways and degrees to default, we simplify by assuming this takes the form of a haircut of a fixed percentage. The benefit of defaulting in this way is that the government can reduce the interest burden on the outstanding debt. As a result, after the default the government will have to apply fewer austerity measures, that is, it will have to reduce spending and/ or increase taxes by less than without the default. Since austerity is politically costly, the government profits from the default.

---

2. See also Gros (2011). The classical article establishing the possibility of multiple equilibria in the bond markets is Calvo (1988). For a more recent analysis, see Corsetti and Dedola (2011).

Figure 4.1 Benefits of default after a solvency shock

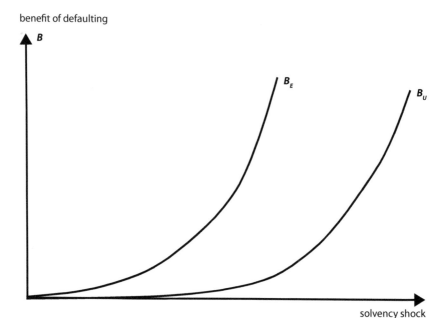

benefit of defaulting

Note: B_U is the benefit of a default that investors do not expect to happen. B_E is the benefit of a default that investors expect to happen.

Source: Authors' illustration.

A major insight of the model is that the benefit of a default depends on whether or not the default is expected. We show two curves representing the benefit of a default. B_U is the benefit of a default that investors do not expect to happen, while B_E is the benefit of a default that investors expect to happen.

Let us first concentrate on the B_U curve. It is upward sloping because when the solvency shock increases, the benefit of a default for the sovereign goes up. The reason is that when the solvency shock is large—that is, the decline in tax income is large—the cost of austerity is substantial. Default then becomes more attractive for the sovereign. We have drawn this curve to be nonlinear, but this is not essential for the argument. We distinguish three factors that affect the position and steepness of the B_U curve:

- *Initial government debt level.* The higher this level, the greater the benefit of a default. Thus with a higher initial debt level the B_U curve will rotate upward.

- *Efficiency of the tax system.* In a country with an inefficient tax system, the government cannot easily increase taxation. Thus in such a country the option of defaulting becomes more attractive. The B_U curve rotates upward.

Figure 4.2 Costs and benefits of default after a solvency shock

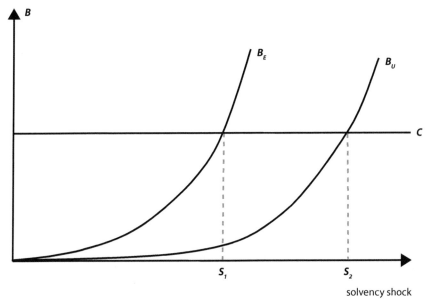

benefit of defaulting

Note: C is the fixed cost. See also note to figure 4.1.

Source: Authors' illustration.

- *Size of the external debt.* When external debt takes a large proportion of total government debt there will be less domestic political resistance against default, making the latter more attractive (the B_U curve rotates upward).

Let us now turn to the B_E curve. This shows the benefit of a default when investors anticipate such a default. It is located above the B_U curve because when investors expect a default, they will sell government bonds. As a result, the interest rate on government bonds increases. This raises the government budget deficit, requiring a more intense austerity program of spending cuts and tax hikes. Thus, default becomes more attractive. For every solvency shock, the benefits of default will now be greater than they were when the default was not anticipated.

We now introduce the cost side of the default. The cost of a default arises from the fact that, when defaulting, the government suffers a loss of reputation. This loss of reputation will make it difficult for the government to borrow in the future. We will make the simplifying assumption that this is a fixed cost in figure 4.2, which presents the fixed cost (C) with the benefit curves.

We now have the tools to analyze the equilibrium of the model. We distinguish between three types of solvency shocks: small, intermediate, and large.

Figure 4.3 Good and bad equilibria

benefit of defaulting

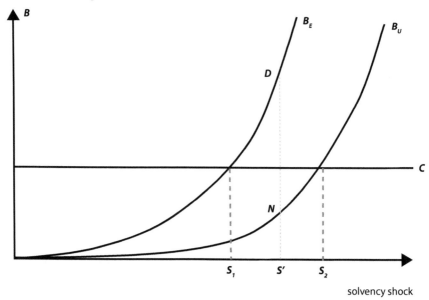

Note: Point *D* is the bad equilibrium point that leads to default; point *N* is the good equilibrium that does not lead to default. See also note to figure 4.2.

Source: Authors' illustration.

Take a small solvency shock, $S < S_1$. This could be, for example, the shocks that Germany and the Netherlands experienced during the debt crisis. For this small shock the costs of a default are always larger than the benefits (of both an expected and an unexpected default). Thus the government will not want to default. When expectations are rational, investors will not expect a default. As a result, a no-default equilibrium can be sustained.

Let us now analyze a large solvency shock, $S > S_2$. This could be, for example, the shock experienced by Greece. For such large shocks, the costs of a default are always smaller than the benefits (of both an expected and an unexpected default). Thus the government will want to default. In a rational expectations framework, investors will anticipate this. As a result, a default is inevitable.

We now turn to an intermediate shock, $S_1 < S < S_2$. This could be, for example, the shocks experienced by Ireland, Portugal, and Spain. For these intermediate shocks we obtain an indeterminacy—that is, two equilibria are possible. Which one will prevail depends on what is expected. To see this, suppose the solvency shock is S' (figure 4.3). In this case there are two potential equilibria, D and N. In the case of point D, investors expect a default (D is located on the B_E line). This has the effect of making the benefit of a default larger than the cost C. Thus, the government will default. D is an equilibrium that is consistent with expectations.

But point N is equally good candidate to be an equilibrium point. In N, investors do not expect a default (N is on the B_U line). As a result, the benefit of a default is lower than the cost. Thus the government will not default. It follows that N is also an equilibrium point that is consistent with expectations.

Thus we obtain two possible equilibria: a bad one (D) that leads to default, and a good one (N) that does not lead to default. Both are equally possible. Which one of these outcomes occurs depends on what investors expect. If they expect a default, there will be one; if they do not expect a default, there will be none. This remarkable result is due to the self-fulfilling nature of expectations.

Since there is a lot of uncertainty about the likelihood of default, and since investors have very little scientific foundation to calculate probabilities of default (there has been none in western Europe in the last 60 years), expectations are likely to be driven mainly by market sentiments of optimism and pessimism. Small changes in these market sentiments can lead to large movements from one type of equilibrium to another. We do not model the dynamics of these changes, which are likely to be influenced by mimicking and herding behavior (Kirman 1993).

The possibility of multiple equilibria is unlikely to occur in a standalone country that can issue sovereign debt in its own currency. Standalone countries can always avoid outright default because the central bank can be forced to provide all the liquidity necessary to avoid such an outcome. This has the effect that there is only one benefit curve. In this case the government can still decide to default (if the solvency shock is large enough). But the country cannot be forced to do so by the whim of market expectations.

Testing the Theory[3]

The theory presented in the previous section leads to a number of testable propositions. We have seen that in a monetary union, distrust about a particular country's solvency leads to an increase in the government bond rate of that country and thus to an increase in the spread (the difference) with the bond rates of other countries. When such distrust occurs, these spreads are likely to significantly increase without much movement of the underlying fundamentals that influence the solvency of the country. More precisely, when market sentiments turn against a country the spreads are likely to exhibit the following features:

- large movements in the spreads over short periods,
- changes in the fundamental variables that cannot account for the total

---

3. This section is based on De Grauwe and Ji (2012).

change in the spreads,[4] that is, movements in the spreads that appear to be dissociated from the fundamentals, and

- changes in the spreads that are clustered in time.

Thus one way to test the theory is first to estimate a model that explains the spreads by a number of fundamental variables. In a second stage we apply a structural break test to see how the model has behaved over time. In a third stage we track the estimated errors of the model, that is, the deviations of the observed spreads from the spreads estimated by the model. More specifically we want to identify periods during which market sentiments drive the spreads away from their underlying fundamentals. We then estimate the model with time dummies that are independent from the fundamentals, and analyze how much of the total variation of the spreads can be accounted for by these time dummies.

In order for such a test to be convincing, it will be important to analyze a control group of countries that do not belong to a monetary union. We will therefore take a sample of standalone countries and analyze whether in this control group one observes similar movements of the spreads away from their underlying fundamentals. Our theory predicts that this should not happen in countries that have full control over the currency in which they issue their debt.

A Basic Fundamental Model

Our specification of the fundamentals model relies on the existing litera-ture.[5] The most common fundamental variables found in this literature are variables measuring the sustainability of government debt. We will use two alternative concepts: the debt-to-GDP ratio and the "fiscal space," which is described below. In addition, we use the current account position, the real effective exchange rate, and the rate of economic growth as fundamental vari-ables affecting the spreads. The effects of these fundamental variables on the spreads are described below.

- When the *government debt-to-GDP ratio* increases, the burden of the debt service increases, leading to an increasing probability of default. This in

---

4. Note that we are not implying that fundamentals do not matter. In fact, small movements of fundamentals can trigger large movements in spreads, because they trigger the fear factor (as in the case of a bank run).

5. See Aizenman and Hutchison (2012), Arghyrou and Kontonikas (2010), Attinasi, Checherita, and Nickel (2009), Beirne and Fratzscher (2012), Caceres, Guzzo, and Segoviano (2010), Caporale and Girardi (2011), Gerlach, Schulz, and Wolff (2010), Gibson, Hall, and Tavlas (2011), and Schuknecht, von Hagen, and Wolswijk (2010). There is of course a vast literature on the spreads in the government bond markets in general. See, for example, the classic papers of Eaton, Gersovitz, and Stiglitz (1986) and Eichengreen and Mody (2000). Much of this literature has been influenced by the debt problems of emerging economies. See, for example, Edwards (1984, 1986), and Min (1999).

turn leads to an increase in the spread, which is a risk premium investors demand to compensate them for the increased default risk.[6]

- *Fiscal space* is defined as the ratio of the government debt to total tax revenues. Aizenman and Hutchison (2012) argue that this is a better measure of debt sustainability than the debt-to-GDP ratio. A country may have a low debt-to-GDP ratio, yet find it difficult to service its debt because of a low capacity to raise taxes. In this case the ratio of government debt to tax revenues will be high, that is, it takes a lot of years to generate the tax revenues necessary to service the debt.

- The *current account* has a similar effect on the spreads. Current account deficits should be interpreted as increases in the net foreign debt of the country as a whole (private and official residents). This is also likely to increase the default risk of the government because if the increase in net foreign debt arises from the private sector's overspending, it will lead to default risk in the private sector. However, the government is likely to be affected because such defaults have a negative effect on economic activity, inducing a decline in government revenues and an increase in budget deficits. If the increase in net foreign indebtedness arises from government overspending, it directly increases the government's debt service, and thus the default risk.

- The *real effective exchange rate* as a measure of competitiveness can be considered an early warning variable indicating that a country that experiences a real appreciation will run into competitiveness problems, which in turn will lead to future current account deficits and debt problems. Investors may then demand an additional risk premium.

- *Economic growth* affects the ease with which a government is capable of servicing its debt. The lower the growth rate the more difficult it is to raise tax revenues. As a result a decline of economic growth will increase the incentive of the government to default, raising the default risk and the spread.

We specify the econometric equation in both a linear and a nonlinear form. The reason why we also specify a nonlinear relationship between the spread and the debt-to-GDP ratio is because each decision to default is a discontinuous one, and one that leads to high potential losses. Thus, as the debt-to-GDP ratio increases, investors realize that they come closer to the default decision, making them more sensitive to a given increase in the debt-to-GDP ratio (Giavazzi and Pagano 1990).

The linear equation is specified as follows:

$$I_{it} = \alpha + z * CA_{it} + \gamma * Debt_{it} + \mu * REE_{it} + \delta * Growth_{it} + \alpha_i + u_{it}, \qquad (4.1)$$

---

6. We also experimented with the government-deficit-to-GDP ratio. But this variable does not have a significant effect in any of the regressions we estimated.

where I_{it} is the interest rate spread of country i in period t,[7] CA_{it} is the current account surplus of country i in period t, $Debt_{it}$ is either the government debt-to-GDP ratio or the fiscal space of country i in period t, REE_{it} is the real effective exchange rate, $Growth_{it}$ is the GDP growth rate, α is the constant term, and α_i is country i's fixed effect. The latter variable measures the idiosyncrasies of a country that affect its spread and that are not time dependent. For example, the fixed effect captures the efficiency of the tax system, quality of governance, and many other variables that are country-specific.

The nonlinear specification is as follows:

$$I_{it} = \alpha + z * CA_{it} + \gamma_1 * Debt_{it} + \mu * REE_{it} + \delta * Growth_{it} + \gamma_2 * (Debt_{it})^2$$
$$+ \alpha_i + u_{it} \tag{4.2}$$

A methodological note should be made here. In the existing empirical literature there has been a tendency to add a lot of other variables on the right-hand side of the two equations. In particular, researchers have added risk measures and ratings by rating agencies as additional explanatory variables of the spreads. The problem with this is that risk variables and ratings are unlikely to be exogenous. When a sovereign debt crisis erupts in the euro area, all these risk variables increase, including the so-called systemic risk variables. Similarly, as rating agencies tend to react to movements in spreads, the ratings also are affected by increases in the spreads. Including these variables in the regression is likely to improve the fit dramatically, but without enhancing the explanation of the spreads. In fact, the addition of these variables creates a risk of false claims that the fundamental model explains the spreads well.

We estimated the linear and nonlinear equations for two groups of countries, the member countries of the euro area and a group of standalone countries. In order to make the two groups comparable we selected among the standalone countries those with GDP per capita greater than or equal to $20,000 and population greater than or equal to 5 million. With these criteria we obtain 14 standalone developed countries[8] (Australia, Canada, Czech Republic, Denmark, Hungary, Japan, South Korea, Norway, Poland, Singapore, Sweden, Switzerland, the United Kingdom, and the United States).

After having established by way of a Hausmann test that the random-effect model is inappropriate, we used a fixed-effect model. A fixed-effect model helps to control for unobserved time-invariant variables and produces unbiased estimates of the fundamental variables. The results of estimating the linear and nonlinear models are shown in table 4.1 for the euro area countries

---

7. The spread is defined as the difference of the government bond rate of each country i with German government bond rate.

8. Saudi Arabia and United Arab Emirates are excluded because their economies are heavily dependent on oil export. Hong Kong, Israel, and Taiwan are excluded because of a lack of some relevant data. Slovakia is a special case as it joined the euro area in 2009 and should not be included in the standalone sample.

Table 4.1   Government bond spreads in euro area countries, 2000Q1–2011Q3

Explanatory variable	(1)	(2)	(3)	(4)
Current-account-to-GDP ratio	0.0243	0.0409	0.0191	0.0356
	[0.0417]	[0.0425]	[0.0442]	[0.0414]
Real effective exchange rate	0.0278	0.0181	0.0206	0.0047
	[0.0179]	[0.0201]	[0.0179]	[0.0136]
Growth rate	−0.0698	−0.0526***	−0.0604	−0.0427***
	[0.0496]	[0.0103]	[0.0411]	[0.0053]
Debt-to-GDP ratio	0.0818***	−0.0553*		
	[0.0148]	[0.0300]		
Debt-to-GDP ratio squared		0.0009***		
		[0.0002]		
Fiscal space			2.7284***	−1.8316***
			[0.4589]	[0.2557]
Fiscal space squared				0.9270***
				[0.0634]
Country fixed effect	Controlled	Controlled	Controlled	Controlled
Number of observations	470	470	470	470
R^2	0.6601	0.7989	0.6960	0.8549

Notes: Cluster at country level and robust standard errors are shown in brackets. * $p < 0.1$, ** $p < 0.05$, *** $p < 0.01$. Columns (1) and (3) are linear specifications; columns (2) and (4) are nonlinear specifications.

Source: Authors' calculations.

and table 4.2 for the standalone countries. The results of tables 4.1 and 4.2 lead to the interpretations below.

First, the debt-to-GDP ratio and the fiscal space variables have significant effects on spreads in the euro area. The fiscal space variable appears to have a slightly higher explanatory power, as can be seen from the fact that the R^2 is higher when we use the fiscal space variable instead of the debt-to-GDP ratio. In contrast, the debt-to-GDP ratio and the fiscal space variables have little impact on the spreads in the standalone countries (the coefficients are much lower and insignificant).

Second, the nonlinear specification for both the debt-to-GDP ratio and the fiscal space variables improve the fit in the euro area countries. This can be seen from the fact that the R^2 in table 4.1 increases in the nonlinear specification. In addition, the squared debt-to-GDP ratio and the fiscal space variables are very significant. Thus, an increasing debt-to-GDP ratio and fiscal space[9]

---

9. The term "fiscal space" is probably a misnomer. It is defined as the ratio of government debt to tax revenues. Thus when this ratio increases fiscal space as defined here increases. The term "fiscal space" suggests that there is then less fiscal space.

Table 4.2 Government bond spreads in standalone countries, 2000Q1–2011Q3

Explanatory variable	(1)	(2)	(3)	(4)
Current-account-to-GDP ratio	0.0184	0.0200	0.0161	0.0137
	[0.0166]	[0.0182]	[0.0183]	[0.0211]
Real effective exchange rate	0.0019	0.0030	0.0013	0.0006
	[0.0082]	[0.0074]	[0.0081]	[0.0081]
Change in exchange rate	−0.0273**	−0.0234**	−0.0274**	−0.0264**
	[0.0098]	[0.0098]	[0.0097]	[0.0095]
Growth rate	−0.0229	−0.0253	−0.0249	−0.0282
	[0.0284]	[0.0286]	[0.0290]	[0.0304]
Debt-to-GDP ratio	0.0102	−0.0164		
	[0.0077]	[0.0124]		
Debt-to-GDP ratio squared		0.0001***		
		[0.0000]		
Fiscal space			0.2258	−0.2155
			[0.2014]	[0.4528]
Fiscal space squared				0.0474
				[0.0444]
Country fixed effect	Controlled	Controlled	Controlled	Controlled
Number of observations	658	658	658	658
R^2	0.8423	0.8504	0.8409	0.8439

Notes: Cluster at country level and robust standard errors are shown in brackets. * $p < 0.1$,
** $p < 0.05$, *** $p < 0.01$. Columns (1) and (3) are linear specifications; columns (2) and (4) are nonlinear specifications.

Source: Authors' calculations.

have a nonlinear effect on the spreads in the euro area, that is, a given increase of these ratios has a significantly higher impact on the spread when these ratios are high. The contrast with the standalone countries is strong. In these countries no such nonlinear effects exist. Financial markets do not seem to be concerned with the size of the government debt and the fiscal space and their effects on the spreads of standalone countries, despite the fact that the variation of these ratios is of a similar order of magnitude as the one observed in the euro area. This result tends to confirm the fragility hypothesis of the euro area, which is that financial markets are less tolerant of high debt-to-GDP ratios and fiscal space in the euro area countries than in standalone countries.

As the theory predicts, the GDP growth rate has a negative impact on the spreads in the euro area. In the standalone countries no significant growth effect is detected. The other fundamental variables (the current-account-to-GDP ratio and the real effective exchange rate) do not seem to have significant effects on the spreads either in the euro area or in the standalone countries. A change in the exchange rate seems to have a significant impact on the spread, but the sign is not expected. The negative sign suggests that "carry trade" has

Table 4.3   Spreads and structural breaks in the euro area, 2000Q1–2011Q3

Explanatory variable	Precrisis	Postcrisis	Precrisis	Postcrisis
Current-account-to-GDP ratio	−0.0057 [0.0056]	0.0521 [0.0592]	−0.0058 [0.0054]	0.0203 [0.0524]
Real effective exchange rate	−0.0144*** [0.0035]	0.2912** [0.1111]	−0.0144*** [0.0034]	0.2961** [0.1044]
Growth rate	−0.0007 [0.0032]	0.0003 [0.0236]	−0.0013 [0.0034]	0.0087 [0.0195]
Debt-to-GDP ratio	0.0032 [0.0019]	0.1485*** [0.0293]		
Fiscal space			0.1412 [0.0831]	4.8318*** [0.8438]
Country fixed effect	Controlled	Controlled	Controlled	Controlled
Number of observations	320	150	320	150
R^2	0.6820	0.7929	0.6888	0.8128

Notes: Cluster at country level and robust standard errors are shown in brackets. * $p < 0.1$, ** $p < 0.05$, *** $p < 0.01$. Precrisis: 2000Q1–2007Q4; postcrisis: 2008Q1–2011Q3.

Source: Authors' calculations.

been a significant factor—that is, countries that have low (high) interest rates tend to experience currency depreciations (appreciations).

Structural Break

We tested whether the emergence of the financial crisis in 2008 may have introduced a structural break. A Chow test revealed that a structural break did indeed occur in the euro area and the standalone countries around 2008. This allows us to treat the precrisis and postcrisis periods as separate. The results are shown in tables 4.3 and 4.4.

In general, the results confirm that since 2008 the markets have become more cautious toward some key economic fundamentals that are associated with higher spreads. To be specific, in both the euro area and standalone countries, the coefficients of the debt-to-GDP ratio and the fiscal space variable are low and insignificant prior to the crisis. In the postcrisis period, these coefficients become larger and are statistically significant.[10] Moreover, the coefficient of the real effective exchange rate is negative prior to the crisis, but this negative effect has disappeared in the postcrisis period.

10. Similar results are obtained by Arghyrou and Kontonikas (2010), Beirne and Fratzscher (2012), Ghosh and Ostry (2012), Gibson, Hall, and Tavlas (2011), and Schuknecht, von Hagen, and Wolswijk (2010).

Table 4.4 Spreads and structural breaks in standalone countries, 2000Q1–2011Q3

Explanatory variable	Precrisis	Postcrisis	Precrisis	Postcrisis
Current-account-to-GDP ratio	−0.0272	0.0078	−0.0299	0.0108
	[0.0230]	[0.0130]	[0.0243]	[0.0137]
Real effective exchange rate	−0.0208*	0.0024	−0.0195*	0.0018
	[0.0101]	[0.0112]	[0.0103]	[0.0116]
Growth rate	−0.0098	−0.0133	−0.0104	−0.0116
	[0.0582]	[0.0193]	[0.0568]	[0.0203]
Debt-to-GDP ratio	−0.0015	0.0246***		
	[0.0139]	[0.0073]		
Fiscal space			0.0657	0.6736***
			[0.3292]	[0.1973]
Change in exchange rate	−0.0555***	−0.0008	−0.0558***	−0.0011
	[0.0127]	[0.0079]	[0.0128]	[0.0077]
Country fixed effect	Controlled	Controlled	Controlled	Controlled
Number of observations	448	210	448	210
R^2	0.8356	0.9493	0.8357	0.9486

Notes: Cluster at country level and robust standard errors are shown in brackets. * $p < 0.1$, ** $p < 0.05$, *** $p < 0.01$. Precrisis: 2000Q1–2007Q4; postcrisis: 2008Q1–2011Q3.

Source: Authors' calculations.

However, the contrast in the postcrisis period between the euro area and standalone countries is striking. The coefficients of the debt-to-GDP ratio and the fiscal space in the euro area are much larger than in the standalone countries. Similarly, the coefficient of the real effective exchange rate in the euro area is significant, while no significant relationship exists in the standalone countries.

Introducing Time Dependency

As will be remembered, an important implication of the fragility hypothesis and its capacity to generate a self-fulfilling crisis is that it can lead to movements in spreads that appear to be unrelated to the fundamental variables of the model. We want to test this hypothesis by measuring the importance of time-dependent effects on the spreads that are unrelated to the fundamentals. In order to do so, we introduce time dependency in the basic fixed-effect model. In the nonlinear specification this yields:

$$I_{it} = \alpha + z * CA_{it} + \gamma_1 * Debt_{it} + \mu * REE_{it} + \delta * Growth_{it} + \gamma_2 * (Debt_{it})^2 + \alpha_i + \beta_t + u_{it},$$
(4.3)

where β_t is the time dummy variable. This measures the time effects that are unrelated to the fundamentals of the model or (by definition) to the fixed

Table 4.5 Government bond spread regressions with time component, 2000Q1–2011Q3

Explanatory variable	(1) Standalone countries	(2) Euro area countries	(3) Core euro area countries	(4) Peripheral euro area countries	(5) Standalone countries	(6) Euro area countries	(7) Core euro area countries	(8) Peripheral euro area countries
Current-account-to-GDP ratio	0.0190 [0.0216]	0.0628 [0.0380]	-0.0099 [0.0133]	0.0381 [0.0541]	0.0149 [0.0208]	0.0544 [0.0343]	-0.0093 [0.0111]	0.0551 [0.0539]
Real effective exchange rate	0.0065 [0.0077]	0.0140 [0.0226]	0.0647** [0.0234]	0.0040 [0.0353]	0.0066 [0.0075]	0.0090 [0.0121]	0.0557** [0.0171]	0.0014 [0.0264]
Growth rate	-0.0245 [0.0425]	-0.1311*** [0.0324]	0.0032 [0.0144]	-0.0958** [0.0247]	-0.0308 [0.0408]	-0.0788** [0.0275]	0.0012 [0.0157]	-0.0885** [0.0247]
Change in exchange rate	-0.0145 [0.0093]				-0.0135 [0.0094]			
Debt-to-GDP ratio	0.0115 [0.0087]	-0.0538* [0.0242]	-0.0610* [0.0256]	-0.0619* [0.0234]				
Debt-to-GDP ratio squared		0.0008*** [0.0002]	0.0004* [0.0002]	0.0008** [0.0001]				
Fiscal space					0.3074 [0.2261]	-2.1116*** [0.3851]	-3.0513* [1.1941]	-2.0340** [0.5729]
Fiscal space squared						0.8667*** [0.0699]	0.8207** [0.3186]	0.7331*** [0.1226]

(continues on next page)

Table 4.5 Government bond spread regressions with time component, 2000Q1–2011Q3 *(continued)*

Explanatory variable	(1) Standalone countries	(2) Euro area countries	(3) Core euro area countries	(4) Peripheral euro area countries	(5) Standalone countries	(6) Euro area countries	(7) Core euro area countries	(8) Peripheral euro area countries
2010Q2	-0.1454 [0.2881]	0.0326 [0.3726]	0.1081 [0.0880]	0.4846 [0.6592]	-0.1690 [0.3156]	0.2263 [0.2407]	0.1847* [0.0872]	0.6809 [0.5280]
2010Q3	-0.1042 [0.2598]	0.3226 [0.4801]	0.1343 [0.1057]	1.2979 [1.0810]	-0.1348 [0.2901]	0.497 [0.4057]	0.2054 [0.1235]	1.5075 [1.0300]
2010Q4	-0.1275 [0.3048]	0.5379 [0.5322]	0.1856 [0.1337]	1.7012** [0.3813]	-0.1582 [0.3322]	0.6920* [0.3332]	0.2665 [0.1531]	1.9527*** [0.3231]
2011Q1	-0.4190 [0.3019]	0.4821 [0.5273]	0.1714 [0.1478]	1.5040** [0.2808]	-0.4517 [0.3284]	0.5814* [0.3140]	0.2571 [0.1699]	1.7363*** [0.2098]
2011Q2	-0.5446 [0.3360]	1.0023 [0.7615]	0.1524 [0.1307]	3.0390** [0.9228]	-0.5906 [0.3599]	1.1379* [0.5739]	0.2468 [0.1496]	3.3287** [1.0161]
2011Q3	-0.2805 [0.2722]	1.4995* [0.7627]	0.7036* [0.3462]	3.5781* [1.2372]	-0.3174 [0.3073]	1.6226** [0.6665]	0.7946 [0.3944]	3.8471* [1.4454]
Other quarterly dummies	Controlled	Controlled	Controlled	Controlled	Controlled	Controlled	Controlled	Controlled
Country fixed effect	Controlled	Controlled	Controlled	Controlled	Controlled	Controlled	Controlled	Controlled
Number of observations	658	470	282	188	658	470	282	188
R^2	0.8602	0.8581	0.8287	0.9566	0.8600	0.9066	0.8288	0.9575

Notes: Cluster at country level and robust standard errors are shown in brackets. * $p < 0.1$, ** $p < 0.05$, *** $p < 0.01$. The core euro area countries are Austria, Belgium, France, Finland, Italy, and the Netherlands. The peripheral euro area countries are Greece, Portugal, and Spain, plus Ireland. Standalone countries are Australia, Canada, Czech Republic, Denmark, Hungary, Japan, South Korea, Norway, Poland, Singapore, Sweden, Switzerland, the United Kingdom, and the United States. Columns (1) to (4) are debt-to-GDP ratio regressions and columns (5) to (8) are fiscal space regressions.

Source: Authors' calculations.

effects. If significant, it shows that the spreads move in time unrelated to the fundamental forces driving the yields.

We estimated this model for both the standalone and the euro area countries. In addition, we estimated the model separately for two subgroups of the euro area, the core and periphery countries.[11] The results are shown in table 4.5. The contrast between standalone and euro area countries is striking. The effect of the time variable in the standalone countries is weak. In the euro area we detect some increasing positive time effect since the second quarter of 2010. Noticeably, there exist significant and positive time effects from the fourth quarter of 2010 to the third quarter of 2011 in the euro area periphery. Thus, during the postcrisis period the spreads in the peripheral euro area countries were gripped by surges that were independent of the underlying fundamentals.

Finally, figures 4.4a and 4.4b plot the time effects obtained from table 4.5. The results suggest that, especially in the periphery, "departures" occurred in the spreads, that is, there was an increase in the spreads that cannot be accounted for by fundamental developments, in particular by the changes in the debt-to-GDP ratios and fiscal space during the crisis.

There can be another interpretation of this result. Before the crisis, the markets did not see any risk in the peripheral countries' sovereign debt. As a result they priced the risks in the same way as they did the risk of core countries' sovereign debt. After the crisis, spreads of the peripheral countries increased dramatically and independent of observed fundamentals. This suggests that the markets were gripped by negative sentiments and tended to exaggerate the default risks. Thus, mispricing of risks (in both directions) seems to have been an endemic feature in the euro area.

Policy Implications

On the whole, the results confirm the fragility hypothesis. A large part of the surge in the spreads of the peripheral countries (Greece, Ireland, Portugal, and Spain) during 2010–11 was not connected to underlying increases in the debt-to-GDP ratios and fiscal space, but was the result of time-dependent negative market sentiments that became very strong after the end of 2010. The standalone countries in our sample have been immune from these liquidity crises and weathered the storm without increases in the spread.

We also find evidence that after years of neglecting high debt-to-GDP ratios, investors became increasingly worried about the high ratios in the euro area, and reacted by raising the spreads. No such worries developed in standalone countries, despite the fact that the debt-to-GDP ratios were equally high and increasing in these countries. This result can also be said to validate the fragility hypothesis that the markets appear to be less tolerant of large public

---

11. The Chow test shows a split between the core and peripheral members. The core euro area countries are Austria, Belgium, France, Finland, Italy, and the Netherlands. The peripheral countries are Greece, Ireland, Portugal, and Spain.

Figure 4.4a   Time component (debt-to-GDP ratio regression), 2000Q1–2011Q3

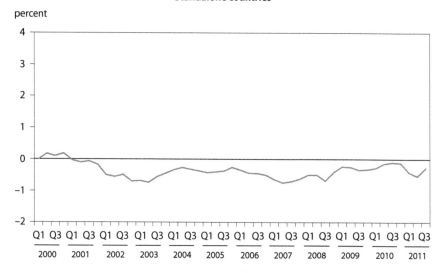

Standalone countries

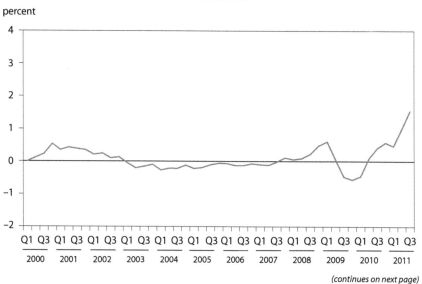

Euro area countries

(continues on next page)

Figure 4.4a Time component (debt-to-GDP ratio regression), 2000Q1–2011Q3 *(continued)*

Core euro area countries

percent

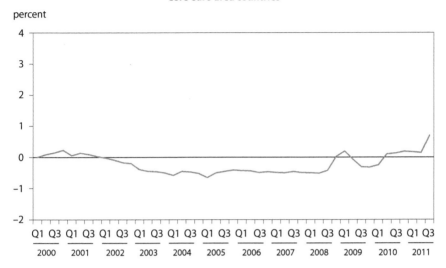

Peripheral euro area countries

percent

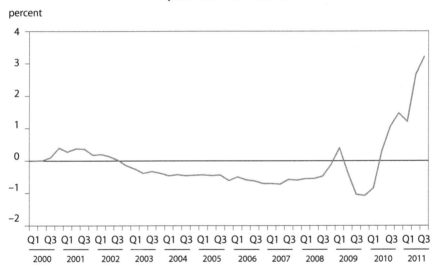

Note: The core euro area countries are Austria, Belgium, France, Finland, Italy, and the Netherlands. The peripheral euro area countries are Greece, Ireland, Portugal, and Spain. The standalone countries are Australia, Canada, Czech Republic, Denmark, Hungary, Japan, South Korea, Norway, Poland, Singapore, Sweden, Switzerland, the United Kingdom, and the United States.

Source: Authors' calculations.

Figure 4.4b   Time component (fiscal space regression), 2000Q1–2011Q3

Standalone countries

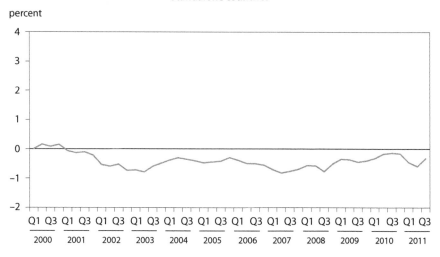

Euro area countries

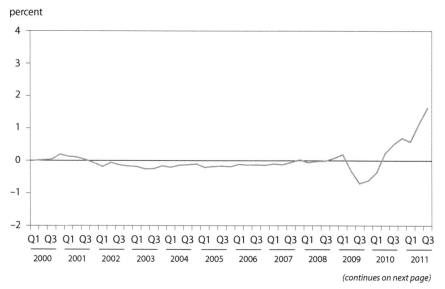

(continues on next page)

Figure 4.4b   Time component (fiscal space regression), 2000Q1–2011Q3
(continued)

Core euro area countries

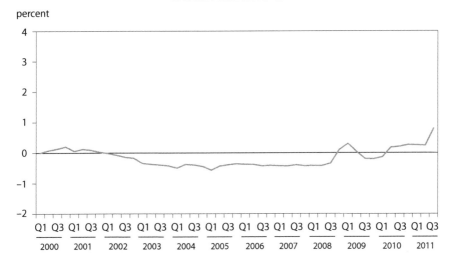

Peripheral euro area countries

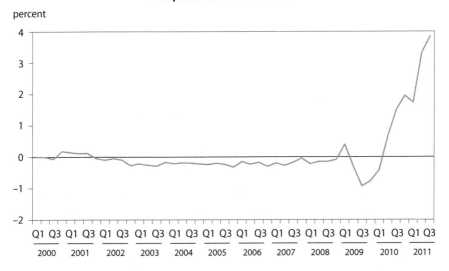

Note: The core euro area countries are Austria, Belgium, France, Finland, Italy, and the Netherlands. The peripheral euro area countries are Greece, Ireland, Portugal, and Spain. The standalone countries are Australia, Canada, Czech Republic, Denmark, Hungary, Japan, South Korea, Norway, Poland, Singapore, Sweden, Switzerland, the United Kingdom, and the United States.

Source: Authors' calculations.

debt accumulation in the euro area than of equally large public debt accumulation in the standalone countries.

Thus, the story of the euro area is also a story of self-fulfilling debt crises, which in turn lead to multiple equilibria. Countries that are hit by a liquidity crisis are forced to apply stringent austerity measures that push them into a recession, thereby reducing the effectiveness of those very same austerity measures. There is a risk that the combination of high interest rates and deep recessions will turn the liquidity crisis into a solvency crisis.

What are the policy implications of these results? We analyze three of them. The first relates to the role of the European Central Bank (ECB); the second has to do with macroeconomic policies in the euro area; and the third relates to the long-run need to move into a fiscal union.

The European Central Bank as a Lender of Last Resort in Government Bond Markets

The ECB is the only institution that can prevent fear and panic in the sovereign bond markets from pushing countries into a bad equilibrium. As a money-creating institution it has an infinite capacity to buy government bonds. The European Financial Stability Facility and the proposed European Stability Mechanism have limited resources and cannot credibly commit to such an outcome. The fact that resources are infinite is key to being able to stabilize bond rates. It is the only way to gain credibility in the market.

The ECB did buy government bonds in 2011 in the framework of its Securities Market Programme. However, it structured this program in the worst possible way. By announcing that the program would be limited in size and time, the ECB mimicked the fatal problem of an institution that has limited resources. No wonder the strategy did not work.

The only strategy that can work is the one that puts the fact that the ECB has unlimited resources at its core. Thus, the ECB should announce a cap on the spreads of Spanish and Italian government bonds, say of 300 basis points. Such an announcement is fully credible if the ECB is committed to use its infinite firepower to achieve this target. If the ECB announcement is deemed credible, it creates an interesting opportunity for investors. The investors obtain a premium on their Spanish and Italian government bond holdings, while the ECB guarantees that there is a floor below which the bond prices will not fall. (The floor price is the counterpart of the interest rate cap.) In addition, the 300 basis points acts as a penalty rate for the Spanish and Italian governments, giving them incentives to reduce their debt levels.

The ECB, however, is unwilling to stabilize financial markets in this way. Many arguments have been given why the ECB should not be a lender of last resort in the government bond markets. Many of them are not credible. Some are serious, such as the moral hazard risk, which should be addressed by institutions responsible for controlling excessive government debts and deficits. These institutions (European Semester, Fiscal Pact, automatic sanctions, etc.)

are in the process of being set up. This disciplining and sanctioning mechanism then should relieve the ECB from its fears of moral hazard (a fear it did not have when it provided 1 trillion euros to banks at a low interest rate) (De Grauwe 2011b, Wyplosz 2011).

The deeper reason for the ECB's reluctance to be a lender of last resort in the government bond market has to do with its business model, whereby the ECB has as a main concern the defense of the quality of its balance sheet—that is, a concern to avoid losses and show positive equity, even if that leads to financial instability.

When the ECB was established it was deemed necessary for it to issue equity to be held by the European Union governments. Thus the idea was that in order to sustain its activities, the ECB needed to obtain the capital of the member countries. This idea was reinforced in 2010 when a decision was taken by the Governing Council to raise the amount of capital by 5 billion euros. It is useful to read the justification of this decision:

> Taking into account the increase of the ECB's balance sheet total over the last years, it is considered necessary to increase the ECB's capital by EUR 5,000 million in order to sustain the adequacy of the capital base needed to support the operations of the ECB. (ECB 2010, L11/53)

It is surprising that the ECB attaches such importance to having sufficient equity. In fact, this insistence is based on a fundamental misunderstanding of the nature of central banking. The central bank's IOUs are legal tender. As a result, a central bank does not need equity at all to support its activities. Central banks can live without equity because they cannot default. All they need is the political support of the sovereign that guarantees the legal tender of the money they issue. This political support does not need any equity stake of the sovereign. In fact it is quite ludicrous to believe that governments that can and sometimes do default should provide the capital for an institution that cannot default. Yet, the ECB seems to have convinced the outside world that this is the case.

All this would not be a problem were it not that the ECB's insistence on having positive equity is in conflict with its responsibility to maintain financial stability. Worse, this insistence has become a source of financial instability. For example, in order to protect its equity, the ECB has insisted on obtaining seniority on its government bond holdings. In doing so, it has made these bonds more risky for the private holders, who have reacted by selling the bonds. This also implies that if the ECB were to take up its responsibility of lender of last resort, it would have to abandon its seniority claim on the government bonds it buys in the market.

The correct business model for the ECB should be to pursue financial stability as its primary objective (together with price stability), even if that leads to losses. There is no limit to the size of the losses a central bank can bear, except the one that is imposed by its commitment to maintain price stability. In the present situation the ECB is far from this limit (Buiter 2008).

Figure 4.5 Relative unit labor cost in peripheral euro area countries and Italy, 1999–2012

index (average 1970–2010 = 100)

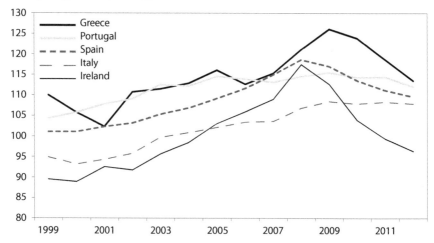

Source: European Commission, Economic and Financial Affairs, Annual Macroeconomic Database, http://ec.europa.eu/economy_finance/db_indicators/ameco/index_en.htm (accessed on July 26, 2012).

Symmetric Macroeconomic Policies

Macroeconomic policies in the euro area have been dictated by financial markets. As argued earlier, financial markets have split the euro area in two, forcing some (the southern European countries) into bad equilibria and others (mainly northern European countries) into good equilibria. The southern European countries (including Ireland) are also the countries that have accumulated current account deficits, while the northern European countries have built up current account surpluses.

The first best policy would have been for the debtor countries to reduce spending and for the creditor countries to increase spending. Thus, the necessary austerity imposed on the southern European countries could have been offset by demand stimulus in the northern countries. Instead, under the leadership of the European Commission, tight austerity was imposed on the debtor countries while the creditor countries continued to follow policies aimed at balancing the budget. This has led to an asymmetric adjustment process where most of the adjusting has been done by the debtor nations. These latter countries have been forced to reduce wages and prices relative to the creditor countries (an "internal devaluation") without compensating wage and price increases in the creditor countries ("internal revaluations"). We show the evidence in figures 4.5 and 4.6.

Figure 4.6 Relative unit labor cost in core euro area countries, 1999–2012

index (average 1970–2010 = 100)

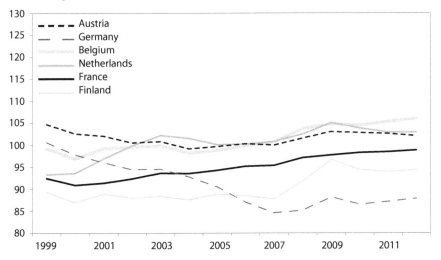

Source: European Commission, Economic and Financial Affairs, Annual Macroeconomic Database, http://ec.europa.eu/economy_finance/db_indicators/ameco/index_en.htm (accessed on July 26, 2012).

Figure 4.5 shows the evolution of the relative unit labor costs of the peripheral countries (for all of which we use the average over 1970–2010 as the base period).[12] Two features stand out. First, from 1999 until 2008–09, one observes the strong deterioration of these countries' relative unit labor costs. Second, since 2008–09, quite dramatic turnarounds of the relative unit labor costs have occurred (internal devaluations) in Ireland, Spain, and Greece, and to a lesser extent in Portugal and Italy.

These internal devaluations have come at a great cost in terms of lost output and employment in these countries. As these internal devaluations are not yet completed (except possibly in Ireland), more losses in output and employment are to be expected.

Is there evidence that a compensating process of internal revaluations is going on in the core euro area countries? Figure 4.6 shows that since 2008–09 there has been very little movement in the relative unit labor costs in these countries. The position of Germany stands out. During 1999–2007, Germany

---

12. We acknowledge that these data are a very imperfect measure of external disequilibria. John Williamson has contributed so much for a better understanding of the fundamental variables that affect the equilibrium exchange rates (Williamson 1983, 2000).

engineered a significant internal devaluation that contributed to its economic recovery and the buildup of external surpluses. This internal devaluation stopped in 2007–08. Since then no significant internal revaluation has taken place in Germany. Figure 4.6 also shows that the other countries remain close to the long-run equilibrium (the average over 1970–2010) and that no significant changes have taken place since 2008–09.

From the preceding analysis one can conclude that the burden of the adjustment to imbalances in the euro area between the surplus and the deficit countries is borne almost exclusively by the deficit countries in the periphery. Surely some symmetry in the adjustment mechanism would alleviate the pain in the deficit countries. The surplus countries, however, do not seem to be willing to make life easier for the deficit countries by taking on their share of the responsibilities to correct external imbalances.

The asymmetry in the adjustment mechanism in the euro area is reminiscent of similar asymmetries in the fixed exchange rate regimes of the European Monetary System. In both these exchange rate regimes, the burden of adjustment to external disequilibria was borne mostly by the deficit countries.

The asymmetry of the fixed exchange rate regimes arose because deficit countries at some point were hit by balance of payments crises that depleted their stock of international reserves. Empty handed, they had to turn to creditor nations that imposed their conditions, including an adjustment process to eliminate the deficits. In short, creditor nations ruled supreme (Williamson 1983).

That the Economic and Monetary Union would change all that appears to be an idle hope. The adjustment process within the euro area seems to be as asymmetric as the adjustment mechanisms of the fixed exchange rate regimes. Why is this? The answer is not because of balance of payments crises. There can be no balance of payments crises in the sense of those that occur in fixed exchange rate systems because in a monetary union internal foreign exchange markets disappear.

Another mechanism is at work in a monetary union, one that arises from the inherent fragility of such a union. When the fiscal position of a particular country in a union deteriorates—for example, due to the deflationary effects of an internal devaluation—investors may be gripped by fear, leading to collective distrust. The ensuing bond sales lead to a liquidity squeeze in the country concerned. This sudden stop in turn leads to a situation in which the government of the distressed country finds it impossible to fund its outstanding debt except at prohibitively high interest rates.

In order to avoid default, the crisis-hit government has to turn hat in hand to the creditor countries that, like their fixed exchange rate predecessors, impose tough conditions. As the creditor countries profit from the liquidity inflow from the distressed country and are awash with liquidity, no pressure is exerted on these countries to do their part of the adjustment. The creditor countries impose their rule on the system.

The European Commission has now been invested with an important responsibility to monitor and correct such imbalances in the framework of the Macroeconomic Imbalance Procedure (MIP). The key idea of the MIP is symmetry, that is, imbalances between surplus and deficit countries should be treated and corrected symmetrically. As our analysis illustrates, the European Commission up until now has not seemed willing (or able) to impose symmetry in the adjustment process.[13] It imposes a lot of pressure on the deficit countries, but fails to impose similar pressure on the surplus countries. The effect of this failure is that the euro area is kept in a deflationary straitjacket.

All of this does not bode well for future enforcement of symmetry in macroeconomic adjustments in the euro area. The MIP is unlikely to work symmetrically for the same reason the European Monetary System did not. In the absence of a lender of last resort in the euro area, deficit countries will remain in a structurally weak position vis-à-vis surplus countries each time market sentiments turn against them. This will continue to make it easier for the European Commission to impose tougher adjustment conditions on the deficit countries than on the surplus countries, thereby becoming the agent representing the interests of the creditor countries. The tyranny of the creditor countries in the euro area will not disappear any time soon.

A Monetary Union Embedded in a Fiscal Union

This diagnosis of the euro area leads us to the idea that some form of pooling of government debts is necessary to overcome this fragility. Pooling government debts shields the weakest in the union from destructive fear and panic that regularly arise in financial markets of a monetary union and that can hit any country. Those that are strong today may become weak tomorrow and vice versa.

Of course, not just any type of pooling of national debts is acceptable. The major concern of the strong countries that are asked to join in such an arrangement is moral hazard, that is, the risk that those who profit from the credibility of the strong countries will exploit this to reduce their efforts to reduce debts and deficits. This moral hazard risk is the single most important obstacle to pooling debts in the euro area. The second obstacle is that, inevitably, the strongest countries will pay a higher interest rate on their debts as they become jointly liable for the debts of governments with less creditworthiness. Debt pooling, therefore, must be designed in such a way as to overcome these obstacles.

Three principles should be followed to design the right type of debt pooling. First, pooling should be partial, that is, a significant part of the debt must remain the responsibility of the national governments so as to give them an ongoing incentive to reduce debts and deficits. Several proposals have been made to achieve this (e.g., the Bruegel and German Debt Redemption Plan). Second, an internal transfer mechanism between the members of the pool

---

13. It is very revealing that the initial "scoreboard" used by the European Commission had the same 4 percent trigger point for the current account imbalance, whether this was a surplus or a deficit. Mysteriously this was later changed to an asymmetric trigger: 6 percent for surplus countries and 4 percent for deficit countries.

must ensure that the less creditworthy countries compensate (at least partially) the more creditworthy ones. Third, a tight control mechanism on the progress of national governments in achieving sustainable debt levels must be an essential part of debt pooling. The Padoa-Schioppa group has recently proposed a gradual loss of control over their national budgetary process for the sinners against budgetary rules.

The euro area is in the midst of an existential crisis that slowly but inexorably could destroy its foundation. The only way to arrest such fears is to convince the financial markets that the euro area is here to stay. Debt pooling that satisfies the principles laid down here gives a signal to the markets that the member countries of the euro area are serious in their intentions to stick together. Without this signal, markets will not quiet down and an end of the euro is inevitable.

References

Aizenman, J., and M. Hutchison, M. 2012. What is the Risk of European Sovereign Debt Defaults? Fiscal Space, CDS Spreads and Market Pricing of Risk. Paper presented at the conference on "The European Sovereign Debt Crisis: Background and Perspectives," sponsored by Danmarks Nationalbank/JIMF, Copenhagen, April 13–14.

Arghyrou, M., and A. Kontonikas. 2010. *The EMU Sovereign-Debt Crisis: Fundamentals, Expectations and Contagion.* Cardiff Business School Working Paper E2010/9. Cardiff, UK: Cardiff University.

Attinasi, M., C. Checherita, and C. Nickel. 2009. *What Explains the Surge in Euro Area Sovereign Spreads during the Financial Crisis of 2007–09?* ECB Working Paper 1131. Frankfurt: European Central Bank.

Beirne, J., and F. Fratzscher. 2012. Pricing and "Mispricing" of Sovereign Debt in the Euro Area during the Crisis. Paper presented at the conference on "The European Sovereign Debt Crisis: Background and Perspectives," sponsored by Danmarks Nationalbank/JIMF, Copenhagen, April 13–14.

Buiter, W. 2008. *Can Central Banks Go Broke?* CEPR Policy Insight 24 (May). London: Centre for Economic Policy Research.

Caceres, C., V. Guzzo, and M. Segoviano. 2010. *Sovereign Spreads: Global Risk Aversion, Contagion or Fundamentals?* IMF Working Paper 10/120. Washington: International Monetary Fund.

Calvo, Guillermo. 1988. Servicing the Public Debt: The Role of Expectations. *American Economic Review* 78, no. 4: 647–61.

Caporale, G., and A. Girardi. 2011. *Fiscal Spillovers in the Euro Area.* DIW Berlin Discussion Paper 1164. Berlin: German Institute for Economic Research.

Corsetti, G. C., and L. Dedola. 2011. Fiscal Crises, Confidence and Default: A Bare-bones Model with Lessons for the Euro Area. Cambridge University. Photocopy.

De Grauwe, P. 2011a. *The Governance of a Fragile Eurozone.* CEPS Working Document 346. Brussels: Centre for Economic Policy Studies. Available at www.ceps.eu/book/governance-fragile-eurozone (accessed on July 26, 2012).

De Grauwe, P. 2011b. The ECB as a Lender of Last Resort. VoxEU, August 18. Available at www.voxeu.org (accessed on July 26, 2012).

De Grauwe, P., and Y. Ji. 2012. *Self-Fulfilling Crises in the Eurozone: An Empirical Test.* CEPS Working Document (June). Available at www.ceps.eu/book/self-fulfilling-crises-eurozone-empirical-test.

Eaton, J., M. Gersovitz, and J. E. Stiglitz. 1986. The Pure Theory of Country Risk. *European Economic Review* 30, no. 3: 521–27.

ECB (European Central Bank). 2010. Decision of the European Central Bank of 13 December 2010 on the increase of the European Central Bank's capital. ECB/2010/26. *Official Journal of the European Union*. Frankfurt.

Edwards, S. 1984. LDC Foreign Borrowing and Default Risk: An Empirical Investigation: 1976–1980. *American Economic Review* 74, no. 4: 726–34.

Edwards, S. 1986. The Pricing of Bonds and Bank Loans in International Markets: An Empirical Analysis of Developing Countries' Foreign Borrowing. *European Economic Review* 30, no. 3: 565–89.

Eichengreen, B., and A. Mody. 2000. Lending Booms, Reserves and the Sustainability of Short-Term Debt: Inferences from the Pricing of Syndicated Bank Loans. *Journal of Development Economics* 63, no. 1: 5–44.

Eichengreen, B., R. Hausmann, and U. Panizza. 2005. The Pain of Original Sin. In *Other People's Money: Debt Denomination and Financial Instability in Emerging Market Economies*, ed. B. Eichengreen and R. Hausmann. Chicago: Chicago University Press.

Gerlach, S., G. Schulz, and W. Wolff. 2010. Banking and Sovereign Risk in the Euro Area. Deutsche Bundesbank. Photocopy.

Ghosh, A., and J. Ostry. 2012. Fiscal Responsibility and Public Debt Limits in a Currency Union. Paper presented at the conference on "The European Sovereign Debt Crisis: Background and Perspectives," sponsored by Danmarks Nationalbank/JIMF, Copenhagen, April 13–14.

Giavazzi, F., and M. Pagano. 1990. Can Severe Fiscal Contractions Be Expansionary? Tales of Two Small European Countries. *NBER Macroeconomics Annual* 5: 75–111.

Gibson, H., G. Hall, and G. Tavlas. 2011. *The Greek Financial Crisis: Growing Imbalances and Sovereign Spreads*. Bank of Greece Working Paper 124. Athens: Bank of Greece.

Gros, D. 2011. A Simple Model of Multiple Equilibria and Default. Centre for Economic Policy Studies, Brussels. Photocopy.

Kenen, P. 1969. The Theory of Optimum Currency Areas: An Eclectic View. In *Monetary Problems of the International Economy*, ed. R. Undell and A. Swoboda. Chicago: University of Chicago Press.

Kirman, A. 1993. Ants, Rationality and Recruitment. *Quarterly Journal of Economics* 108, no. 1: 137–56.

McKinnon, R. 1963. Optimum Currency Areas. *American Economic Review* 53, no. 4: 717–25.

Min, H. 1999. *Determinants of Emerging Market Bond Spread: Do Economic Fundamentals Matter?* World Bank Working Paper 1889. Washington: World Bank.

Mundell, R. 1961. A Theory of Optimal Currency Areas. *American Economic Review* 51, no. 4: 657–65.

Obstfeld, M. 1986. Rational and Self-fulfilling Balance-of-Payments Crises. *American Economic Review* 76, no. 1: 72–81.

Schuknecht, L., J. von Hagen, and G. Wolswijk. 2010. *Government Bond Risk Premiums in the EU Revisited: The Impact of the Financial Crisis*. ECB Working Paper 1152. Frankfurt: European Central Bank.

Williamson, John. 1983 (revised in 1985). *The Exchange Rate System*. Policy Analyses in International Economics 5. Washington: Institute for International Economics.

Williamson, John. 1990. What Washington Means by Policy Reform. In *Latin American Adjustment: How Much Has Happened?* ed. John Williamson. Washington: Institute for International Economics.

Williamson, John. 1999. Implications of the East Asian Crisis for Debt Management, Paper presented at the conference on "External Debt Management," sponsored by the Reserve Bank of India, Indian Ministry of Finance, and the World Bank, Kovalam, Kerala, January 7–9. Available at www.piie.com (accessed on July 26, 2012).

Williamson, John. 2000. *Exchange Rate Regimes for Emerging Markets: Reviving the Intermediate Option*. Policy Analyses in International Economics 60. Washington: Institute for International Economics.

Wyplosz, C. 2011. They Still Don't Get It. VoxEU, October 25. Available at www.voxeu.org.

5

Target Zones and Monitoring Bands

MARCUS MILLER

> *Paradoxically, by intervening in the foreign exchange market,*
> *the central bank makes the market look more efficient.*
> —Paul De Grauwe and Marianna Grimaldi (2006)

Well before the demise of the Bretton Woods system of pegged but adjustable exchange rates, John Williamson was concerned with the risk of speculative attack. He proposed a "crawling peg" regime that would be less vulnerable to speculative pressures (Williamson 1965). Though the name has entered the English language as a term describing exchange rate regimes "in which a currency's value is allowed to go up or down frequently by small amounts within overall limits," the idea was not widely adopted.

So when the Bretton Woods system finally collapsed in 1973, "the world... stumbled into a regime of laissez faire in exchange rate policies, with most of the major currencies (and subsequently many of the minor ones as well) floating. For several years the only reasonable question to ask was whether there was a need for some rules to govern the way in which floating rates were managed" (Williamson 2000, 6).

It seemed, in fact, that the power of stabilizing speculation was far weaker than Milton Friedman had imagined in his celebrated defense of floating exchange rates (Friedman 1953, part 3). So weak indeed were the forces of mean reversion that econometricians came to treat the behavior of real exchange rates as indistinguishable from a random walk—a process with an asymptotic variance of infinity! This widespread view was successfully challenged some time later by James Lothian and Mark Taylor (1996), who showed it had low

Marcus Miller is a professor of economics at Warwick University.

Author's Note: Editorial guidance from Randy Henning and comments from other contributors to this volume are gratefully acknowledged, those of Joseph Gagnon and Olivier Jeanne in particular. Thanks also to Katie Roberts for research assistance funded by the UK Economic and Social Research Council's Competitive Advantage in the Global Economy Centre at Warwick University. My intellectual indebtedness to John Williamson will hopefully be clear from the narrative.

power against the alternative hypothesis of nonlinear mean reversion. But in the early years of floating the random walk perspective held sway.

As for the policy implications, John went on to note:

> By the early 1980s...the repeated appearance of major exchange rate misalignments among the floating currencies had led some of us to the conviction that the problem was not the way in which rates were managed, but what happened when they were not managed. It seemed that the markets displayed at best only a very weak tendency to pull exchange rates back toward any plausible concept of a medium term equilibrium rate. Hence we began to explore the possibility of designing a more structured regime. This search resulted in the development of proposals for target zones. (Williamson 2000, 6)

The idea was first floated in the volume on *Trade Policy in the 1980s*, edited by William Cline, where, in chapter 3, Fred Bergsten and John collaborated to propose a target zone for exchange rates (Bergsten and Williamson 1983). John promptly elaborated the concept in one of the earliest Institute for International Economics Policy Analyses, *The Exchange Rate System* (Williamson 1983, revised 1985), arguing that rates be kept within broad bands around fundamental equilibrium exchange rates (FEERs), which were defined and calculated for the major G-7 countries (with macroeconomic implications developed later in Williamson and Miller 1987). These calculations and ideas surely played an important intellectual role in the policy debate that led to coordinated efforts first to devalue then to stabilize the overvalued dollar (in the Accords of Plaza 1985 and Louvre 1987, respectively).[1] Subsequent calculations of FEERs revealed overvaluation for the United Kingdom and Italy, before both were unceremoniously ejected from the Exchange Rate Mechanism (ERM) in 1992.

When the problems of the ERM in Europe were followed by the peso crisis in Mexico, Maurice Obstfeld and Kenneth Rogoff (1995) argued that exchange rate options were "hollowing out," leaving no effective intermediate regime between currency union at one end of the spectrum and free floating at the other, as is indicated in figure 5.1, which gives a timeline of significant developments for exchange rates since the end of Bretton Woods.

Most of the European countries that had suffered the ERM crisis did, of course, resolve to proceed toward monetary union, with inflation targets to be pursued by the European Central Bank and a floating euro currency finally launched in 1999. This approach—of inflation targets assigned to an independent central bank with a floating exchange rate—also became the fashion for many countries outside mainland Europe, including the United Kingdom, for example, and Commonwealth countries like Canada and New Zealand. Indeed,

---

1. A vivid personal memory of how radical it seemed to challenge market forces then comes from a meeting convened—high up in one of the Twin Towers of the World Trade Center—by Henry Kaufman to discuss the behavior of the dollar in the early 1980s. For a US exporter complaining bitterly that the freely floating dollar threatened to drive him out of business, the idea that implementing a target zone might help restore the forces of mean reversion seemed little short of a providential miracle.

Figure 5.1 Timeline of key international economic events

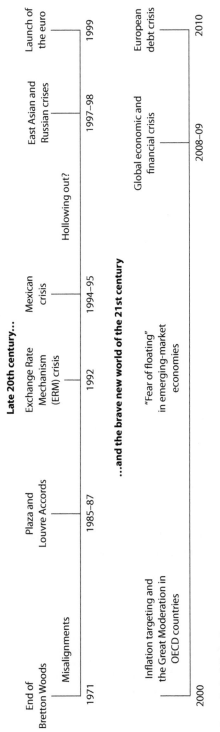

Source: Author's illustration.

the macroeconomic framework developed by Michael Woodford (2003), which analyzes the control of inflation by "Taylor rules" for interest rates, became the new macroeconomic orthodoxy. So successful was the policy stance in delivering stable inflation and low unemployment in OECD countries that the period from 1987 to 2007 came to be known as the "Great Moderation."[2]

For emerging-market economies, however, exchange rate crises continued: in East Asia in 1997–98, then Russia, and then Latin America, with Argentina forced to leave its dollar peg and "pesify" its overseas debts. A key feature of these episodes was the abrupt shift in capital flows that triggered devaluation—what Guillermo Calvo called "sudden stops." The balance sheet effects of dollarized liabilities were so adverse that they induced a "fear of floating," and countries that left a dollar peg did not float freely but managed their exchange rates to mitigate these effects.[3]

Consequently, in *Exchange Rate Regimes for Emerging Markets*, John advocated the revival of intermediate options as a viable and superior alternative:

> Let us be realistic enough to accept the fact that few countries feel comfortable abandoning their exchange rate to either the workings of the free market or permanent fixity. Most governments and central banks believe they can bring to bear something that markets lack, namely a focus on long term issues.... But then one needs to ask whether exchange rate policy should be subject to public scrutiny. If one regards that as desirable, managed floating is ruled out. In addition to providing transparency, a reference rate or monitoring band has the potential to strengthen the incentive for stabilizing speculation, and thus ease the problem posed by excessive capital mobility.
>
> Hence, my recommendation is to move to one of the more formal intermediate regimes. The key step would be to make a public announcement of their reference rate, or parity (center of the band). (Williamson 2000, 51)

The idea of giving a key role to the International Monetary Fund (IMF) in sustaining an intermediate regime was spelled out later in a Special Report of the Institute for International Economics, *Reforming the IMF for the 21st Century*, edited by Edwin Truman (2006). To revamp the international monetary system, Williamson (2006) proposed a system of reference rates,[4] succinctly described by Joseph Gagnon (2011, 234) as follows:

> Under the "monitoring zone" version of this proposal, the International Monetary Fund (IMF)—in consultation with member countries—would establish

---

2. On the bold assumption of financial market efficiency, the complex dynamic stochastic general equilibrium models adopted to guide monetary policy dispensed with any detail of financial institutions. Central banks in the United States and the United Kingdom liberalized financial markets subject to "light touch" regulation that took financial stability for granted. The resulting credit boom was destined to lead to the worst banking crisis seen since the 1930s.

3. Eloquently described in Calvo and Reinhart (2002).

4. See also Williamson (2007).

relatively wide zones around estimated equilibrium values of each economy's effective exchange rate. When the exchange rate is within this zone, the central bank would not be allowed to intervene in the foreign exchange market. When the exchange rate is above the zone, the central bank would be encouraged to sell domestic currency for foreign currency to put downward pressure on the exchange rate. Similarly, when the exchange rate is below the zone, the central bank would be encouraged to sell foreign currency to put upward pressure on the exchange rate. These operations would be aimed at damping wide swings in exchange rates and would not prevent central banks from setting their interest rate instrument as needed to achieve inflation and output stability. Most important, *central banks would not try to limit the value of the exchange rate*; the monitoring zone would be considered a guide for when the central bank should start and stop intervening, not as a limit to exchange rate movements. [italics added]

As this account makes clear, the position taken is not that flexible rates are bad, it is that the stabilizing speculation that Friedman appealed to is far too weak and needs strengthening.

The extent to which problems of collective action (and the failures of "collective cognition" discussed by Augusto de la Torre and Alain Ize [2011, 2]) might explain why an international organization like the IMF can play a useful role is left for further discussion elsewhere in this volume. Here I take up four specific topics of direct relevance to my theme: the popular target zone model developed by Paul Krugman (1991) and why it failed to excite John's enthusiasm; how adding behavioral factors can help to account for currency misalignments; how John's reference rate proposal fares in the recent assessment of floating rates by Gagnon (2011), with an aside on issues of implementation; and how that proposal might play a role in the future of the international monetary system.

Paul Krugman's Target Zone Model: Turning Friedman on His Head

After studying the monetary history of the United States—and the financial collapse of the 1930s, in particular—Milton Friedman concluded that steady growth of the money supply[5] was essential for macroeconomic stability. Keeping financial intermediation on a steady track would, he believed, help to control inflation and avoid financial crises. He also believed that floating exchange rates would allow individual countries the freedom to choose their own monetary policy—floating down if there was high money growth, and vice versa.

Friedman's policy recommendation depended crucially on a stable velocity of money—that is, a stable relationship between the size of the banking system and money income. What if that were not so? What if the velocity of money were unstable? Then (in a constant employment setting, for example), keeping

---

5. Defined to include bank deposits as well as notes and coins.

Figure 5.2 Exchange rate in a currency band

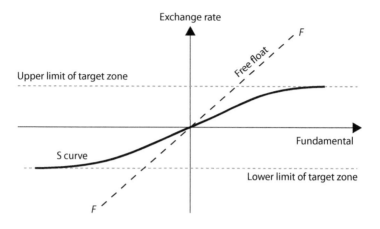

Source: Author's illustration.

the supply of money on a constant trajectory would involve instability of prices and the exchange rate.

This was the scenario that Paul Krugman (1991) chose as the setting for his analysis of target zones. For good measure, he assumed that the velocity of money followed a random walk. It's not difficult to see the broad conclusion that emerged. For price stability, policy would have to adjust the money supply so as to offset the velocity shocks, with absolute price stability involving continuous, stochastic adjustment. This turned Friedman's monetary rule on its head.

As Krugman explored this topsy-turvy world of wandering velocity, like Alice in Wonderland he came across the unexpected. He found, for example, that one could stabilize prices and the exchange rate without intervening, so long as one promised to intervene as and when the price level and the exchange rate reached the edges of preannounced bands. Credible promises to intervene so as to maintain target zones for prices and exchange rates would keep them stable inside these intervention bands.

Plotting the relationship between the exchange rate and velocity variable, Krugman found it was S shaped for a credible band with infinitesimal marginal intervention, with "smooth-pasting" at the edge of the band as shown in figure 5.2 (where a free float would lead to a matching random walk in the price of the foreign exchange rate along the "free float" line shown as FF, and a peg to no movement in the exchange rate).

Excited by this discovery, others joined in to see what would happen if the intervention was, for example, discrete or not fully credible. What emerged was a literature on "target zones" or, more technically, "regulated Brownian motion," with contributions showing the links with the theory of financial options, as a monetary authority that promises to redeem its currency when it reaches a

Table 5.1 Testing the predictions of Paul Krugman's (1991) target zone model

	Prediction	Result of test	Extension to accommodate findings
Distribution of rates inside band	U shaped	Hump shaped, normal	Mean-reverting fundamentals
Relation to fundamentals	Flatter than float	Little discernible difference	Mean-reverting fundamentals
Expected currency movements	To center of band	Outside the band	Lack of credibility

Source: Driffill (2008).

floor price is effectively giving a "put" option to holders.[6] As Paul Krugman and Julio Rotemberg (1992) showed, however, an adequate level of foreign currency reserve holdings would be crucial for the credibility of such promises.[7]

After the intellectual excitement came a dawning realization that this analysis of efficient asset pricing in a world of Brownian motion populated by rational agents and central banks with deep pockets was not suitable for addressing the problems for which John Williamson had proposed target zones as a solution. Moreover, key predictions of the target zone model were soon found to be rejected by European data (see columns 2 and 3 in table 5.1).

Attempts were made to explain this rejection (see column 4), but they did not convince Lars Svensson, who concluded that it was "a beautiful hypothesis slain by an ugly fact" (Driffill 2008, 3). As Krugman (1992, 14) confessed:

> There is an irony here: many of the target zone modellers have in other work taken to heart extensive evidence against rational expectations...in asset markets in general and foreign exchange markets in particular. Yet the target zone models assume rational expectations.... [T]here is a major tension in all analysis of financial markets between the clean analytics of efficient market theory and the growing evidence that efficient market theory is an inadequate empirical description.

This probably explains why John was not enamored of this strand of the literature. As he remarked later, "If one believes the market is forward-looking and rational, then one would not want to intervene at all: free floating is the preferred policy" (Williamson 2000, 49).

What could account for deviations from fundamentals? Does it leave a role for target zones or monitoring bands?

---

6. The collection of papers in Krugman and Miller (1992) gives a flavor of the research results.

7. A point emphasized by Mr. Sakakibara (aka Mr. Yen) when John and I visited him in Tokyo in 1987 and he assured us that "We have the greatest stash of cash in Asia."

Why Have a Target Zone? Four Parables

George Akerlof once observed that "economic theorists, like French chefs in regard to food, have developed stylized models whose ingredients are limited by some unwritten rules…. I disagree with any rules that limit the ingredients in economic models" (Akerlof 1994, 2). He went on to note that "the absence of psychological-anthropological-sociological behaviors in economic theory allows a whole new field of potential interest…[where] the economic theorist [can] ask what the consequences of these behaviors will be for the usual economic results" (Akerlof 1994, 3).

In this vein, four different parables of how traders in foreign exchange markets may behave are recounted to see what light they may throw on the role for policy interventions.

Target Zones to "Stop Loss Stoppers" (Paul Krugman and Marcus Miller 1993)

The idea in this paper was to offer a simple model of excess volatility in exchange rates that seem to correspond to the concerns of policymakers, and then to see what target zones might accomplish. The model used involve two groups of participants: traders who require a risk premium to shift the currency composition of their portfolios but do not employ trigger strategies to limit their exposure; and a group of "stop loss" traders who are much less risk averse, but exit (and enter) at given trigger points imposed to limit principal/agent problems in trading firms.

Stop loss traders who exit when prices fall and enter when prices rise make the market more sensitive to economic fundamentals than rational expectation models imply. Between the triggers for entry and exit, the exchange rate therefore has an inverse S-shaped relationship (see schedule TT in figure 5.3).

This sets the stage for considering what target zones might accomplish. The principal result is that if they assure informed traders that stop loss order will not be triggered, then speculation switches from being destabilizing to stabilizing. Instead of sell orders when prices are low and buy orders when prices are high, the market anticipates stabilizing intervention by the central bank. Graphically, the inverse S-shaped curve reverts to the more familiar target zone solution.

Target Zones to Silence Noise Traders (Olivier Jeanne and Andrew Rose 2002)

The authors of this study also draw a contrast between prevailing theories of exchange rate determination and the perception of policymakers. The former, they argue, rely on models with rational expectations where exchange rate volatility is the reflection of shocks in the fundamentals, and the choice of an

Figure 5.3 Target zone with informed investors

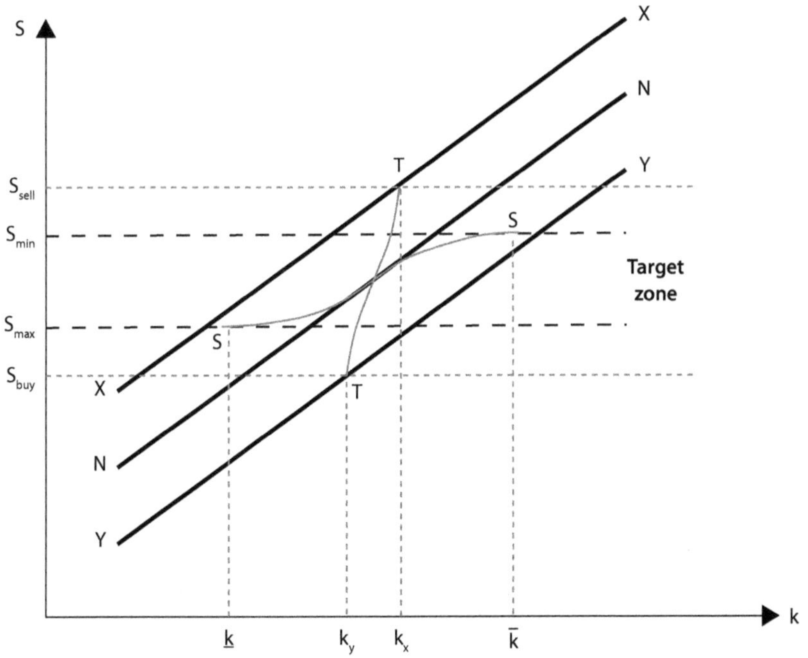

Source: Author's illustration.

exchange rate regime or a target zone involves the allocation of a given amount of fundamental volatility between the exchange rate and domestic variables. Real-world policymakers, on the other hand, seem to believe that exchange volatility may include a "nonfundamental" component, which is large under floating rates, but disappears when the currency is fixed.

This nonfundamental element in the market is captured by introducing "noise traders"—irrational actors who create exchange rate volatility if they choose to enter the foreign exchange market in order to diversify their portfolios and buy foreign bonds. The model generates a fascinating result the authors describe as follows:

> For a range of fundamental macroeconomic volatility, our model generates multiple equilibria; the noise traders can either be present or absent from the markets. If they are present, they generate exchange rate volatility; we think of this as being a floating rate regime. But there is another, "fixed rate," equilibrium without noise traders and with a more stable exchange rate. With a suitable policy stance, the policy authorities can coordinate activity to this equilibrium. In fact, an appropriate exchange rate target zone can lower exchange rate volatility without any macroeconomic cost at all. (Jeanne and Rose 2002)

The authors conclude that exchange rate policy works by affecting the composition of traders in the foreign exchange market, not by the traditional mechanism of subordinating monetary policy to an exchange rate target.[8]

Herd Dogs and Stampeding Cattle (Christopher Kubelec 2004)

Some attribute the proximate cause of misalignments to herding in asset markets by participants tempted to buy overvalued assets or sell undervalued ones. Kubelec (2004, 245) uses an analogy from Katherine Dominguez and Jeffery Frankel (1993) to suggest how in this context policy intervention can act like herd dogs:

> Clearly, a small number of dogs cannot always sustain control of the steers. So when a stampede gets under way because each panicked steer is following its neighbors, the herd can wander off quite far from its initially desired direction. However, the dogs can be helpful in a stampede because, by turning a few steers around, they might induce the herd to follow.

As indicated by Martin Evans in his discussion published in the same volume, Kubelec's study, which focused on Japan, involves an extension of the early insights of Jeffrey Frankel and Kenneth Froot (1990), with the idea that traders choose between "chartist" and "fundamentalist" forecasting rules for spot rates depending on their past and expected future profitability. On the basis of this decision, they then make trading decisions, which in aggregate determine the spot exchange rate. Intervention plays a role in this model via its effect on the forecasting choice made by traders. In particular, it is argued that intervention will be most effective in states of the world where the current spot rate is viewed as being far from some long-run level. Essentially, intervention can more easily persuade traders following "destabilizing" strategies to change their plans in these states than when the spot rate is close to its long-run level.

Because sterilized intervention changes the excess return on foreign bonds, it also affects the realized profits from investing in them. In this way, it can be used by the authorities to reduce the profitability of destabilizing forecasting strategies. Kubelec uses his estimated model to calculate the value for the Japanese yen that would have prevailed with a free float, which is shown in figure 5.4, as compared with the actual path. If the model is correct, it would suggest that the Japanese authorities were really rather successful in limiting erratic and persistent movements in the exchange rate.

A key implication of this research is that sterilized intervention can affect the exchange rate.[9] When traders choose between trend chasing and stabilizing

---

8. Writing earlier in the *European Economic Review* (Miller and Williamson 1988), John and I had tried to articulate a similar view; but—lacking the analytical elegance of Jeanne and Rose—we failed to convince our discussant, Stanley Fischer.

9. Kubelec's analysis, like the monograph of De Grauwe and Grimaldi (2006) from which the quotation at the beginning of this chapter is taken, involves transferring to the foreign exchange market

Figure 5.4   Simulated path of the yen-dollar exchange rate in the absence of intervention, 1991–2003

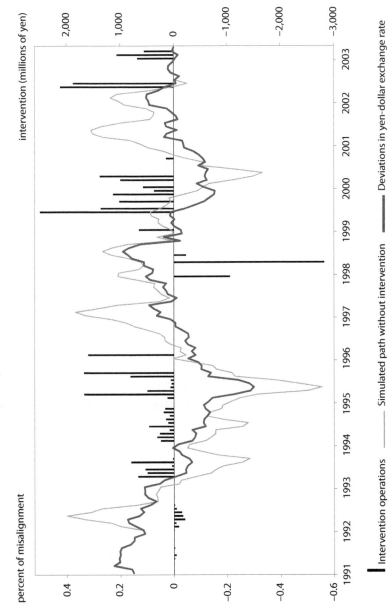

Source: Kubelec (2004).

forecasting rules on the basis of the profitability of these competing strategies, sterilized intervention that pushes the rate toward equilibrium can coordinate traders to help stabilize the exchange rate.

Bulls and Bears (Luisa Corrado, Marcus Miller, and Lei Zhang 2007)

In financial markets where portfolio management is delegated to agents with private information, traders will be subject to monitoring rules, such as the "draw-down rules" discussed by Sanford Grossman and Zhongquan Zhou (1993) that involve firing traders who lose more than a given percent of a previous peak value of the portfolio. The Corrado, Miller, and Zhang paper analyzes the interaction between these monitoring rules and the policy actions of the monetary authority.

It is assumed that traders are either speculative "bulls" or "bears" with different expectations about the rate of appreciation/depreciation of a currency. At any one time the market is dominated by one or the other group. Which group is currently in the ascendant depends on the historical evolution of the exchange rate. Because the speculators are subject to drawdown constraints, the exchange rate displays excess volatility in the absence of any intervention, as the rules lead to the repeated switching ("churning") of traders.

This excess volatility can be reduced when a monitoring band in the exchange rate interacts with the monitoring rules in the market. In particular, official action can have self-fulfilling effects if market composition shifts in ways that support official stabilization.

The contrast between volatility with a free float and the possible effect of imposing a monitoring band can be seen visually by comparing figures 5.5 and 5.6. In figure 5.5, the slope of the exchange rate is always greater than one (indicating high volatility) and the elliptical, lozenge-shaped solution for exchange rate outcomes slides up and down the 45 degree line as drawdown limits are reached.[10] In figure 5.6, however, the elliptical shape is much flatter and is anchored by the reference rate (at the center of the band) as official intervention affects traders' choice of belief. The decline in volatility is indicated by the fact that the slope of the exchange rate is everywhere less than one.[11]

---

the treatment of equities by William Brock and Cars Hommes (1997). I focus on Kubelec's study here because it is more familiar to me, being one of his PhD supervisors at Warwick University, and because Paul De Grauwe discusses his own research in chapter 4 of this volume.

10. The bulls will be those who believe that the exchange rate has an upward trend, and vice versa for bears.

11. Note that while official intervention can have self-fulfilling properties in this model, it does involve assigning monetary policy to external targets, albeit on a state-contingent basis.

Figure 5.5   Excess volatility with repeated switching

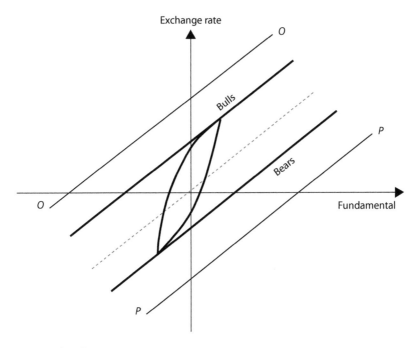

Source: Author's illustration.

Figure 5.6   Bulls and bears in a monitoring band

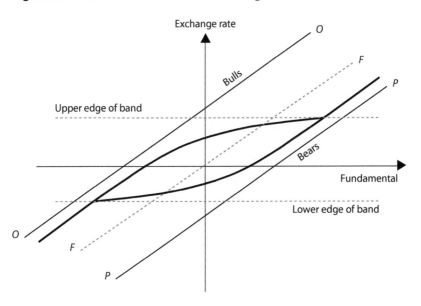

Source: Author's illustration.

A Contemporary Assessment of Floating Rates, and Issues of Implementation

Flexible Exchange Rates for a Stable World Economy (Joseph Gagnon 2011)

The target zones literature was found wanting because it failed to allow for exchange rates to deviate from fundamentals. Various stylized accounts of how and why such deviations might occur have been described. But these, it could be argued, are just stories. What of the real world of policy in action? What can one learn from recent experience?

Take, for example, the study by Gagnon (2011), entitled *Flexible Exchange Rates for a Stable World Economy*. He begins with the assertion that "a return to fixed or tightly managed exchange rates would not serve the best interests of households or businesses or governments" (p. 2) and ends with the conclusion that "on purely economic terms, and assuming that the central bank is capable of conducting sound monetary policy aimed at stabilizing inflation and output, a free float is the most desirable regime" (p. 233). But how convincing is the analysis that comes between? How persuasive would this case for free floating appear to, say, an observer like Zhou Xiaochuan, governor of the People's Bank of China? I believe three points would give cause for doubt.

First is the fact that the data used to demonstrate that exchange rate volatility does not impede steady growth with low inflation end with the global financial crisis of 2008-09; and little attention is given to the implications of that crisis. Figures presented in chapter 1 of Gagnon (2011, 3, 4), for example, show that real GDP in the euro area and the United States grew reasonably steadily during 1999-2004 and that the average inflation rate during this period was close to 2 percent in both economies. But what of the financial chaos and convulsions that have beset these economies since then, Governor Zhou might well ask?

Second, it is conceded that the standard economic model of exchange rates—consisting of uncovered interest rate parity and purchasing power parity—is not consistent with the data. Gagnon (2011, 43) writes that "studies show that the vast majority of monthly or annual changes in exchange rates cannot be explained by changes in relative interest rates, by changes in expected future exchange rates, or by expected future relative price levels." To remedy the deficiencies of the standard economic model, however, a missing factor is introduced, namely the currency "risk premium."[12] But it turns out that this simply denotes the residual in the uncovered interest rate parity equation

---

12. In bilateral comparisons involving both the United Kingdom and the United States, for example, Gagnon (2011, 58) notes that "almost all the movement in the RER [real exchange rate] is accounted for by movement in the risk premium; very little of the movement in the RER remains to be explained by the standard model. This pattern is common across most floating RERs."

(Gagnon 2011, 57). In short, the so-called risk premium is not an explanatory variable: It is what Robert Solow would call a "label for our ignorance."[13]

Third, the "modern economic model" used to generate floating rate simulations is in fact a type of dynamic stochastic general equilibrium (DSGE) model, replete with infinitely lived consumers, endowed with rational expectations, and served by efficient financial markets. Models of this variety flourished during the Great Moderation and were used by central banks on both sides of the Atlantic as a basis for setting interest rates to control inflation. But because the efficiency of financial markets was assumed as a matter of course, the models failed to pick up the growing threats to financial stability that led ultimately to a major financial crisis.[14] Could one blame Governor Zhou if he were to conclude that DSGE modeling is another case of a beautiful theory slain by ugly facts?

Gagnon's bold policy recommendation for free floating would seem to contradict John Williamson's concerns about misalignments (and promotion of intermediate regimes for managing them). But those who expect the book to end with a decisive duel between the free floating of Milton Friedman and intermediate regimes advocated by John Williamson are in for a surprise. As if recognizing some of the criticisms just made, Gagnon in his policy conclusions expresses doubts about free floating without intervention or guidance: "Given that the extreme of perfect capital mobility does not exist in the real world, is there a role for foreign exchange intervention...? [M]ight central banks be able to damp exchange rate volatility without sacrificing their primary objective of stabilizing inflation and output?" (Gagnon 2011, 234).

He then goes on to cite the reference rate proposal by John as "a framework for foreign exchange intervention that may be helpful in reducing and stabilizing volatile risk premiums. Under the "monitoring zone" version of this proposal, the International Monetary Fund (IMF)—in consultation with member countries—would establish relatively wide zones around estimated equilibrium values of each economy's effective exchange rate" (Gagnon 2011, 234), and he proceeds to consider the implementation of reference rates in a straightforward, business-like manner: "Because of the uncertainties involved in estimating equilibrium exchange rates...it would be essential to establish a wide monitoring zone around the reference rate, at least +/-10 percent and possibly as much as +/-20 percent. Notably, one set of estimates of the disequilibrium among exchange rates of G-20 countries in early 2011 ranged from –22 percent to +30 percent, with most estimates under 10 percent in absolute percentage points (Cline and Williamson 2011)" (Gagnon 2011, 235).

More than that, Gagnon adduces two powerful arguments of his own in favor of reference rates: that the central bank will make a profit and that the

---

13. Interestingly enough, risk premium volatility may exhibit the same multiplicity of equilibrium as discussed above. See the reference to Flood and Rose (1995) on page 60 of Gagnon (2011).

14. In particular, those posed by excess risk taking by financial institutions backed by government guarantee but subject only to "light-touch" regulation.

setting is good for cooperation. In more detail, first, he states that "it is possible that central banks and the IMF have a better view of long-run exchange rate fundamentals than market participants, who can get caught up in short-run fads" (Gagnon 2011, 236), for which he cites as supporting evidence the research of Kubelec (2004) on Japanese intervention. He argues that "if central banks apply a strategy of buying low and selling high consistently over time, they should be able to make extra profits, which would gradually increase the credibility of their exchange rate pronouncements among market participants," citing as evidence the profits made by the Reserve Bank of Australia and the US Federal Reserve (Gagnon 2011, 237). Second, he points out that "the element of international cooperation inherent in the proposed reference rate system makes it a natural vehicle with which to counter the recent tendency of many developing economies to deliberately hold down the value of their currencies through massive purchases of foreign exchange. The reference rate rules would forbid these purchases of foreign exchange by central banks whose currencies were not judged by the IMF to be overvalued" (Gagnon 2011, 237).

How does Gagnon reconcile support for free floating with recommendations for explicit exchange rate management? The explanation is that sterilized exchange rate intervention is seen as a separate policy tool, and given the evident failure of efficient market theory (EMT), he sees a useful role for sterilized intervention to affect the exchange rate. Proponents of the "impossible trinity" may well argue that, with perfect capital mobility, one has to choose between an independent monetary policy and exchange rate management, but Gagnon's study suggests that this is actually a false dilemma. He makes the crucial point that the failure of EMT means we don't have perfect capital mobility: hence the scope for exchange rate management without abandoning independent monetary policy. So purveyors of simple parables can, it seems, take comfort from this detailed study of exchange rates in practice.

Issues of Implementation

While John has proved continuously creative in coming up with proposals to remedy the deficiencies of unregulated markets, it is probably fair to say that he has been less concerned intellectually with issues of implementation. Like John Maynard Keynes on the problem of reparation payments after World War I, John often seems to think it is enough to sketch a sensible, Pareto-efficient, technocratic solution for all concerned gratefully to take it up.[15]

---

15. I recall Fred Bergsten once chided him—apropos of the Blueprint of 1987, if memory serves me—saying, "John, you never told me that we would have to rewrite the US Constitution to implement your ideas!" Perhaps making Gagnon's point about sterilized intervention being a separate policy tool would have helped here! Later, it should be said, Williamson and Henning (1994) did specifically address the politics of implementing target zones and the Blueprint.

But what about vested interests, one could well ask? If, for example, hedge funds and investment banks in the United States (or United Kingdom), riding shot-gun with the authorities in Washington, can regularly make a killing from their operations during currency crises, why will they want to change things? And if Wall Street is as close to the US Treasury as some critics allege, will that not go for the US government too?[16] In short, I believe that there are often important problems of implementation that need to be addressed. More than good economics may be necessary to "save capitalism from the capitalists." As Daron Acemoglu and James Robinson (2005) have shown historically, it may take political action too.

To illustrate this point, I look in the next section at a simple game of how to improve the future of the international monetary system. John's ideas seem to offer a promising way forward here, where both protagonists can improve their lot. But the Nash equilibrium is the status quo!

A Glimpse of the Future? China and the International Monetary System

It could be that China wants to sit back now, especially as a G20 member, and think afresh after the crisis about how the world monetary system might evolve better, with fewer unpredictable, chaotic financial movements occurring. Until then, China may not want fresh movement of their currency adding to their problems.

—Jim O'Neill (2010)

In discussing Joseph Gagnon's monograph we have imagined how it might appear to a Chinese central banker. Let us take this a little further. As the above citation from Jim O'Neill suggests, Governor Zhou may have been thinking of a system of managed exchange rates and IMF-created reserves as an alternative to the current system of flexible exchange rates with national currencies as reserves (particularly the dollar). The motivation for this could be that the flexible exchange rate system has been associated with global financial crisis—with the biggest losses occurring in those countries like the United States and the United Kingdom, which had "been keen supporters of very flexible and free financial markets, including floating exchange rates. This fact cannot be lost on developing countries, including China. There is evidence that countries with more tightly regulated financial systems, including some in the developed world, have fared better in this crisis" (O'Neill 2010, 44).

What of the strategic issues currently involved and how they might pan out in the future? Consider a "great game" played between two great powers—a game in which the European Union plays no significant part. Under the status

---

16. The same goes for banking crises: Stiglitz (2012) emphasizes how the incentive of powerful players to defend economic rents can stand in the way of social progress.

Table 5.2   Actions and notional payoffs in the "great game"

		Is the United States willing to be flexible about the international monetary system?	
		Floating rates with the dollar as reserve currency	Reference rates with special drawing rights as reserve currency
Will China cooperate on adjusting global imbalances?	Peg to dollar with export surplus	0, 0	+1, −1
	Revaluation and rebalancing	−1, +3	+2, +2

Note: The first payoff number shown in each cell is for China, the second for the United States.

Source: Miller (2011b).

quo, China pegs its currency against the dollar and runs a low-consumption economy (and seems deaf to US rhetoric calling for revaluation of the renminbi and rebalancing of domestic demand, even though this offers more consumption for its citizens). Meanwhile, the United States, reluctant to give up the "exorbitant privilege" of printing the world's money, dismisses any suggestion of an alternative reserve asset. Can this persist as equilibrium? Assume each player has a choice of two actions, and chooses a best response to the other's action. Specifically, China can either stay with the status quo or revalue its currency and rebalance its aggregate demand (in favor of domestic consumption). For its part, the United States can either persist with the current floating rate international monetary system based on the dollar or participate in the development of a reference rate system based on the IMF's special drawing rights (SDR) (table 5.2).

What are the payoffs to each party? Normalizing payoffs to zero for the status quo, assume that China would be happy to revalue and rebalance in the context of an SDR-based system with reference rates (table 5.2, column 4), but not when this involves perpetuating the dollar-based system (column 3). The United States, on the other hand, may be reluctant to give up the dollar (a loss of one unit of welfare), but this could be more than compensated by China agreeing to the revalue and rebalance demand.

One might hope that equilibrium will involve a shift from the current status quo in the top left-hand corner of table 5.2 (0, 0) to a reformed international monetary system without global imbalances, as shown in the bottom right corner (+2, +2). This will, after all, make both parties better off. But without coordination and commitment, the status quo is the only Nash equilibrium (as is indicated by the arrows that show how each party will respond to the other's choice of action, converging on the status quo).

What is the moral of the "great game"? It is that, despite the possibility of extra consumption, China will offer reciprocity and flexibility in policy adjustment only if the United States and others are credibly willing to redesign the international monetary system. Or, putting it bluntly, the emerging-market economies of Brazil, Russia, India, and China will agree to play ball only if they have a role in drawing up the rules of the game.[17]

Conclusion

In a recent debate on the future of macroeconomics chaired by John Driffill (2011), three suggestions were put forward to improve the current state of the discipline. First, that macroeconomists—freed from the chokehold of DSGE modeling—be more eclectic in their choice of theory; second, that more respect be given to data relative to preconceived assumptions; and third, that economists be able to use biological rather than physical models of behavior—drawing inspiration from Charles Darwin, say, rather than Isaac Newton (Miller 2011a, 23).

Happily, it seems that John Williamson scores well on all three dimensions. On the last of these, indeed, I recall that he once said that if not economics, he would have chosen to study biology. Not coincidentally, he has a legendary enthusiasm for bird watching, which has taken him all over the world—with trips to economic conferences overseas sometimes doubling as ornithological opportunities!

Could it be, as Akerlof (1994) suggests, that a biological perspective helps in analyzing exchange rate regimes and the various intervention rituals that are practiced within them? That a behavioral perspective has helped John detect powerful disruptive forces in action, analyze how they might be controlled, and challenge the academic orthodoxy of the day on the basis of careful study of markets and institutions? Whatever the reason, John Williamson's insights into the behavior of currency markets—and his creative policy suggestions for improvement—seem to be as perceptive and relevant today as they have been since 1965.

References

Acemoglu, Daron, and James Robinson. 2005. *Economic Origins of Dictatorship and Democracy*. New York: Cambridge University Press.

Akerlof, George. 1994. *An Economic Theorist's Book of Tales*. Cambridge: Cambridge University Press.

Bergsten, Fred, and John Williamson. 1983. Exchange Rates and Trade Policy. In *Trade Policy in the 1980s*, ed. William R. Cline. Washington: Institute for International Economics.

Brock, William, and Cars Hommes. 1997. A Rational Route to Randomness. *Econometrica* 65, no. 5: 1059–95.

Calvo, Guillermo A., and Carmen M. Reinhart. 2002. Fear of Floating. *Quarterly Journal of Economics* 117, no. 2: 379–408.

---

17. Further discussion is provided in Miller (2011b).

Cline, William, and John Williamson. 2011. *Estimates of Fundamental Equilibrium Exchange Rates, May 2011.* Policy Briefs in International Economics 11-5. Washington: Peterson Institute for International Economics.

Corrado, Luisa, Marcus Miller, and Lei Zhang. 2007. Bulls, Bears and Excess Volatility: Can Currency Intervention Help? *International Journal of Finance & Economics* 12, no. 2: 261–72.

De Grauwe, Paul, and Marianna Grimaldi. 2006. *The Exchange Rate in a Behavioral Finance Framework.* Princeton, NJ: Princeton University Press.

de la Torre, Augusto, and Alain Ize. 2011. *Containing Systemic Risk: Paradigm-Based Perspectives on Regulatory Reform.* World Bank Policy Research Working Paper 5523. Washington: World Bank.

Dominguez, Katherine, and Jeffrey Frankel. 1993. *Does Foreign Exchange Intervention Work?* Washington: Institute for International Economics.

Driffill, John. 2008. Exchange Rate Target Zones. In *The New Palgrave Dictionary of Economics,* second edition, ed. Steven N. Durlauf and Lawrence E. Blume. London: Palgrave Macmillan.

Driffill, John. 2011. The Future of Macroeconomics. *Manchester School* 79, no. 2: 1–38.

Flood, Robert, and Andrew Rose. 1995. Fixing Exchange Rates: A Virtual Quest for Fundamentals. *Journal of Monetary Economics* 36, no. 1: 3–37.

Frankel, Jeffrey, and Kenneth Froot. 1990. Chartists, Fundamentalists and Trading in the Foreign Exchange Market. *American Economic Review* 80, no. 2: 181–85.

Friedman, Milton. 1953. *Essays in Positive Economics.* Chicago: University of Chicago Press.

Gagnon, Joseph. 2011. *Flexible Exchange Rates for a Stable World Economy.* Washington: Peterson Institute for International Economics.

Grossman, Sanford, and Zhongquan Zhou. 1993. Optimal Investment Strategies for Controlling Drawdowns. *Mathematical Finance* 3, no. 3: 241–76.

Jeanne, Olivier, and Andrew Rose. 2002. Noise Trading and Exchange Rate Regimes. *Quarterly Journal of Economics* 117, no. 2: 537–69.

Krugman, Paul. 1991. Target Zones and Exchange Rate Dynamics. *Quarterly Journal of Economics* 106, no. 3: 669–82.

Krugman, Paul. 1992. Exchange Rates in a Currency Band: A Sketch of a New Approach. In *Exchange Rate Targets and Currency Bands,* ed. P. Krugman and M. Miller. Cambridge, UK: Cambridge University Press.

Krugman, Paul, and Marcus Miller, ed. 1992. *Exchange Rate Targets and Currency Bands.* Cambridge, UK: Cambridge University Press.

Krugman, Paul, and Marcus Miller. 1993. Why Have a Target Zone? *Carnegie-Rochester Series on Public Policy* 38, no. 1: 279–314.

Krugman, Paul, and Julio Rotemberg. 1992. Speculative Attacks of Target Zones. In *Exchange Rate Targets and Currency Bands,* ed. Paul Krugman and Marcus Miller. Cambridge, UK: Cambridge University Press.

Kubelec, Christopher. 2004. Intervention When Exchange Rate Misalignments Are Large. In *Dollar Adjustment: How Far? Against What? Special Report 17,* ed. Fred C. Bergsten and John Williamson. Washington: Institute for International Economics.

Lothian, James, and Mark Taylor. 1996. Real Exchange Rate Behavior: The Recent Float from the Perspective of the Past Two Centuries. *Journal of Political Economy* 104, no. 3: 488–509.

Miller, Marcus, 2011a. Macroeconomics: A Discipline Not a Science. *Manchester School* 79, no. 2: 21–24.

Miller, Marcus. 2011b. Macro-governance. *Queries* 1, no. 4: 39–46.

Miller, Marcus H., and John Williamson. 1988. The International Monetary System: An Analysis of Alternative Regimes. *European Economic Review* 32, no. 5: 1031–48.

Obstfeld, Maurice, and Kenneth Rogoff. 1995. The Mirage of Fixed Exchange Rates. *Journal of Economic Perspectives* 9, no. 4: 73–96.

O'Neill, Jim. 2010. A Twenty First Century IMS. In *Beyond the Dollar,* ed. P. Subacchi and J. Driffill. London: Chatham House.

Stiglitz, Joseph. 2012. *The Price of Inequality.* New York: W. W. Norton.

Truman, Edwin, ed. 2006. *Reforming the IMF for the 21st Century.* Special Report 19. Washington: Institute for International Economics.

Williamson, John. 1965. *The Crawling Peg.* Princeton Essays in International Finance 50. Princeton, NJ: Princeton University Press.

Williamson, John. 1983 (revised in 1985). *The Exchange Rate System.* Policy Analyses in International Economics 5. Washington: Institute for International Economics.

Williamson, John. 1998. Crawling Bands or Monitoring Bands: How to Manage Exchange Rates in a World of Capital Mobility. *International Finance* 1, no. 1: 59–79.

Williamson, John. 2000. *Exchange Rate Regimes for Emerging Markets: Reviving the Intermediate Option.* Policy Analyses in International Economics 60. Washington: Institute for International Economics.

Williamson, John. 2006. Revamping the International Monetary System. In *Reforming the IMF for the 21st Century,* ed. Edwin M. Truman. Special Report 19. Washington: Institute for International Economics.

Williamson, John. 2007. *Reference Rates and the International Monetary System.* Policy Analyses in International Economics 82. Washington: Peterson Institute for International Economics.

Williamson, John, and Marcus Miller. 1987. *Targets and Indicators: A Blueprint for the International Coordination of Economic Policy.* Policy Analyses in International Economics 22. Washington: Institute for International Economics.

Williamson, John, and C. Randall Henning. 1994. Managing the Monetary System. In *Managing the World Economy: Fifty Years after Bretton Woods,* ed. Peter B. Kenen. Washington: Institute for International Economics.

Woodford, Michael. 2003. *Interest and Prices.* Princeton, NJ: Princeton University Press.

II

FINANCE

6

International Finance

AVINASH D. PERSAUD

The diversity of the chapters in this volume is a reminder that John Williamson has made a mark on a broad canvas of subjects. He is an expert on the International Monetary Fund (IMF) and World Bank, the economic development of Latin America and Asia, and the political economy of policy reform, and he is a towering figure in the field of exchange rate policy, financial crises, and capital account convertibility. If there is a common theme across this epic it is the development of policy rules that limit the boom-bust cycle at the national, regional, and international levels.

From the cauldron of today's global crisis, which had as its origin a parochial subsector of the US housing market, that common theme seems a disarmingly obvious focus of attention. Today, policymakers busy themselves developing macroprudential regulations, promoting stricter regulation of globally significant financial institutions, ring-fencing local capital at international banks from capital calls made by head offices, considering currency transaction taxes, and developing a European banking union. All of these policies are designed to better insulate the domestic economy from the quick tides of international capital flows.

However, during the international financial crises of the last 30-odd years, which mostly centered on emerging-market economies, the Washington-based multilateral institutions such as the IMF and World Bank tended to downplay the external conduit of instability. Attempts to restrict this channel of instability through capital controls and exchange rate arrangements were at best

Avinash D. Persaud is chairman of Elara Capital Plc, chairman of PBL, chairman of Intelligence Capital Limited, and board director of Beacon Insurance and RBC Latin America and the Caribbean. He thanks William R. Cline for valuable comments on this chapter.

frowned upon. At worst, those who promoted such efforts were dismissed as relics of a past era. Domestic fiscal policy was the focus of policy prescriptions, earning the IMF its moniker "It's Mostly Fiscal."

Rapid liberalization of exchange and capital controls was often thrown in with other conditions of emergency lending by the multilateral institutions. The pace of capital liberalization in the 1980s and 1990s intensified the depth and breadth of emerging-market crises, culminating in the Asian financial crisis, which started in Thailand in July 1997, and ended only with the Brazilian devaluation of January 1999. It is in this context that John Williamson, along with a handful of others (well represented among the authors of this volume), have been engaged in seeking a new international financial architecture to help reduce the amplitude of the international boom-bust cycle and assist in managing the sudden stops of international capital flows (Williamson 1977, 2005).

John Williamson's focus on policy solutions to real-world problems has led him to design and promote international financial architecture that finds a middle road. He rejects the notion of a bipolar world with only full floats or full fixes (Williamson 2000), with either complete liberalization or complete autarky, or with omnipotent international institutions or impotent ones. The IMF need not be all-powerful to be all-helpful. Crawling exchange rate pegs are neither fixed nor floating and are designed to bring some of the benefits of both fast and slow capital mobility (Williamson 1965). His experience leads him to reject rapid liberalization of the capital account (Williamson and Mahar 1998), and to pin substantial blame for the Asian financial crisis on overhasty deregulation, but not to accept tardy deregulation of trade and subsidies.

The enduring challenge for this vision of a new international architecture that reduces the egregiousness of the booms and the devastation of the busts has been to rekindle that Bretton Woods "moment" when countries were prepared to constrain their domestic freedom for a greater international good. I begin this chapter by looking at the structural obstacles to international cooperation on international finance and how countries have responded to a world without rules. I then argue that the current international financial crisis has provided an unexpected, but achievable, route toward a world of more stable capital flows, through the increased emphasis on macroprudential regulation as opposed to microprudential regulation. I examine some practical proposals to better manage national and international cycles of boom and bust. I go on to argue that macroprudential regulation is not just about domestic counter-cyclical policies but a more structural approach to better matching risk taking to risk capacity, nationally and internationally. I assess the right role for international decision making on financial regulation and local decision making. My starting point is one of pessimism on traditional attempts at international policy cooperation, but I conclude optimistically that John Williamson's goal of a stronger, more stable, more sustainable system of international financial flows is within reach, if through less traditional routes.

The Difficulty of Reaching Meaningful Agreements on International Economic Rules

The evolutionary success of humanity is partly related to our ability to cooperate for a greater good (Axelrod and Hamilton 1981). However, there are many challenges to cooperation in the field of macroeconomic policymaking. The dismal science predicts that there will always be an underinvestment in global public goods, such as international financial stability, where it is easy to free-ride the investments made by others (Kaul et al. 2003, Barrett 2010). Yet hope remains, perhaps because of the knowledge that a successful effort in this field has indeed happened before—over three weeks in July 1944 at Bretton Woods. Since then there have been some surprising albeit more modest successes. Much was wrong with the international accords on the regulation of international banks, referred to as Basel I and Basel II, but Revised Basel II is much better, and at least there is an accord. International rules on money laundering and antiterrorist financing are becoming stricter and more readily enforced. Today, previously uncooperative jurisdictions such as Liechtenstein and Andorra are no longer considered facts of life, but instead face excommunication from international banking flows. Innovative forms of financing global public goods are being developed, such as the duty on airline tickets that helps to finance the Global Alliance for Vaccines and Immunization.

Despite modest successes elsewhere, progress in macroeconomic policy coordination has been slight in recent years. On October 20, 2011, ahead of the Seoul G-20 meeting, a proposal by US Treasury Secretary Timothy Geithner in a letter to G-20 leaders echoed John Maynard Keynes' proposals 67 years ago, urging countries to agree to pursue domestic policies that limit their current account imbalances to less than 4 percent of GDP and to accept penalties if these limits are breached, in order to shift the burden of adjustment away from deficit countries to surplus countries. In 1944, with the horrors of World War II still being revealed, Keynes's Great Britain was a major deficit country, and the main surplus country, the United States, rejected his idea of binding rules. In 2011, Tim Geithner's America was the major deficit country and the surplus nations of China, Germany, and Japan rejected the idea of binding rules.

The inability to reach agreement is not just about deficit and surplus countries having different interests. It is also about the political economy of international policy coordination. We need international rules to address situations when countries do things that are neither in their own interests nor in the interests of others, or when countries acting in their own national interests can have a powerfully negative impact on others. Countries are generally incentivized to act in their own national interest—more so the healthier the democracy (Rodrik 1999). There are in fact very few countries or circumstances where size or magnitude is such that the pursuit by a country of its own interests could destabilize the rest of the world. Japan's "lost decade" of growth in the 1990s occurred at a time when it was the second-largest economy in the world, and while its near-zero interest rates, big deficits, and stagnant growth had unmistakable effects in its region, the gravitational effects were weak elsewhere.

The most likely cases of self-interest hurting others would be unneighborly policies in the world's largest economy, the United States, which in market terms is still around twice the size of today's next-largest economy (China), three times the size of the third-largest economy (Japan), and four times the size of the fifth largest (Germany). The European Union would be near equal to the United States in economic size if it were operating as a single political and fiscal force. But it is not—at least not yet.

Given that the United States also issues the world's reserve currency and therefore faces a far looser budget constraint than other nations, it is even more likely that it is the United States whose policies need to be constrained by international policy rules for the greater good, not China, Japan, or Germany.

Indeed, on at least three separate occasions in the modern era, US policy initiatives have led to twin deficits in both fiscal and trade accounts, larger than any other country could sustain, and big enough to create substantial policy problems for the rest of the world. President Lyndon Johnson's "Great Society" and Vietnam War spending triggered inflationary pressure abroad that would later destabilize Bretton Woods. President Ronald Reagan's "Star Wars" program and tax cuts fostered overseas inflationary pressures and such exchange rate misalignments that it provoked the Plaza Accord.[1] President George W. Bush's tax cuts, alongside fighting a war and accommodative monetary and regulatory policy, presaged the current crisis. US Treasury Secretary John Connally's famous remark to European finance ministers in 1971 that the dollar "is our currency but your problem" well captures the challenge.

Yet, being the most powerful country, the United States is unwilling to let international rules constrain its fiscal and monetary policies. (Congress is hardly willing to even let domestic rules constrain fiscal policy.) Some Americans may consider this an anti-American comment, but such behavior is not unique to the United States—most large and powerful countries would probably act in the same way. Outside the United Kingdom, the British Empire was not considered a charitable foundation. To most non-Americans, there is little evidence that the United States would constrain itself on matters of strategic importance. The United States has opted out of the International Criminal Court; unlike most other nations, its Congress decides at will which UN agencies it will fund and which it will not; and it stands virtually alone outside international financial accounting standards. When the United States loses at World Trade Organization (WTO) tribunals, it tries to bypass the judgments and negotiate alternative settlements to the ones set by the WTO decision.

While the United States is not so powerful today that it can impose its will on anyone other than small and medium-sized economies, it is sufficiently so

---

1. The Plaza Accord was an agreement to depreciate the dollar in relation to the yen and Deutsche mark through joint intervention in the currency markets and supportive monetary policies. The accord was signed by the governments of France, West Germany, Japan, the United States, and the United Kingdom on September 22, 1985, at the Plaza Hotel in New York City.

that it can reject constraints that bind its policymakers. And without meaningful constraints on the systemically most important economy the exercise of international policy rules and coordination would be futile. It would be like regulating the financial sector by regulating every financial institution except the largest, which happened to be larger than the second and third put together.

Creating Safe Harbors in Troubled Seas

In a world mainly devoid of effective rules on unruly capital flows and exchange rates, small to medium-sized economies adapted a wide range of sea defenses to create safe harbors against the volatile tides of capital. Many policymakers were emboldened to do so by John Williamson's writings. At a time when capital controls were a taboo, the European Union's Economic and Monetary Union was one such response. The buildup of large international reserves in Asian countries was another. Different countries in Latin America, such as Argentina, Brazil, Chile, and Colombia, played with different forms of exchange rate arrangements and capital taxes (Williamson 1996). Many of these policies had or have the same objective—to tame the ebb and flow of cross-border capital—and many of these different tools could be calibrated so as to be equivalent to one another. In the cold light of the current financial crisis, these individual and uncoordinated responses appear to have delivered some safety and some risk to the international financial system, contributing to the character of the current crisis and reminding us of John Williamson's call for an overhaul of the entire system.

There is fresh hope from an unlikely quarter for those seeking a system less prone to feast and famine. The crisis itself has given momentum to new regulatory initiatives, collectively referred to as macroprudential rules, that could have an effect at dampening the boom-bust cycle nationally and internationally. These macroprudential rules are finding more international acceptance than other policy tools, such as capital and exchange controls, in part because the fault lines are not foreign versus domestic, and in part because there is space for domestic policy as well as internationally binding minimums. It should be no surprise that this is the very kind of middle path with which John Williamson finds merit (Subramanian and Williamson 2009).

Why Financial Regulation Needed Reform

It seems banal today to point out that the reason why policymakers try to prevent financial crises is that the costs to society are enormous and exceed the private cost to individual financial institutions. Policymakers regulate in order to internalize these externalities on to the behavior of financial institutions. A significant tool used by regulators to achieve this is capital adequacy requirements, but the previous approach proved too narrow and too microprudential. It implicitly assumed that we can make the whole system safe by ensuring the safety of individual banks. This sounds like a truism, but it is a fallacy of composition. In trying to make themselves safer, banks and other highly leveraged financial intermediaries can and do behave in ways that collectively undermine the system.

Selling an asset when the price of risk increases is a prudent response from the perspective of an individual bank. But if several banks act in this way, the asset price will collapse, forcing risk-averse institutions to sell more. The cycle spins round and round, leading to contagious declines in asset prices, enhanced correlations and volatility across markets, spiraling losses, and collapsing liquidity. Liquidity risk is not a solid to be measured and easily categorized; rather, it is endogenous to market behavior.

I have previously described these horizons where liquidity appears abundant before vanishing as a liquidity black hole, and there are strong parallels between the nature and drivers of liquidity black holes and sudden stops in international crises. Through a number of avenues—some regulatory, some not, and often in the name of sophistication, transparency, and modernity—the increasing role of current market prices on behavior has deepened the endogeneity of the financial system. These avenues include mark-to-market valuation of assets; regulatory-approved, market-based measures of risk, such as the use of credit default swaps prices in internal credit models or price volatility in market risk models; and the increasing use of credit ratings where the signals are slower moving but positively correlated with financial markets (ratings tend to be upgraded during a boom and downgraded during a bust). Where measured risk is based on market prices, or on variables that are correlated with market prices, it becomes procyclical, falling in the boom and rising in the bust (Persaud 2002, 2003)

In the up phase of the economic cycle, when price-based measures of asset values rise, price-based measures of risk fall, and competition to grow bank profits increases, most financial institutions spontaneously respond by (1) expanding their balance sheets to take advantage of the fixed costs of banking franchises and regulation; (2) trying to lower the cost of funding by using short-term funding from the money markets; and (3) increasing leverage. Those resisting such measures are seen as underleveraging their equity and are duly punished by the stock markets. As Citigroup CEO Chuck Prince poignantly said, "When the music is playing you have to get up and dance."[2]

When the boom ends, asset prices fall and short-term funding to institutions with impaired and uncertain assets or high leverage dries up. Forced sales of assets drive up their measured risk and, inevitably, the boom turns to bust.

One of the key lessons of the current crisis and previous ones is that market discipline is insufficient in booms and excessive during busts. It is significant that those institutions most resilient to the crisis to date, such as HSBC, had

---

2. Michiyo Nakamoto and David Wighton, "Citigroup Chief Stays Bullish on Buy-Outs," *Financial Times*, July 10, 2007.

a lower equity rating (lower price-earnings ratios) than those that proved least resilient, such as Northern Rock, Bear Stearns, Fortis, and Lehman Brothers. Let us not throw out the baby with the bath water. But although market discipline has a substantial role to play in financial sector development more generally, it cannot play a frontline role in our defense against financial crises, domestically or internationally.

One of the reasons why market discipline was seen as such a key pillar in the previous approach to banking regulation is that the implicit crisis model regulators had in their minds was that financial crashes occur randomly as a result of a bad institution failing, and that failure then becoming systemic. Our experience domestically and internationally is different. Crashes follow booms. In the boom, financial institutions (or countries) almost all look good, and in the bust they almost all look bad. Differentiation is poor. This current crisis is nothing but yet another instance of this all-too-familiar boom-bust cycle.

If crises repeat themselves, banning the individual products, players, and jurisdictions that were circumstantially at the center of the current crisis will do little to prevent the next one. Moreover, the notion that some financial products are safe and some are not, and that the use of unsafe products is the problem, also looks suspect in a boom-bust world. Booms are the result of things appearing safer than they are. Anointing seemingly safe products during the boom is certain to lead to their use in a manner, or to such excessive use, that makes them unsafe. Securitization, for example, was originally viewed as a way to make banks safer. Diversified portfolios of subprime mortgages were viewed as having safely low delinquency rates. Strong microprudential regulation is necessary to weed out the truly reckless institutions and behavior and to create an environment of greater certainty. But what is most needed to soften the inevitable busts is to supplement microprudential regulation with macroprudential regulation in order to calm the booms that a static, institution-by-institution view inevitably lets slip through.

Introducing Micro- and Macroprudential Regulation

Microprudential regulation—comprising measures such as the certification of workers in the financial sector, know-your-customer rules and requirements on how financial products are sold, reporting standards for financial institutions, and capital adequacy for loans issued by banks—concerns itself with the stability of individual institutions and the protection of individuals. By contrast, macroprudential regulation concerns itself with the stability of the financial system as a whole. This is familiar territory for John Williamson (Williamson 2005, Subramanian and Williamson 2009).

Microprudential regulation examines the responses of an individual bank to exogenous risks. By construction it does not incorporate endogenous risk. And although there is much scope to converge microprudential regulation to an international standard, such regulation ignores the systemic importance of individual institutions in terms of size, degree of leverage, and interconnectedness with the rest of the system (Persaud 2002).

One of the key purposes of macroprudential regulation is to act as a countervailing force to the decline of measured risks in a boom (which would otherwise trigger levels of risk taking that would later be considered excessive) and the subsequent rise of measured risks in the bust that follows (which makes loan officers excessively conservative). It is countercyclical and goes against the market.

On paper, bank supervisors have plenty of discretion but find it hard to use it because of the politics of booms. Almost everyone wants a boom to last. Politicians are looking to reap electoral benefit from the sense of well-being and prosperity. Policy officials convince themselves and try to convince others that the boom is not an unsustainable credit binge, but rather the positive result of structural reforms they have put in place. Booms also have social benefits. Not only does philanthropy rise, but because there is the perception that risks have fallen, access to finance for the unbanked and underinsured rises. Booms are not quite a conspiracy of silence, but there are few who gain from the early demise of a boom. Booms are accommodated, growing larger and larger and thus reaping more damage when they eventually collapse. (John Williamson [1998] has been a keen observer of these political challenges to policy, challenges often neglected by mainstream economists.)

Countercyclical Charges and Liquidity Buffers: Some Practical Suggestions

There is growing consensus around the idea that capital requirements need to be countercyclical in order to dampen rather than amplify the financial and economic cycle. This can be achieved by requiring buffers of resources to be built up in good times. There is also growing consensus around the related idea of limits to leverage and liquidity buffers. Dependency on short-term external funding is a source of weakness for banks as well as countries. How countercyclical capital charges and liquidity buffers should be implemented has not been addressed in great detail to date. Given the politics of booms discussed above, the "how" is almost as important as the "whether."

In practical terms, Charles Goodhart and I have recommended that regulators increase the existing microprudential or base capital adequacy requirements (based on an assessment of inherent risks) by two multiples.[3] The first is related to above-average growth of credit expansion and leverage. Where they are separate, regulators and monetary policy officials should meet as part of a Financial Stability Committee. The outcome of that meeting would be a fore-

---

3. To see the presentation of the original idea of the two multiples, see Charles Goodhart and Avinash Persaud, "How to Avoid the Next Crash," *Financial Times*, January 30, 2008; and "The Party Pooper's Guide to Financial Stability," *Financial Times*, June 4, 2008. The ideas were expanded upon in Geneva Report 11 (Brunnermeier et al. 2009).

cast of the degree of growth of the average bank's assets that is consistent with the central bank's target for inflation (or some other nominal macro target). The forecast would have a reasonable band around it. If an individual bank's assets grow above this band it will have to put aside a higher multiple of its base capital charge for this new lending, and if its assets grow less than the lower bound, it may put aside a lower multiple.

For instance, let us suppose the Financial Stability Committee concluded that 10 percent growth in aggregate bank assets was consistent with its inflation target of 3 percent, and that, given uncertainty about the velocity of money and credit in the economy, this target would have a reasonable degree of uncertainty of +/-2.5 percent. The growth in a bank's assets by 25 percent, or twice the 10 percent +/-2.5 percent upper band, could lead to a doubling of the minimum capital adequacy level from 8 to 16 percent of risk-weighted assets. An alternative approach, which the Swiss authorities announced in 2010, is to pursue a base capital adequacy requirement in "bad" times, and a level twice that in "good" times, with good and bad being determined by bank profitability. This is worth considering for its simplicity to calculate and implement, but it does reduce the time-varying element in the proposals above with a potentially oversimplified two-state world. The credit mistakes are made in the late part of the boom.

It is important to note that Financial Stability Committees already exist in many countries. They generally have not worked because while worthy people meet and fret together, there is no consequence to their deliberations. A consequence, such as agreeing on the level of sustainable bank asset growth, would focus these committees in a more productive way.

The second multiple on capital charges should be related to the mismatch in the maturity of assets and liabilities. One of the significant lessons of the crash of 2007–08 is that the risk of an asset is largely determined by the maturity of its funding. Northern Rock and other casualties of the crash might well have survived with the same assets if the average maturity of their funding had been longer. The liquidity of banks' assets had fallen far more than the credit quality of these assets had deteriorated.

However, if regulators make little distinction between how assets are funded, financial institutions will rely on cheaper, short-term funding, which increases systemic fragility and interconnectivity. This private incentive to create systemic risks can be offset by imposing a capital charge that is inversely related to the maturity of funding of assets that cannot normally be posted at the central bank for liquidity.

The idea of liquidity buffers, with the size of the buffer related to maturity mismatches between assets and liabilities, is increasingly supported by policymakers and academics. However, there is little discussion of methodology and plenty about outstanding issues. For instance, measuring the liquidity maturity of assets and liabilities is not straightforward. A 10-year, AAA government bond has almost immediate liquidity. Bankers, who vigorously dislike these new liquidity buffers, will prey on the minutiae in an attempt to persuade the authorities to delay such initiatives. In the framework set out in the *Geneva Report on the World Economy 11*, assets that cannot be posted at the central bank for liquidity can be assumed to have a minimum liquidity maturity of two years or more (Brunnermeier et al. 2009). If a pool of these assets were funded by a pool of two-year term deposits, there would be no liquidity risk and no liquidity charge. If, on the other hand, the pool of funding had a maturity of one month and so had to be rolled over every month, the liquidity multiple on the base capital charge would be near its maximum—say two times—so the minimum capital adequacy requirement would rise from 8 to 16 percent. In a boom when the countercyclical multiple is also at two times, the final capital adequacy requirement would be 32 percent of risk-weighted assets (8 percent x 2 x 2). We recognize that liquidity multiples will make lending more costly given that banks traditionally fund themselves short and lend long. However, the liquidity multiple will give banks an incentive to find longer-term funding, and where they cannot, it will address a real systemic risk. It is important to recall that reported bank capital in excess of 20 percent of risk-weighted assets was common in the industry before the crash and proved insufficient.

Role of Value Accounting in the Promulgation of Crises

Accounting issues are often considered to be central to the crisis. It is argued that mark-to-market accounting has added to the illusion of wealth in the boom, validating excessive lending and then triggering a spiral of sales in the crisis as asset values collapsed. It is a major fuel line into the boom-bust cycle. Value accounting even found its way into the G-20 Communiqué. Detractors have called for a suspension of mark-to-market accounting during a crisis, arguing in part that this is how such past events as the Latin American debt crisis in the 1980s were successfully worked out. But the genie is out of the bottle and suspending market valuations that previously existed could be counterproductive in a world gripped by panic and uncertainty.

I propose that regulators allow financial institutions to move toward what I call "mark-to-funding" accounting (Persaud 2008a, 2008b). Under mark-to-funding valuations, there are essentially two alternative prices for an asset: today's market price and the present discounted value of the future earnings stream. In normal times, these two prices are usually similar. In a liquidity crisis, the market price falls substantially below the present discounted value of the future earnings stream. If an institution has short-term funding, the relevant price for it is the market price. If it has long-term funding, the present discounted value of the future earnings stream price is a better measure of the risks faced by the institution than the market price. In mark-to-funding accounting, a weighted average of the market price and present discounted value of the future earnings stream is taken depending on the weighted average maturity of the funding. It is a Williamson-style "middle way" that points us in a better direction than the alternatives of mark-to-market valuations or historic cost valuations. The combination of liquidity charges and mark-to-funding value accounting incentivizes institutions to seek longer-term funding and encourages ownership of illiquid assets by institutions with longer-term funding, bringing greater systemic resilience.

To Each According to Their Risk Capacity

A big idea is hidden in the practical approach to liquidity charges described above. Placing a charge on the degree of maturity mismatch between assets and funding discourages institutions without a capacity for liquidity risk from holding it and encourages institutions to develop such capacity through long-term funding, reducing some of the more systemically dangerous interconnectivity of the financial system. The response of financial regulators to the crisis has been to require that banks set aside more capital, in part because of the previous underestimation of systemic risks. If risk is allocated to places without a capacity for that risk, the amount of capital required to protect the financial system from systemic crisis is beyond the economics of banks. This is when governments step in. However, an alternative approach that would minimize the need for taxpayer support is to incentivize risks to flow to places with a capacity for that risk. If this could be done, the system could be safer with less capital than otherwise (Warwick Commission 2009). But what does this mean?

Broadly, there are three types of financial risks: credit risk (the risk of a default); market risk (the risk that market valuations fall sustainably); and liquidity risk (the risk that the previous market price can be achieved only over some period of time). In thinking about risk capacity, it is useful to think how these risks are best hedged.

Credit risk rises the more time there is for a default to occur. The best hedge is by diversifying credit risks and trying to find those that are supported by circumstances that undermine other credit risks. Banks have the greatest capacity for credit risks because they generally have the greatest access to differing credits and expertise in credit. A pension fund or insurance company has much less capacity for credit risk.

Liquidity risk is best hedged across time. Pension funds, insurance companies, and other investment vehicles with long-term funding or liabilities therefore have the greatest capacity for liquidity risk because they can hold on to assets that cannot be sold straight away and wait for buyers to return. Market risk is best hedged through a combination of diversification across other market risks and over time.

In a financial system where risks are allocated to capacity, one should therefore expect to see banks holding most credit risks, least liquidity risk, and some market risk, and long-term investors holding most liquidity risk, least credit risk, and some market risk. However, the previous approach to financial regulation ignored issues of capacity, often in the name of level playing fields and a singular view of risk. As a result, credit risk sailed to long-term investors and liquidity risk sailed to banks, increasing the system's interconnectivity and aggregate fragility. Requiring margins or capital charges for liquidity mismatches and separately analyzing the risks of a portfolio of credits could go a long way to pushing risk to where there is a capacity for it, reducing systemically dangerous interconnectivity of the financial system, and ultimately reducing the amount of deadweight capital required for there to be confidence in the system.

A system with high capital mobility, domestic macroprudential regulation, and countries with very different demographics could produce a much better allocation of resources globally. Countries that are aging, and therefore accumulating savings naturally in long-term savings institutions, could invest those funds in long-term investments abroad (and not in short-term government paper that is ill suited to their requirements). If the borrower could lock in the maturity of these funds (perhaps through long-term bonds or preference shares) and the investor could lock in the credit quality (perhaps through government guarantees for infrastructure projects), the systemic risk from this cross-border capital flow would be modest on both sides, without substantial set-asides of reserves and capital.

How Can You Tame Boom-Bust if You Don't Know Whether You Are in a Boom?

One of John Williamson's important contributions has been to create numerical estimates of a concept: fundamental equilibrium exchange rates. Policymakers cannot take the necessary steps if they do not know where they are. Many, most notably Alan Greenspan, voiced the concern that it was difficult to act countercyclically if you did not know where you were in the cycle and estimating that position was impossible. I beg to disagree. Measuring the cycle is what inflation-targeting central banks do daily. But this misses the point a little. If the purpose of countercyclical capital charges were to end boom-bust cycles, then I would accept that we would need to be more confident about the calibration of booms than we are today. However, if the purpose is to lean against the wind, calibrations can be less precise. Recall that without countercyclical charges the natural inclination in a boom is to lend even more because measured risks fall. The previous approach took the economic cycle and amplified it. Macroprudential regulation would, at worst, squeeze the financial cycle back to the magnitude of the economic cycle and, at best, serve to moderate that economic cycle by changing the cost of lending through the cycle. The goal is to moderate the worst excesses of the cycle, not to kill it. A world without economic cycles may not be good. Cycles are often a source of stretched ambitions and large-scale projects that provide benefits through many cycles in the future, such us building out railways or the channel tunnel or the fiber-optic network.

Systemically Important Institutions, Behavior, and Instruments

Not all financial institutions pose the same systemic risks. It stands to reason that regulation should acknowledge that some banks are systemically important and others are less so. In each country, supervisors should establish a list of systemically important institutions subject to closer scrutiny and greater containment of behavior. The key factors that determine the extent to which an institution, instrument, or trade is systemic are (1) size of exposures, especially where those exposures are to the core banking system and retail consumers; (2) degree of leverage and maturity mismatches; and (3) correlation or interconnectivity with the financial system. Where instruments are declared systemic because of these factors, they should be required to be centrally cleared. Today, interconnectivity can also be included in the homogeneity of behavior of institutions that on their own appear small relative to the size of the financial system.

All banks, and any other financial institution subject to deposit insurance, should be required to hold a minimum capital requirement as protection for the deposit insurance fund. Systemically important institutions and, where appropriate, systemically important instruments would be subject to both microprudential and macroprudential regulation in accordance with their contribution to systemic risk. This can be done by adjusting the microprudential ratio of capital, margin, or other requirements by a coefficient corresponding to an institution's macroprudential risk.

Great attention is being placed today on dealing with the incentives of individual bankers and traders. There is a movement toward requiring banks to disclose remuneration arrangements of traders and others. I do not share the zeal of some for governments to be involved in the decisions of private firms in matters of executive compensation. While I would not argue against measures to lengthen bankers' horizons, I place greater hope in macroprudential regulation pushing banks to develop incentive packages that are more encouraging of through-the-cycle behavior. However, if that fails, regulators should do more. Incentives are important. If a bank supervisor believes an institution has set incentives in a manner that is conducive to excessive risk taking, the supervisor should raise that institution's capital adequacy requirements. This is something the United Kingdom's Financial Services Authority has confidently announced that it will do and it will be interesting to see if it is able to do so.

International Policy Coordination

A strongly held view is that financial institutions are global and so financial regulation needs to be global. This equivalency does not add up. More international meetings would not have averted the crisis. Indeed, the crisis has taught us that there is plenty that needs to be done at the national level to strengthen regulation.

In terms of macroprudential rules for bank capital and liquidity, my expectation is that there will be a switch back from "home-country" to "host-country" regulation. The degree of macroprudential risk depends on conditions on the ground. This apparent retreat from internationalism should not be resisted, as it has two systemic benefits. First, under nationally set macroprudential rules, foreign banks regulated by their home regulator abroad would be required to set up their local presence as independent subsidiaries that can withstand the default of an international parent and be regulated locally. This would reduce exposure to lax jurisdictions more effectively than trying to force all to follow a standard that is likely to be inappropriate for all.

Second, while this may seem counterintuitive, nationally set countercyclical charges could give the euro area, other common currency areas, and fixed or managed exchange rate countries a critical additional policy instrument that provides a more differentiated response than does a single interest rate to a boom in one member state and deflation in another. Capital adequacy for bank lending to the real estate markets in Ireland and Spain should have been far higher than for Germany. I fear the fashionable idea of a "European banking union" could work against this desirable possibility.

If there were a boom in Ireland and no boom in Germany, and as a result national regulators raised capital adequacy for lending in Ireland and not Germany, international banking flows would come out of Ireland into Germany, which is exactly what would be desirable until the Irish property market cooled down or the German market heated up.

Capital adequacy requirements are not attached to the jurisdiction of the head office of the bank but to the location of the subsidiary doing the lending. The Irish subsidiary of a German bank would have to set aside capital required by the Irish authorities. No lending would take place outside local subsidiaries and, if it did, the authorities could make such contracts unenforceable, which would be effective deterrence. Macroprudential regulation, alongside a requirement for subsidiarization of branches of foreign banks, provides the kind of insulation from this feast and famine of international capital flows that capital controls and exchange rate arrangements try to do. Moreover, it does so without drawing a distinction between foreign or domestic lending—a distinction so easily exploited by protectionist impulses. Rather it simply asks whether there is a boom of lending or a dearth, not whether or not that lending is from domestic sources. Macroprudential is the new capital control with the advantage that it is less prone to national discrimination and protectionism.

Although, as mentioned, the thrust of regulation will likely see a greater role for host-country macroprudential regulation, there are a number of procedures that are best regulated internationally, where risks are less endogenous to national circumstances. In addition, under certain circumstances international regulation would facilitate acceptance of certain regulations by international institutions and their capital. These regulations are primarily of a microprudential nature, such as standards for directors, general corporate governance, financial reporting, anti-money laundering, know-your-customer rules, consumer protection, and minimum capital adequacy

The framework used to raise and lower national macroprudential targets and limits should be as international and transparent as possible. And there should be extensive information sharing between regulators on the activities of international banks. This agenda for policy cooperation is sufficiently modest and nonthreatening to domestic policy choices as to be well within our reach.

Conclusion

The task, so well identified by John Williamson, is to redesign the international financial system so that it is fit to allocate surplus savings to investments that need it, thereby raising global growth, and so that it does so in a smooth and predictable manner that facilitates long-term investment and reduces the need for expensive short-term insurance mechanisms.

The tools with which the policy community has tried to reshape the financial system—exchange rates, degree of capital account liberalization, and monetary and fiscal policy—have required a level of policy coordination that is not currently available and may never be. There was a moment at the end of 2008, amid the debris of the collapse of Lehman Brothers, when policymakers were most open to a new system. But that moment has passed.

More lasting has been the recognition that financial regulation must play a part in avoiding financial crashes—all cannot be left to monetary and fiscal policy alone—and that for it to do so, it must be far more proactively macroprudential long before the next crash. We cannot avoid crashes without limiting the booms.

Microprudential regulation—which concerns the certification, reporting, operation, and governance of individual institutions—can be put on an internationally agreed-upon path of convergence. But while the framework for macroprudential policy can be established internationally, the calibration of macroprudential policy—levels of capital adequacy, leverage and liquidity levels that vary with the economic cycle, and the degree of maturity mismatch—must be set locally.

This hybrid approach—internationally agreed-upon microprudential regulation administered by the home-country regulator of an international bank, along with nationally set macroprudential limits and targets administered by the host-country regulator—is likely to be both internationally palatable and as effective as any other approach in taming boom-bust cycles. It is not the whole-scale redesign of the financial system that many imagined. Some would view it as unambitious—one might lament that we are no longer returning to the moon, so to speak. But with so much at stake, function beats form.

References

Axelrod, Robert, and William D. Hamilton. 1981. The Evolution of Cooperation. *Science* 211, no. 4489: 1390–96.

Barrett, Scott. 2010. *Why Cooperate? The Incentive to Supply Global Public Goods.* Oxford: Oxford University Press.

Brunnermeier, Markus, Andrew Crockett, Charles Goodhart, Avinash Persaud, and Hyun Shin. 2009. *The Fundamental Principles of Financial Regulation.* Geneva Report on the World Economy 11. London: Centre for Economic Policy Research.

Kaul, Inge, Pedro Conceição, Katell Le Goulven, and Ronald U. Mendoza. 2003. *Providing Global Public Goods: Managing Globalization.* New York: Oxford University Press for the United Nations Development Programme.

Persaud, Avinash. 2002. Sending the Herd off the Cliff Edge: The Disturbing Interaction between Herding and Market-Sensitive Risk Management Systems. In *Market Liquidity: Proceedings of a Workshop Held at the BIS,* volume 2. Geneva: Bank for International Settlements.

Persaud, Avinash, ed. 2003. *Liquidity Black Holes.* London: Risk Books.

Persaud, Avinash. 2008a. Reason with the Messenger, Don't Shoot Him: Value Accounting, Risk Management and Financial System Resilience. VoxEU, October 12. Available at www.voxeu. org/article/problems-suspending-mark-market-accounting-rules (accessed on July 31, 2012).

Persaud, Avinash. 2008b. Valuation, Regulation and Liquidity. *Financial Stability Review,* no. 12 (October). Paris: Bank of France.

Rodrik, Dani. 1999. Democracies Pay Higher Wages. *Quarterly Journal of Economics* 114, no. 3: 707–38.

Subramanian, Arvind, and John Williamson. 2009. The World Crisis: Reforming the International Financial System. Peterson Institute for International Economics essay prepared for publication in *Economic and Political Weekly* (Mumbai, India), March 5. Available at www.piie.com/ publications/papers/subramanian-williamson0309.pdf (accessed on July 31, 2012).

Warwick Commission. 2009. *The Warwick Commission on International Financial Reform: In Praise of Unlevel Playing Fields.* Warwick University. Available at http://www2.warwick.ac.uk/research/ warwickcommission.

Williamson, John. 1965. *The Crawling Peg.* Princeton Essays in International Finance 50. Princeton, NJ: Princeton University Press.

Williamson, John. 1977. Transferência de Recursos e o Sistema Monetário Internacional. In *Estudos Sobre Desenvolvimento Econômico,* ed. John Williamson et al. Rio de Janeiro: BNDES.

Williamson, John. 1996. *The Crawling Band as an Exchange Rate Regime: Lessons from Chile, Colombia, and Israel.* Washington: Institute for International Economics.

Williamson, John. 1998. Economists, Policy Reform, and Political Economy. Keynote address to a conference on the political economy of policy reform, Rajiv Gandhi Institute, New Delhi, December.

Williamson, John. 2000. *Exchange Rate Regimes for Emerging Markets: Reviving the Intermediate Option.* Policy Analyses in International Economics 60. Washington: Institute for International Economics.

Williamson, John. 2005. *Curbing the Boom-Bust Cycle: Stabilizing Capital Flows to Emerging Markets.* Policy Analyses in International Economics 75. Washington: Institute for International Economics.

Williamson, John, and Molly Mahar. 1998. *A Survey of Financial Liberalization.* Princeton Essays in International Finance 211. Princeton, NJ: Princeton University Press.

7

Growth-Linked Securities

STEPHANY GRIFFITH-JONES AND DAGMAR HERTOVA

Though this chapter is focused on GDP-linked securities—and John Williamson's contribution to the discussion of this potentially valuable instrument—it must be placed in a broader context of countercyclical policies and mechanisms. John shared this concern with several of us (but, alas, not with most economists) about the need for more stable capital flows, increasingly broadened now to the need for more stable national and international financial systems. We can see two great strengths of John's contributions: first is the focus on broad analytical and theoretical issues—in this case the need to stabilize the boom and bust of capital flows to emerging economies; and second is the attention to detailed policy proposals that could help deal with the issues raised, including the design of GDP-linked securities to help stabilize capital flows.

While much thought has been given to flows to developing economies, we see now that such mechanisms would have been equally or even more relevant for lending to developed countries. Indeed, it is interesting when analyzing the euro area crisis to note how little emphasis there has been on the role that capital flows played in causing it. In addition, the US government would have benefited from issuing GDP-linked securities, as this would have lowered debt service in difficult times. But when John and one of us (Griffith-Jones) raised

Stephany Griffith-Jones is the financial markets director of the Initiative for Policy Dialogue at Columbia University in New York and associate fellow at the Overseas Development Institute. Dagmar Hertova is an economist at the Development Policy and Analysis Division of the Department of Economic and Social Affairs at the United Nations in New York. The authors thank Jorge Carrera and Guillermo Mondino for providing estimates on Argentine GDP-linked warrants. Thanks go as well to Paolo Mauro for insightful comments on an early version of the paper presented at the organizational meeting for this volume in April 2012. The authors also thank Edward Griffith-Jones for excellent research assistance.

this possibility with the US Treasury before the subprime crisis, we got a rather cold reception.

So how did John Williamson conceptualize the problem of curbing the cycle of booms and busts? This is most clearly shown in Williamson (2005):

> If one goes back in history, one finds that these (the Latin American and East Asian crises) are only the most recent of a succession of booms in lending to emerging markets that have given way to busts that impoverished both those who lent money and those who borrowed from them....

> In recent years, the flow of foreign capital has become the prime driver of the business cycle in a number of emerging markets, especially in Latin America. That the process is driven primarily by variations in the availability of foreign capital rather than by developments in the host countries seems strongly indicated by the large size of the variations in the overall flow.... It seems that, as José Antonio Ocampo (2003) has emphasized, the variations in capital flows are driven primarily by changes in risk evaluation. When foreign investors develop an appetite for risk (Ocampo points out that this should more properly be called an underestimation of risk), there is a boom in capital flows; the bust is marked by a flight to quality (risk aversion).

> External financing crises are far from being a novel feature of the international financial system: they have recurred at various times during the past two centuries.... The issue that is addressed in this study is whether it has to be this way or whether feasible policy actions could curb the sequence of boom and bust and thus permit both investors and emerging markets to tap the potential benefits of capital mobility without the costs of the crises that have so often ensued. (Williamson 2005, 2)

In the same book, John outlines the historical sequence:

> The Bretton Woods years were the only lengthy period since the birth of capitalism in Holland in the 17th century that lacked major banking or debt crises. The Bretton Woods years were also, not coincidentally, the period when financial repression was practically ubiquitous. The end of that period was heralded by Carlos Diaz-Alejandro, who presciently titled a 1984 paper on the debt crisis, *Goodbye Financial Repression, Hello Financial Crash*. (Williamson 2005, 4)

Finally, the policy implications John draws from these historical trends are clear and prescient:

> The process of financial liberalization needs to be approached with a great deal of caution and with a lot of care to install an effective system of prudential supervision that will deter bankers from acting in the interests of their cronies rather than their ostensible principals, depositors, and shareholders. (Williamson 2005, 5)

John then develops in his 2005 study a range of policy actions for debtors, creditors, and the international community to try to curb the boom-bust cycle of capital flows. He stresses that some of the actions that would seem most likely to be effective would require the agreement of the general international community, including the source countries, to change the international rules of the game. The emphasis on source countries and on international action seems particularly important to us (one of us had been working on these issues for a long time, with very limited company from other economists). Griffith-Jones (1998, 171) described the "need for measures to be taken by source countries to discourage excessive surges of easily reversible capital inflows to emerging countries' capital flows from the source countries."

John's proposals to try to curb the boom-bust pattern of capital flows include a range of measures, such as forward-looking (or countercyclical) banking provisions and capital controls by emerging countries, which he stresses could be particularly effective. He also emphasizes measures such as GDP-linked securities and local currency bonds. Again, here John was well ahead of the curve. Very few economists before the global financial crisis starting in 2007 argued for countercyclical provisions. That short list included José Antonio Ocampo and Bank for International Settlements economists Claudio Borio and Phillip Turner (Griffith-Jones and Ocampo 2008). Now of course countercyclical regulation is very mainstream. Similarly, on capital controls, John was clear on their potential important net benefits as a tool to deal with volatile capital flows, provided countries followed good macroeconomic policies. Today this position is also much more accepted, with the International Monetary Fund (IMF), for example, quite clearly arguing that capital controls may be a valuable instrument if surges of capital are significant.

In summary, John's contribution to the broad subject of curbing boom-bust cycles was important and prescient. He was often ahead of the curve and even swam against the tide. In rereading carefully his excellent 2005 text, we found only one disagreement, though this does benefit in part from hindsight. John writes:

> Some cyclical fluctuations seem to be an inherent feature of the financial markets of capitalist economies, but their relatively benign form in the industrial countries in the 60 years since World War II demonstrates that they do not have to be as destructive as they have been in the emerging markets. The action program that has been developed in this study is intended to facilitate a process of financial maturing similar to the one that has already occurred in the industrial countries. (Williamson 2005, 115)

Our disagreement is with the final sentence, because we now know that underregulated financial markets can be as, if not more, disruptive in developed countries as in developing countries, and that the latter should not aspire to "mature" to financial sectors similar to developed ones. On the contrary, developing countries need to rethink carefully how they can shape their financial sectors and regulation to serve the needs of their economies and avoid costly crises. The challenge is even deeper for the developed countries, having just endured major crises. The instrument we now discuss—GDP-linked securities—could be valuable for both developed and developing countries.

Overview of Growth-Linked Securities

The present global economic and financial crisis has focused attention on policies and instruments that would allow countries to manage and minimize the risks associated with increasing international financial integration. In light of this, there have been a variety of ideas and proposals put forth relating to innovative financial instruments. Some of these proposals have been put into practice, albeit to a limited degree and under special circumstances.

The idea of GDP-linked bonds falls into this category. The proposal for such an instrument is not new, and a first wave of interest in indexing debt to GDP emerged in the 1980s, propounded by economists such as John Williamson (2005). The practice has been encouraged by economists such as Robert Shiller (1993, 2005),[1] Eduardo Borensztein and Paolo Mauro (2004) at the IMF, and the US Council of Economic Advisers (CEA 2004). At the United Nations, one of us coauthored a study (Griffith-Jones and Sharma 2009) and organized a series of meetings to promote the idea. John Williamson was a key and valued supporter of this endeavor.

Though the idea of GDP-indexed debt has so far been implemented only to a limited extent—and unfortunately only by countries that were having difficulties in servicing their debts—it received new impetus after the wave of debt crises in a number of developing countries in the 1990s. In particular, GDP-indexed bonds have attracted discussion in recent years, since a variant of this instrument played a role in Argentina's debt restructuring (see below).

A key point is that it would be ideal for governments to issue growth-linked securities in a precautionary way when their macroeconomic fundamentals are strong and investors are keen to invest in their bonds. At such a moment any novelty premium would be relatively low. The problem is that in good times, governments have less incentive to issue such bonds, as they see downturns or crises as unlikely, especially during their mandate. However, the global financial crisis, as well as all preceding ones, have made the case for these bonds far stronger.

The Benefits of GDP-Indexed Bonds

The introduction of GDP-indexed bonds could have a number of benefits for borrowing countries and investors, as well as broader benefits for the global economy and financial system. Those benefits are detailed in the following sections.

---

1. Shiller proposed the creation of "macro markets" for GDP-linked securities that were to be perpetual claims on a fraction of a country's GDP.

Gains for Borrowing Countries

GDP-indexed bonds provide two major benefits to borrowers: First, they stabilize government spending and limit the procyclicality of fiscal pressures by requiring smaller interest payments at times of slower growth, providing space for higher spending or lower taxes, and vice versa. This runs counter to the actual experience of borrowing countries often forced to undertake fiscal retrenchment during periods of slow growth. The bonds could also curb excessively expansionary fiscal policy in times of rapid growth.

Second, by allowing debt-service ratios to fall in times of slow or negative growth, GDP-indexed bonds reduce the likelihood of defaults and debt crises. Crises are extremely costly, both in terms of growth and production and in financial terms. The extent of this benefit is of course determined by the share of debt that is indexed to GDP.

Simulations show that the gains for borrowers can be substantial. If half of Mexico's total government debt had consisted of GDP-indexed bonds, it would have saved about 1.6 percent of GDP in interest payments during the 1994–95 financial crisis (Borensztein and Mauro 2004). These additional resources would have provided the government with space to avoid sharp spending cuts, and might even have provided some leeway for additional spending that could have mitigated some of the worst effects of the crisis. Countries experiencing volatile growth and high levels of indebtedness, and particularly those undergoing debt restructuring, find GDP-indexed bonds particularly attractive.

Gains for Investors

Investors would likely receive two main benefits from the introduction of GDP-indexed bonds. First, the bonds would provide an opportunity for investors to take a position on countries' future growth prospects, offering them equity-like exposure to a country. Though this is made possible to some degree through stock markets, such opportunities are often not representative of the economy as a whole. In this respect, GDP-indexed bonds would also provide a diversification opportunity, for example by giving investors in countries or regions with low growth rates an opportunity to have a stake in countries with higher growth rates. Moreover, since growth rates across countries tend to be uncorrelated to some extent, a portfolio including GDP-indexed bonds for several economies would have the benefits of diversification, thus increasing the ratio of returns to risks. If GDP-linked bonds were to become widespread across countries, investors could take a position on growth worldwide—the ultimate risk diversification.

The second main benefit for investors from GDP-indexed bonds would be a lower frequency of defaults and financial crises, which often result in costly litigation and renegotiation and sometimes in outright large losses.

Broader Benefits to the Global Economy and Financial System

On a larger scale, GDP-indexed bonds can be viewed as desirable vehicles for international risk-sharing and as a way of avoiding the disruptions arising from formal default. They can be said to have the characteristics of a public good in that they generate systemic benefits over and above those accruing to individual investors and countries. For example, by reducing the likelihood of a default by the borrowing country, these instruments would benefit not just their holders but also the broader categories of investors, including those who hold plain vanilla bonds. Similarly, the benefits of a lesser likelihood of financial crises extend to those countries that may be affected by contagion as well as to economies and multilateral institutions that may have to finance bailout packages. As elaborated below, these externalities provide an additional compelling explanation of why it is not sufficient to expect markets to develop these instruments on their own, which indeed they have not. Rather, there exists a justification for the international community, using public international institutions and especially the multilateral and regional development banks, to coordinate efforts to achieve such an end.

John Williamson's Important Contributions to Growth-Linked Securities

Besides John Williamson's pioneering role in advocating the use of GDP-linked bonds as a valuable instrument, he has made several more specific contributions, especially in his 2008 paper entitled *Is There a Role for Growth-Linked Securities?* (Williamson 2008).

Analysis of Variants of Growth-Linked Securities

John has strongly emphasized that the distinct implications of the different structures of growth-linked securities have yet to be recognized. Here we present the main variants of growth-linked securities and John's analysis of the difference between them (without going into as much detail as he did).

Robert Shiller (1993) proposed what will be referred to as a "Shiller security" as one of several new instruments intended to offer investors a broader range of investment possibilities. This security would represent a permanent fraction of the issuer country's nominal GDP. It could pay, for example, one-trillionth of a nation's nominal GDP, leading Shiller to propose the name "trill" for this kind of security (Kamstra and Shiller 2009).

A second variant was suggested by Borensztein and Mauro (2004). A "Borensztein-Mauro security" would be very similar to a standard bond but would pay an interest rate that would vary proportionately with the issuer country's real growth rate. Take, for example, a country that, based on past experience, is expected to grow at an annual rate of 3 percent and can issue conventional bonds with fixed annual interest payments of 10 percent. A

Borensztein-Mauro security would pay 1 percent of additional interest for each 1 percent of growth above expectations, and 1 percent less interest for each 1 percent of growth below expectations. If the economy grows at 5 percent, then the payment would increase to 12 percent; and with growth of 2 percent the security would pay 9 percent.

A third variant was suggested by Daniel Schydlowsky at a meeting at the United Nations in 2005 convened by one of us, and where John Williamson was a speaker.[2] This security would make payments just as the Borensztein-Mauro security, but the difference between this proposed payment and the payment that would occur under a conventional bond would be added or subtracted from the principal, rather than being transferred between the debtor and creditor. Using the example above, when the economy grows at 5 percent, the extra 2 percent in payment would be subtracted from the country's debt. In this case, the debtor country would still benefit from the countercyclical element of the growth-linked security, but its debt would be decreased if it were to grow above the threshold and vice versa.

Having described the proposed variants, Williamson (2008) turns to analyzing the effects of varying economic performance on the debt-servicing of these securities. It is clear that there are substantive and economically significant differences between the three variants. First, the Shiller security is the only one that indexes for inflation, although it would be relatively easy to adjust the other two variants to do so.

Second, changes in real growth rate have varying effects on the payments of the different securities. An increase in the real growth rate has no effect on the payment of the Schiller security in the short run. In the long run, thanks to capital appreciation, the value of the security increases and implies higher servicing payments. On the other hand, a higher growth rate implies higher servicing of the Borensztein-Mauro security in the short run, but the value of the principal would be unaffected. Under the Schydlowsky variant, interest payments would increase in the short run but the country's debt would be decreased in the long run. It is evident that the Borensztein-Mauro security would be the most effective in providing fiscal stabilization benefits and in reducing the risk of debt default.

Potential Role of Muslim Investors

John Williamson argues that growth-linked bonds could be very attractive for Muslim investors "because they do not imply the payment of a fixed rate of interest irrespective of the ability to pay of the debtor, [and] one can hope that sharia law will take a benign view of such instruments" (Williamson 2008, 10). According to John, four criteria are described by Islamic law for financial instruments to be deemed "Islamic." First, financial assets should avoid *riba*,

2. GDP-Indexed Bonds: Making It Happen, New York, October 31, 2005.

meaning interest payments. Since growth-linked securities offer the opportunity to avoid conventional interest payments, while earning a competitive rate of return through payments that vary with the borrower's ability to pay, they are consistent with this principle.

Second, financial assets should avoid *gharar*, which can be understood as unnecessary uncertainty. Growth-linked securities reduce uncertainty for borrowers, but may increase uncertainty for lenders. John argues that as long as lenders are able to diversify away their uncertainty, growth-linked securities can be deemed Islamic in this sense.

Third, Islamic finance must not promote sinful activities prohibited by Islam, such as drinking or gambling. Since by investing in growth-linked securities Islamic creditors would invest in positive growth prospects of non-Islamic countries, the prohibited activities would be a part of the faster growth. In this sense, it would be difficult to envisage growth-linked bonds, much like most sovereign bonds, as being Islamic, unless an acceptable maximum level of sinful activities were specified.

Lastly, Islamic finance covers real activities, not financial speculation; for example, bonds that are backed by collateral are acceptable. Growth-linked securities are not likely to satisfy this condition, as they are not designed, like most sovereign borrowing, to be backed by real collateral.

Overall, growth-linked securities clearly satisfy the first condition of Islamic finance. Compliance with the other three conditions is not as clear; however, other forms of sovereign borrowing face the same problems. Therefore, John argues that Islamic investors should not be reluctant to hold growth-linked securities, which are closer to Islamic philosophy than normal sovereign bonds.

Why Moral Hazard Is Not Important

John Williamson believes that the fears of moral hazard risks are "vastly overdone" (Williamson 2008, 9). It does not make sense for governments to suppress growth just so that their debt servicing bill will be lower, as the benefits would be very small compared to the costs of curbing growth. Underreporting of growth may be of more concern. Again, this is not likely for political and technical reasons. First, politicians like to report that the economy has been growing during their time in office. It would not be beneficial for them to underreport growth. Second, from the technical perspective, substantially underreporting growth for extended periods of time would be very difficult. Finally, any misreporting by governments would come to the attention of markets and most probably be punished. Markets would allow for such behavior in pricing of new issues of securities, and it would become more costly for the country to borrow in the way of growth-linked securities in the future.

GDP Revisions

Even though John does not think moral hazard risks are important, he does believe governments may be reluctant to pay more on growth-linked securities when GDP data are statistically revised. He describes three possible sources of revisions of GDP data that may cause concern (Williamson 2008).

First, there are routine adjustments to GDP data, usually prompted by additional information becoming available following the publication of data. A second source of revisions comes from manipulation of data by the issuer. However, as discussed above, it would be very difficult to continuously misreport growth.

Third, there are GDP revisions resulting from modifications of the structure of national income estimates reflecting the changing structure of the economy. To analyze the scope of this problem, John Williamson, with the help of one of us (Dagmar Hertova), conducted rigorous analysis of historical GDP revisions published in the IMF's *International Financial Statistics* yearbooks of 1983 until 2006 for some 66 countries (Williamson 2008). The vast majority of GDP revisions were found to be small adjustments to nominal GDP and the GDP deflator that normally occur following the initial publication of statistics. In total, over 80 percent of all revisions were within 1 percent of the values reported in the previous year, and almost 90 percent were within 3 percent.

The authors examined nonroutine adjustments to real GDP—those larger than 3 percent—in more detail. In total, between 1981 and 2000 (the years with adequate data) there were 41 apparent GDP revisions in 38 countries (out of 740 observations). These revisions averaged 6.7 percent.

Williamson (2008) has proposed several approaches to designing securities that would resolve the problem of GDP revisions. One approach would incorporate into the contract of the securities the exact formula for measuring GDP, which would then always be used when calculating the payment. However, in the case of long-term securities, such a measure could become outdated and would not account for changes in the structure of the economy. Another approach, applicable for the Borensztein-Mauro security but not the Shiller one, would be to simply add to the old GDP formula the increase in real GDP that results from the latest updated formula. Lastly, payments could simply reflect the impact of any and all revisions. If a revision is made to the way national accounts data are calculated, and subsequently GDP is reported higher, then the payment increases based on the revision. Under a Borensztein-Mauro bond, payment would be higher for the year of the revision and then return to normal. In order not to jeopardize the countercyclical element of the security in such a year, the excess GDP could be capitalized, that is, added to the value of the debt. The securities would still provide the countercyclical element but incorporate GDP revisions.

Would These Securities Really Be Countercyclical?

Experience with growth-linked securities, however limited, has highlighted the fear that their countercyclical element may be limited by lags in publication of GDP data. In the case of both the Argentine and Greek warrants discussed below, payment in a given year is based on the growth reported in the previous year. The fear is that this lag in payment may imply a procyclical effect rather than the intended countercyclical effect. Williamson (2008) has acknowledged that there may be cases when lags could wipe out the countercyclical benefits of these instruments, but it is important to look at what happens generally.

Since the Borensztein-Mauro security is the one that offers the most countercyclical benefits in principle, it is also more susceptible to the problem at hand. Hertova (2006) analyzed the timing of payments and its effects on Colombia and Malaysia had half of their sovereign debt been swapped for Borensztein-Mauro-type securities. The study compared the interest payments under different timing scenarios. In one scenario, growth rates are measured annually, with payments lagging one year. In a second scenario, growth rates are measured semiannually with a six-month lag from the end of the reporting period to payment.

The results suggest that the second scenario, with only a six-month lag in payments, would have had substantial countercyclical benefits for the issuing countries. In contrast, with a lag in payments of one year, there would be very little, if any, countercyclical benefit. For example, the savings resulting from Colombia's 1999 recession would only have been realized at the end of 2000 when growth had already picked up again. In contrast, if the payments had been based on semiannual growth with a lag of six months, then savings would have been realized in 1999, expanding the country's fiscal space when needed. Malaysia would have also benefited from growth-linked securities, if to a lesser extent, with payments based on semiannual growth during the 1997 Asian crisis.

Lessons Learned

Argentine GDP-Linked Securities

GDP-linked securities were included in the Argentine debt restructuring package in 2005 that aimed to exchange $82 billion in bonds on which the country had defaulted four years earlier. With a creditor participation rate in the debt swap of 76 percent, the notional value of the GDP-linked securities, which were initially attached to every restructured bond, was $62 billion. At the end of November 2005, 180 days after the issue date, the warrants became detachable and started trading separately. The securities were issued in different currencies: Argentine pesos (under Argentine law), dollars (one under the New York law and one under Argentine law), euros (under English law), and yen (under Japanese law). More GDP-linked securities were issued as part of the 2010 restructuring, when $12.9 billion of debt was swapped in a settlement with creditors who rejected the 2005 offering.

Initially, the GDP-linked warrants were viewed by Argentina's creditors as well as by the financial markets as having very little value (Griffith-Jones and Sharma 2009), so they represented little gain for the country. Some commentators have argued that the existence of the warrants helped make the overall package (which was favorable to Argentina) somewhat more acceptable to creditors, and therefore could have had intangible benefits. Nevertheless most observers and participants in the deal agree that the market gave little value to the warrants when they were issued. However, thanks to the country's booming growth in the following years, and the corresponding higher payments made on the warrants (as well as the expected higher payments in future), the warrants substantially outperformed expectations and their prices soared. At the time of the exchange, the price of the securities suggested by major investment banks was about $2 per $100 of notional value. At the time they became detached, the dollar-denominated securities were trading at $4.25 (Costa, Chamon, and Ricci 2008). In the following years, the market price of the Argentine GDP-linked securities skyrocketed, with the dollar-denominated warrant reaching a peak of $15.82 in June 2007. As of July 4, 2012, the dollar-denominated warrant was trading at $14.65.[3]

It is likely that markets charged a premium for the Argentine warrants due to the apparent poor prospects of the Argentine economy at the time, the novelty of the instrument, the complexity of its pricing, and concerns about data accuracy. However, this premium declined substantially, especially in the first three months of trading (Costa, Chamon, and Ricci 2008). More importantly, from the Argentine perspective, payments on the warrants have started to become rather high (see below).

Payments have been made to the holders of the Argentine GDP-linked securities on December 15 of each year starting in 2006 under the following conditions:[4]

- Real GDP exceeds base-case GDP.
- Real annual GDP growth exceeds base-case GDP growth. Based on the set levels of base-case real GDP levels, the threshold for real GDP growth starts at 4.26 percent for 2005, falling to 3.55 percent for 2006, and then gradually falling to 3 percent for 2015 and onward.
- Total payments on the warrants do not exceed the payment cap, which has been set at 0.48 per unit of currency of the warrants. The warrants

---

3. Using the Bloomberg exchange rate as of July 4, 2012. See Ken Parks, "Argentina Bonds Retreat, Peso Steady on Low Volume; Merval +0.5%," *Wall Street Journal*, July 4, 2012.

4. Republic of Argentina, Prospectus Supplement (to Prospectus dated December 27, 2004), January 10, 2005, www.mecon.gov.ar/finanzas/sfinan/english/download/us_prospectus_and_prospectus_supplement.pdf (accessed on July 28, 2012).

will expire no later than December 15, 2035. If the payment cap has been reached prior to this date, the warrant will be deemed to have expired then.

When the above conditions are met, the government will make a payment as follows:

Payment = ((0.05 x excess GDP) x unit of currency coefficient) x notional value of GDP-linked securities,

where *excess GDP* is the amount by which actual GDP exceeds the base-case GDP, expressed in billions of nominal pesos, and the *unit of currency coefficient* represents the proportion of a GDP-linked security with a notional amount of one unit of currency in the total amount of eligible securities available at the time of exchange (i.e., $81.8 billion).

Given a lag in publishing GDP data, the payment based on the GDP performance in a given year is paid at the end of the following year. The warrants will not provide any principal payments.

An important feature of the warrants is that the payment is not in itself based on GDP growth, but rather on the level of GDP. Since Argentina grew rapidly in the years following the debt exchange (figure 7.1), the base GDP level has been exceeded early, resulting in high payments on the warrants. High early growth also means that the level of GDP is more likely to stay above the base level, increasing the chance of future payments and their value and thus raising the value of the warrant.

As a result, payments on the warrants have proved very costly for Argentina, rising from a total of $395 million in 2006 to almost $2.5 billion in 2011 and an estimated $3.8 billion at the end of 2012 (table 7.1). The government did not make any payment in 2010, as growth in the previous year was below the threshold of 3.29 percent. However, the missed payment in 2010 was effectively made up for in 2011. Furthermore, with the level of GDP rising at a much faster pace than the expected base GDP due to exceptional growh in 2010–11, projected payments for 2012 have shot up.

It is clear that the GDP-linked securities are starting to be a burden for the Argentine government and economy. The payments represented over 0.5 percent of Argentine GDP and over 2.5 percent of exports in 2011, compared with just 0.18 percent and 0.72 percent in 2006, respectively. The payments are projected to rise quite significantly in 2012. Up to 2011, payments on the warrants were between 10 and 30 percent of the total servicing of interest on public sector debt. In 2012, however, this ratio is estimated to rise to 34 percent, a very high level indeed (table 7.1).

As mentioned above, the government made no payments on the GDP-linked securities at the end of 2010. However, looking at the fiscal balances, it seems that the temporary relief would have benefited Argentina more in the previous year. By 2010, growth had already picked up again and the fiscal balance had improved compared to 2009. This suggests that in this instance, the countercyclical element of the warrants may have been lost.

Figure 7.1   Argentine base-case GDP level and GDP growth versus actual GDP level and GDP growth, 2005–34

a. Level of real base-case GDP versus actual and estimated GDP

billions of 1993 Argentine pesos

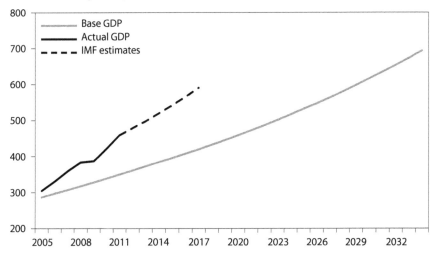

b. Base-case annual real GDP growth versus actual and estimated GDP growth

percent

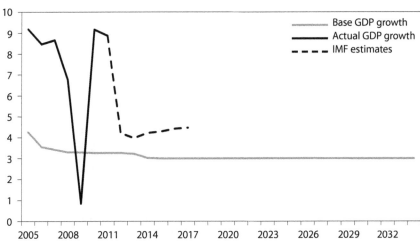

IMF = International Monetary Fund

Sources: Ministry of Finance of the Republic of Argentina, www.mecon.gov.ar (accessed on July 18, 2012); IMF, *World Economic Outlook* database, April 2012, www.imf.org/external/pubs/ft/weo/2012/01/weodata/index.aspx (accessed on July 27, 2012).

Table 7.1 Argentina: Servicing of GDP-linked securities, 2005–12

Indicator	2005	2006	2007	2008	2009	2010	2011[a]	2012[a]
Payments on GDP-linked warrants								
Billions of dollars	—	0.395	0.812	0.996	1.416	0	2.481	3.787[b]
As share of total servicing of interest on public sector debt (percent)	—	10.5	15.6	24.8	22.1	0	30.0	34.2
As percent of GDP	—	0.18	0.31	0.30	0.46	0	0.55	0.80
As percent of exports	—	0.72	1.22	1.21	2.12	0	2.52	n.a.
GDP growth (percent)	9.18	8.47	8.65	6.76	0.85	9.16	8.87	4.22
Fiscal balance (percent of GDP)	–1.56	–0.89	–2.08	–0.81	–3.62	–1.58	–3.29	–3.07
Primary fiscal balance (percent of GDP)	4.65	4.18	2.47	2.76	0.21	1.68	–0.36	–0.19

n.a. = not available; — = not applicable

a. Economic indicators data for 2011 and 2012 are estimates from IMF, *World Economic Outlook* database, April 2012.

b. Unofficial estimate from Central Bank of Argentina. Original estimated payments in 2012 expressed in Argentine pesos were converted to dollars using exchange rate as of July 11, 2012, as reported by the Central Bank of Argentina.

Sources: Authors' calculations using data from the Ministry of Finance of the Republic of Argentina, www.mecon.gov.ar (accessed on July 18, 2012); Central Bank of Argentina, www.bcra.gov.ar/index_i.htm (accessed on July 18, 2012); Argentine National Statistics Institute (INDEC), www.indec.mecon.ar (accessed on July 18, 2012); and IMF, *World Economic Outlook* database, April 2012 (fiscal balances), www.imf.org/external/pubs/ft/weo/2012/01/weodata/index.aspx (accessed on July 27, 2012).

Table 7.2   Argentina: Annual and accumulated payments on GDP-linked securities (per 100 units, unless otherwise specified)

| | Annual payment | | | | |
Currency	December 15, 2006	December 15, 2007	December 15, 2008	December 15, 2009	December 15, 2011
US dollars (New York law)	0.62	1.32	2.28	3.17	4.38
US dollars (Argentine law)	0.62	1.32	2.28	3.17	4.38
Euros (English law)	0.66	1.26	1.99	2.84	4.19
Argentine pesos (Argentine law)	0.65	1.38	2.45	3.72	5.98
Yen (Japanese law)	0.68	1.46	2.42	2.66	3.39
	Accumulated payment				
US dollars (New York law)	11.77				
US dollars (Argentine law)	11.77				
Euros (English law)	10.94				
Argentine pesos (Argentine law)	14.18				
Yen (Japanese law)	10.60				
	Accumulated payment (percent of total cap)				
US dollars (New York law)	24.53				
US dollars (Argentine law)	24.53				
Euros (English law)	22.79				
Argentine pesos (Argentine law)	29.55				
Yen (Japanese law)	22.09				

Source: Ministry of Finance of the Republic of Argentina, www.mecon.gov.ar (accessed on July 28, 2012).

Overall, Argentina had paid out about $6 billion on the warrants as of end-2011. Given that the total cap on payments has been set at 48 percent of the value of the securities, Argentina has already paid around a quarter of its total GDP warrants payments within the first six years (table 7.2). If Argentina were to continue to pay the warrants (and grow) at the same speed as in the last six years, the GDP warrants could expire before their set maturity of 30 years.

Given current GDP projections, payment for the warrants in 2013 and 2014 may not happen, as the economy is expected to slow substantially in 2012 and 2013. Growth would need to be above 3.26 percent in 2012 and 3.22 percent in 2013 to trigger payment on the warrants. But since the payment is based on the level of excess GDP above the base level (which is now substantial), growth that is just slightly above the threshold (at, say, 3.3 percent) would result in substantial payment on the warrants, whereas growth of, say, 3.1 percent would imply no payment at all. Thus, the Argentine government could be tempted to underreport growth in order to avoid a payment.

However, this risk is paradoxically practically eliminated by the fact that, if anything, Argentina has been criticized for allegedly overreporting growth and underreporting inflation. If the government were to do this (a bad practice for any number of other reasons), it would increase the likelihood of servicing on the warrants, an undesirable result from the Argentine perspective and a very fortunate one for investors and creditors. Some private estimates of GDP suggest that Argentina's official statistics have overreported GDP growth by 1.9 percentage points on average since 2008 (JP Morgan 2012), and by as much as 3 percentage points in 2011 alone (Barclays Capital 2012b). At the same time, some sources allege inflation has been underreported since 2006 on average by 14.5 percentage points compared to private measures (JP Morgan 2012).

Greek GDP-Linked Securities

In February 2012, Greece issued GDP-linked securities as part of what is considered the biggest sovereign debt restructuring in history. The deal, which was agreed to as part of Greece's €130 billion bailout from the European Union and the IMF, along with Greece's massive austerity measures, erased about €100 billion from the country's staggering debt. Greece's sovereign debt still stands at 160 percent of its GDP, the highest in Europe. In the deal, private sector bond holders agreed to a loss of 53.5 percent of nominal value and over 70 percent of the net present value of the Greek bonds they are holding.

In total, €172 billion of Greek private debt has been swapped in the deal, with a participation rate of 85.8 percent for bonds issued under Greek law (€152 billion) and 69 percent for foreign-law bonds and bonds issued by state enterprises (€20 billion). Overall, the participation rate would reach 95.7 percent, following the use of collective action clauses.[5]

Participating holders received detachable GDP-linked securities, with a notional amount equal to the face amount of new bonds.[6] The securities will provide an annual payment on October 15 of every year starting in 2015 until 2042 under the following conditions (Morgan Stanley 2012):

- Nominal GDP equals or exceeds the reference nominal GDP.

- Real GDP growth is positive and in excess of specified targets. Based on the set levels of reference GDP levels, the threshold for real GDP growth starts at 2.9 percent for 2015, and then gradually falls to 2 percent for 2021 and onward (Morgan Stanley 2012).

- Each annual payment will not exceed 1 percent of the notional value of the bonds.

---

5. Ministry of Finance of Greece, PSI Press Release, March 9, 2012, www.minfin.gr/portal/en/resource/contentObject/id/baba4f3e-da88-491c-9c61-ce1fd030edf6 (accessed on July 28, 2012).

6. Ministry of Finance of Greece, PSI Launch Press Release, February 21, 2012, www.minfin.gr/portal/en/resource/contentObject/id/7ad6442f-1777-4d02-80fb-91191c606664 (accessed on July 28, 2012).

If the above conditions are met, the government will make a payment as follows:

Payment = (1.5 x (real GDP growth rate – reference real GDP growth rate)) x notional value of the GDP-linked securities

As in the case of Argentina, payment based on growth in a given year will not be made until the following year and the securities will not pay out a principal.

Differences between Argentine and Greek GDP-Linked Securities

Structural differences between the Greek and Argentine warrants imply differences in the payout. First, the Greek securities have an annual payment cap whereas the Argentine warrants have a total payment cap. While the payment cap of 1 percent of the value of the Greek warrants limits that country's obligations (a very positive circumstance, given the country's huge debt overhang), it may not be so attractive to investors. On the other hand, the Argentine analysis in this chapter has shown that while the GDP-linked warrants have been a very attractive investment, they have recently become a large burden for the government. In addition, the payments on Argentine warrants were made in the early stages of the warrants' maturity and any payment missed in any given year due to slow growth would be made up further out in the stream of payments. In contrast, any missed payment in the case of the Greek warrants would be "lost" to the investors and creditors (Barclays Capital 2012a). This difference has important implications for both creditors and debtors. It would seem to offer some protection for Greece, which is in any case still overburdened by an excessive debt overhang. However, the annual payments cap is rather high.

Second, the Argentine warrant payments are related to nominal GDP performance and thus indexed to inflation (as under the Schiller security).[7] In contrast, the payment on the Greek securities is a function of real growth.

Given Greece's bleak economic situation and future prospects, will the Greek GDP-linked securities lead to significant payments? It remains to be seen. But it seems that at the moment markets and investors are attaching very little value to the Greek warrants and do not expect them to be as valuable as the Argentine warrants (Barclays Capital 2012a, Whittall 2012). For example, Morgan Stanley (2012) projects a fair value for the Greek warrant at around 1 cent, and even under a positive scenario the value remains below 2 cents. The cap on annual payments of the Greek warrants also restricts the possibility of large payouts for the investors.

However, we should remember that investors also initially attached very little value to the Argentine warrants, yet their prices then shot up. The Greek

---

7. Joseph Cotterill, "The Worlds Inside a Greek GDP Warrant," *Financial Times* blog, February 24, 2012.

warrants seem to have been better designed from the country's perspective, and unfortunately, growth prospects in the short term look pretty grim for Greece, so large payments seem unlikely in the near future. On the other hand, because Greece has seen such a large decline in GDP, it may see a rebound of growth, which could generate warrant payments that may not be desirable at a time of fragile and highly needed recovery. Having a reference GDP may offer some protection, but further study is required on this.

Conclusion and Next Steps

As has been argued in this chapter and in John Williamson's 2008 paper, it would be most desirable for countries to issue GDP-linked securities in normal times, as this has clear benefits for all parties and for the international financial system. Issuing GDP-linked warrants as part of a debt restructuring process, as Argentina and Greece have done, can be costly from the debtor perspective and not attract much attention from investors and creditors, who tend to under-value the future benefits of those warrants.

If the advantages of issuing GDP-indexed bonds in normal times can be significant, as suggested above, why have financial markets not yet adopted them? To put it a bit provocatively, if markets can create so many "socially useless" or even harmful financial innovations, why can they not create innovations that could be beneficial?

A key point is that the systemwide benefits provided by these instruments are greater than those realized by individual investors. Hence, there are externalities that do not enter the considerations of individual financial institutions. Other factors that dissuade beneficial financial innovation from taking place include the fact that the markets for new instruments may be illiquid. There is therefore a need for a concerted effort to achieve and ensure a critical mass so as to attain market liquidity. Related to this are coordination problems, whereby a large number of borrowers have to issue a new instrument in order for investors to be able to diversify risk.

Given the existence of positive externalities in issuing these kinds of instruments, as well as coordination problems, there is a clear case for involving multilateral institutions. Concretely, multilateral or regional development banks could play an active role as "market makers" for GDP-linked bonds. They could begin by developing a portfolio of loans, the repayments on which could be indexed to the growth rate of the debtor country. Once the institutions have a portfolio of such loans to different developing countries, they could securitize and sell them on the international capital markets. Such a portfolio of loans could be particularly attractive for private investors, as it would offer them the opportunity to take a position on the growth prospects of a number of economies simultaneously. Given the low correlation among these countries' growth rates, the return-risk ratio would be higher. As correlations tend to be lower at the global level, the World Bank may be best placed to do such securitization. However, the European Investment Bank could offer a portfolio of developed and developing countries' GDP-linked securities. Other regional development banks could also play a role, including the Islamic Development Bank.

Alternatively, the multilateral development banks could buy GDP-linked bonds that developing countries would issue via private placements. The active involvement of those banks in this type of lending would serve to extend the benefits of adjusting debt service to changes in economic growth to countries that do not have access to international bond markets. The Agence Française de Développement has started making such loans to low-income countries with a very simple formula that gives debtor countries the option to take a total debt service holiday in years when their projected exports are below 95 percent of their previous average exports.

This brings us to a final point: it is important that the design of these growth-linked securities be simple, well thought through, and, ideally, standardized. Again, here, public financial international institutions or the United Nations could play an important role.

References

Barclays Capital. 2012a. Greek PSI 2: Valuation and Timeline. *Interest Rates Research* (February 24). Available at www.scribd.com/doc/84986988/Barclays-Capital-GREEK-PSI-2 (accessed on July 30, 2012).

Barclays Capital. 2012b. Argentina: Pro-growth GDP Print Supports GDP Warrants. *Emerging Markets* (March 27).

Borensztein, Eduardo, and Paolo Mauro. 2004. The Case for GDP-indexed Bonds. *Economic Policy* 19, no. 38: 166–216.

CEA (Council of Economic Advisers). 2004. *GDP-Indexed Bonds: A Primer.* Washington.

Costa, Alejo, Marcos Chamon, and Luca Antonio Ricci. 2008. *Is There a Novelty Premium on New Financial Instruments? The Argentine Experience with GDP-Indexed Warrants.* IMF Working Paper 08/109. Washington: International Monetary Fund.

Griffith-Jones, Stephany. 1998. *Global Capital Flows: Should They Be Regulated?* Basingstoke, UK: Palgrave Macmillan.

Griffith-Jones, Stephany, and José Antonio Ocampo. 2008. Building on the Counter-Cyclical Consensus: A Policy Agenda. Paper prepared for the High-level Roundtable on "Towards Basel III? Regulating the Banking Sector after the Crisis," Brussels, October 12. Available at www. stephanygj.net/papers/Counter-Cyclical-Regulation.pdf (accessed on July 28, 2012).

Griffith-Jones, Stephany, and Krishnan Sharma. 2009. GDP-Indexed Bonds: Making it Happen. In *Innovative Financing for Development,* ed. Suhas Ketkar and Dilip Ratha. Washington: World Bank.

Hertova, Dagmar. 2006. Fiscal Implications of GDP-Linked Bonds. Photocopy (August).

JP Morgan. 2012. Argentina Economic Outlook: Deep Inside of a Parallel Universe.... *Emerging Markets Research* (June). Available at http://quantfinanceclub.com/wp-content/uploads/2012/06/Argentina-research-June-2012.pdf (accessed on July 28, 2012).

Kamstra, Mark, and Robert J. Shiller. 2009. *The Case for Trills: Giving the People and Their Pension Funds a Stake in the Wealth of the Nation.* Cowles Foundation Discussion Paper no. 1717. New Haven, CT: Yale University.

Morgan Stanley. 2012. *Greece: Trading After the PSI* (March 8). Available at http://linkback.morganstanley.com/web/sendlink/webapp/BMServlet?file=bonq7288-3ob9-g000-85a7-001a64f 36000&store=0&d=UwBSZXNlYXJjaAA0MTIzNDA%3D&user=nd54zuh9cp-268&__gda__ =1457382936_5fb99d9fa43eb48efd58fc760ec9e45c (accessed on July 28, 2012).

Ocampo, José Antonio. 2003. Capital Account and Countercyclical Prudential Regulations in Developing Countries. In *From Capital Surge to Drought: Seeking Stability for Emerging Economies*, ed. Ricardo Ffrench-Davis and Stephany Griffith-Jones. Basingstoke, UK: Palgrave Macmillan.

Shiller, Robert J. 1993. *Macro Markets: Creating Institutions for Managing Society's Largest Economic Risks*. Oxford: Clarendon Press.

Shiller, Robert J. 2005. In Favor of Growth-Linked Bonds. *Indian Express*, March 10.

Williamson, John. 2005. *Curbing the Boom-Bust Cycle: Stabilizing Capital Flows to Emerging Markets*. Policy Analyses in International Economics 75. Washington: Institute for International Economics.

Williamson, John. 2008. Is There a Role for Growth-Linked Securities? Peterson Institute for International Economics, Washington. Photocopy (April 15).

Whittall, Christopher. 2012. Investors Eye GDP Warrants Dubiously. *International Financing Review*, no. 1922 (February 26 to March 2). Available at www.ifre.com/investors-eye-gdp-warrants-dubiously/21001925.article (accessed on July 28, 2012).

8

Capital Mobility and Regulation

OLIVIER JEANNE

"Capital flow management" has become a buzzword to talk about policy measures aimed at smoothing the boom-bust cycle in capital flows to emerging-market economies. Although John Williamson is perhaps better known for his ideas and proposals about exchange rate regimes and for having coined the term "Washington Consensus," a significant part of his work has been about capital flow management.

This chapter addresses the current analytical and policy questions on capital mobility and regulation and draws links to John Williamson's work in the area. First, I review the evolution of John's ideas on international capital flows and their management, and put them in the context of the events and debates of the time. As background for this discussion, figure 8.1 reports the net capital inflows to upper-middle-income countries since 1978. I then review the current research agenda on capital mobility and regulation, which is becoming increasingly active, and discuss how it relates to the themes developed in John's work.

The 1990s

John Williamson's work in the 1960s, 1970s, and 1980s touched on capital flows, of course, but it was focused mainly on other topics such as exchange rate regimes and reform of the international monetary system. John seems to have taken increased capital mobility as a fact of life for advanced econo-

Olivier Jeanne has been a senior fellow at the Peterson Institute for International Economics since 2008. He thanks José Antonio Ocampo and Ted Truman for very useful comments on a first draft of this chapter.

Figure 8.1 Net capital inflows to upper-middle-income countries, 1978–2010

billions of US dollars

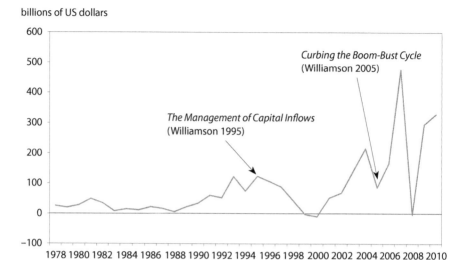

Note: Capital inflows were measured as the current account balance net of the accumulation of reserves (minus gold).

Source: World Bank, World Development Indicators, http://data.worldbank.org/data-catalog/world-development-indicators (accessed on July 31, 2012).

mies.[1] One theme that pervades his work on exchange rates—and that would later pervade his work on capital flows—is that they should not be left entirely to market forces and should be managed by governments.

John's first papers that were specifically dedicated to capital flows appeared in the early 1990s: "On Liberalizing the Capital Account" in 1991 and two papers published in Spanish, "Acerca de la liberalización de la cuenta de capitales" in 1992 and "El manejo de los flujos de entrada de capitales" in 1995.[2] Since these papers provide an early version of John's views on capital flows (and these views have not substantially changed since), I dedicate a substantial part of my discussion to summarizing them. My discussion is based mainly on the 1995 paper, which gives the most complete exposition of John's ideas.

---

1. In private correspondence, John tells me that he did not have strong opinions on the issue of capital mobility until his writing in the 1990s. He pointed out early on that increasing capital mobility would make it increasingly difficult for adjustable pegs to survive (Williamson 1965). "When Thatcher opened the UK capital account in 1979, I approved (but not publicly)," he wrote.

2. The 1992 paper is a Spanish translation of the 1991 paper, "On Liberalizing the Capital Account." The 1995 paper, which is translated as "The Management of Capital Inflows," is available in English on the Peterson Institute for International Economics website, www.piie.com/publications/papers/paper.cfm?ResearchID=277 (accessed on July 31, 2012).

In these papers, John developed an early analysis of the problems that may be caused by excessive capital inflows to emerging-market economies. In retrospect, he was one of the rather few mainstream economists to have expressed serious reservations about unfettered emerging-market finance and to have opposed the pressure for capital account liberalization in the emerging markets during the first half of the 1990s.

The 1995 paper ("The Management of Capital Inflows"), more specifically, was written as a warning to countries in Asia and central Europe that were receiving large volumes of capital inflows at the time. Capital inflows can be excessive, as shown by the experience of Latin America in the 1970s and 1980s. John was strongly in favor of the Chilean attempt to repel excessive inflows rather than the decision of Mexico, for example, to absorb the inflows and let them finance an increase in domestic spending.

John's case against unfettered capital mobility relied on several arguments. First, large capital inflows lead to a real appreciation of the currency that erodes the competitiveness of the domestic tradable goods sector (Dutch disease). This may be a problem if and when there is a capital flow reversal because the country will not be able to rely on a robust tradable goods sector to repay the external debt. And even if the capital inflow is permanent, the damage to the tradable goods sector caused by the real appreciation can harm the country's prospects for long-term growth—a view, John notes, that lacks a sound theoretical foundation but is "held quite strongly by many economists" (Williamson 1995).

As a rule of thumb, John proposed that the external liabilities of a country should be limited to 40 percent of its GDP, but he notes that the composition of capital inflows also matters. Equity-like liabilities such as foreign direct investment are less likely to generate a capital account crisis than debt, and the maturity of debt matters. As a second rule of thumb, he proposed to "treat a dollar of a foreign non-debt claim as something less than a dollar's worth of debt, e.g., to give it a 50 percent weight" (Williamson 1995).

Another problem with a surge in capital inflows is that it may lead to domestic imbalances, including bubbles in asset prices:

> One undesirable consequence of such a bubble is typically a decline in the local savings rate, as individuals discover that their asset accumulation objectives are being achieved without the need for anything so tedious as abstaining from consumption. Another undesirable consequence can be a financial crisis, and the danger of a recession, when the bubble bursts. (Williamson 1995)

Although John wrote this in 1995 with emerging-market economies in mind, it would be difficult to find a more apt and succinct description of the link between current account deficits and the boom-bust in credit and asset prices in the United State observed before and during the Great Recession (Obstfeld 2012).

"The Management of Capital Inflows" also contains a list of 12 possible policy actions for curbing the effects of a surge in capital inflows. The list includes currency appreciation (number 1), the accumulation of reserves (number 2), and several measures that would now be called "macroprudential" (such as increasing regulatory bank reserves). These policy actions are not listed by order of preference, but rather in the order that a policymaker would typically consider them. John noted the costs associated with letting the currency appreciate (mentioned above) as well as the quasi-fiscal costs of holding large stocks of international reserves. The imposition of controls on capital inflows was ranked 11th on the list not because it was viewed as one of the least desirable measures, but because John thought that capital controls would typically be considered by default, after other measures have been tried and proved insufficient. This being said, it is fair to say that John did not see capital controls as a panacea or even as a frontline defense.

At the same time, however, the Washington Consensus was moving toward a view of the gains that emerging-market economies can derive from capital inflows that was less burdened than John's with caveats and qualifications.[3] In his famous characterization of the Washington Consensus given at a conference held at the Institute for International Economics in 1989 (and published in Williamson 1990), there was some emphasis on the benefits of foreign direct investment inflows, but liberalization of foreign financial flows was "not regarded as a high priority" for developing economies. But the 1990s started to see a strong push for capital account liberalization coming from the investor community and the official sector, including the International Monetary Fund (IMF). This culminated in the debate over giving the IMF jurisdiction over its member countries' capital accounts in order to promote their orderly liberalization.

The 1994–95 Mexican crisis did not change the prevailing optimism about capital account liberalization in emerging-market economies as much as it perhaps should have. The crisis could be seen as an isolated case due to problems that were specific to Mexico, and one whose international repercussions were contained by official crisis lending. There was volatility in Mexico and in the countries subsequently affected by the so-called Tequila crisis, but an outright default was avoided, and by contrast with the debt crisis of the 1980s, the Mexican crisis marked nothing like the beginning of a "lost decade" of growth.

In a speech at the IMF's Annual Meetings in 1997, Stanley Fischer made the case for financial globalization and advocated an amendment to the IMF's articles, the purpose of which "would be to enable the Fund to promote the orderly liberalization of capital movements."[4] Around the same time, Rudiger Dornbusch declared capital controls "an idea whose time is past" and that "the correct answer to the question of capital mobility is that it ought to be unrestricted" (Dornbusch 1998, 20).

---

3. A history of the Washington Consensus is presented in Williamson (2008).

4. Stanley Fischer, "Capital Account Liberalization and the Role of the IMF," speech at the Annual Meetings of the International Monetary Fund, Washington, September 19, 1997.

The enthusiasm for capital account liberalization was dampened by the next bout of capital flow volatility in Southeast Asia, which John observed from a good vantage point as chief economist for the South Asia Region at the World Bank in 1996–99. He examined the lessons from that crisis in Williamson (1998, 1999). Although the crisis was to some extent a vindication of the fears that he had expressed in "The Management of Capital Inflows," John did not claim credit for having told us so (he actually does not cite his 1991 or 1995 pieces in his post–Asian crisis papers). That being said, consistent with his earlier work he laid the blame for the crisis mainly at the door of premature and excessive capital account liberalization, leading to the accumulation of short-term foreign currency external liabilities (Williamson 1998). And he took the crisis as an opportunity to refine his earlier insights on the desirable composition of capital flows (Williamson 1999).

The 2000s

The Southeast Asian crisis opened a debate (that is still going on) about reforming the international financial architecture, but it did not make capital controls come back into vogue. In fact, it is at the time of the Southeast Asian crisis that Chile abandoned the system of capital controls that John Williamson had been praising earlier in the decade.[5] The Central Bank of Chile had grown tired of administering these controls and during the 1990s had been producing a steady stream of research that was skeptical or hostile toward them. In his defense of the intermediate option for exchange rate regimes, John argued that this new research was too negative and somewhat inconsistent because it claimed at the same time that the controls were both ineffective and distortionary (Williamson 2000). But the debate on the international financial architecture tended to focus on other measures, such as collective action clauses in sovereign debt, the creation of a new sovereign debt restructuring mechanism (Krueger 2001), measures to relieve the "original sin" of foreign currency borrowing in emerging-market economies (Eichengreen and Hausmann 2003), and the "bipolar view" that balance of payments crises could be avoided by having exchange rates that were either floating or irrevocably fixed (Summers 2000).

Be that as it may, capital flows to emerging-market economies started to boom again in 2003. John restated and refined his analysis of the need to regulate and manage capital flows in *Curbing the Boom-Bust Cycle: Stabilizing Capital Flows to Emerging Markets* (2005).[6] There he compared the contribution of different types of capital flows to economic volatility, and emphasized that the flows that are the most dangerous (such as short-term foreign currency

---

5. Chile phased out its system of controls on capital inflows (the *encaje*) in September 1998.

6. Some of the analysis in Williamson (2005) was prefigured in a chapter that John wrote for a book edited by Ricardo Ffrench-Davis and Stephany Griffith-Jones entitled *From Capital Surges to Drought* (Williamson 2003). Similar themes were developed by José Antonio Ocampo (2003).

debt) are also the ones that seem to contribute the least to economic development, since (unlike foreign direct investment) they finance little investment and bring no access to intellectual property.[7] John concluded by proposing an action program with seven measures, including macroprudential measures to reduce the procyclicality of bank lending, measures to reduce foreign currency borrowing by emerging-market economies and encourage the development of equity-like financial instruments, and prudential capital controls on inflows.

Meanwhile, emerging-market economies responded to the surge in capital inflows not by using capital controls but by accumulating international reserves to an unprecedented extent.

A new period of capital flow volatility came with the Great Recession and the financial turmoil caused by the collapse of Lehman Brothers in the fall of 2008. Bank flows to emerging-market economies suddenly dried up, but this sudden stop did not last long. One year later, many emerging-market economies had to deal with the opposite problem—a new surge in capital inflows. This time, the type of prudential capital controls that John had advocated for almost 20 years came back into use. These controls were now more in the spirit of the times, with its emphasis on countercyclical macroprudential regulation to smooth the effects of booms and busts in credit and asset prices.

Brazil, rather than Chile, was the new poster child for prudential capital controls. Brazil introduced a 2 percent tax on all capital inflows except direct investment in October 2009. The tax rate was increased to 6 percent in October 2010, and the coverage of the controls was extended to derivatives. The controls seem to have been successful in stopping the appreciation of the real, although this effect may also have resulted from other concomitant factors. The tax is paid rather than evaded, in large part because it has remained relatively small. Several other emerging-market economies, including Korea, Taiwan, Thailand, and Indonesia, experimented with controls on capital inflows in 2009 and 2010.

At the same time, the official community started to show more tolerance, and even sympathy, toward the use of prudential capital controls (IMF 2011; Ostry et al. 2010, 2011). Capital controls were presented as legitimate instruments in the policy "toolbox" that emerging-market economies can use to reduce the impact of volatile capital flows (Ostry et al. 2011). As IMF Chief Economist Olivier Blanchard put it in his summary remarks at the end of a conference on managing capital flows coorganized by the IMF and the Brazilian authorities: "While the issue of capital controls is fraught with ideological overtones, it is fundamentally a technical one, indeed a highly technical one" (Blanchard 2011).

---

7. The large empirical literature on the impact of international financial integration on growth and development generally fails to detect a robust connection between the two, except perhaps for foreign direct investment and equity market liberalization. See Rodrik and Subramanian (2009) for a review of that literature, and Cline (2010) for an interpretation of the evidence that is more optimistic about the gains from integration.

In a monograph entitled *Who Needs to Open the Capital Account?* that I coauthored with John Williamson and Arvind Subramanian, we observe an asymmetry between international trade in goods and trade in assets: there is no international rule or discipline for capital account policies but there is (most notably with the World Trade Organization) a strong international regime for trade policies (Jeanne, Subramanian, and Williamson 2012). We find this asymmetry problematic and propose to develop international rules for capital account policies. On the one hand, the lack of commonly agreed-upon rules implies that capital controls are still marked by a certain stigma, so the appropriate policies may be pursued with less than optimal vigor. On the other hand, certain capital account policies may have harmful multilateral effects and negative spillovers on the global economy. This is particularly the case with policies that repress domestic demand and, through a combination of reserve accumulation and restrictions on inflows, maintain a current account surplus, as in China. Those policies have the same economic effects as trade protectionism and undermine the global public good that is free trade. Thus, we see a need for an international regime that would legitimize the use of capital account policies that are appropriate and discourage the use of those that are not.

Research Questions

John's writings about capital flow management contain many insights, some of which have been incorporated into the modern research literature, and some of which have not. The way open macroeconomics is taught to graduate students today is very different from the way it was taught when John was a student of Fritz Machlup at Princeton in the early 1960s. Modern macroeconomic theory is grounded in the behavior of rational and intertemporally optimizing agents. This marks progress in some respects, but it has come at an important cost: valuable insights about the economy have been downplayed or even forgotten because they do not fit neatly into the new framework. I will review how John's insights about capital flow management are captured (or not) by the modern literature, and how these insights can provide inspiration for new research.

One thing that we are starting to better understand is the welfare case for curbing the boom-bust cycle in capital flows. The research agenda on the new welfare economics of prudential capital controls is reviewed, for example, by Anton Korinek (2011a). This literature explains the need for regulating capital flows by systemic externalities generated by financial frictions. It explains precisely in which sense capital inflows can be deemed to be "excessive" from the point of view of the country's welfare, which occurs when private agents do not internalize the contribution of their own borrowing to the risk and severity of a systemic crisis. This literature also provides models that can be used to quantify the optimal countercyclical Pigouvian taxation of capital inflows (Bianchi 2011, Korinek 2010). This literature validates John's insight that different types of capital flows should be regulated in a differentiated way that takes into account their contribution to systemic risk.

Stephanie Schmitt-Grohé and Martín Uribe (2012) make a slightly different case for prudential controls.[8] These authors consider a small open economy with downward nominal rigidity that pegs its nominal exchange rate (they have euro area members in mind). The nominal wage (and so the real wage, given the fixed nominal exchange rate) increases during a boom in capital inflows. But the wage does not fall when there is a reversal, leading to unemployment. The externality in this case is that agents do take into account the impact of increasing their nominal wages on future unemployment. A tax on capital inflows helps to contain the increase in nominal wage during the boom and raises average employment. The magnitude of these effects is potentially large. Under plausible calibrations, the optimal capital controls are shown to lower the average unemployment rate by 10 percentage points, reduce average external debt by 10 to 50 percent, and increase welfare by 2 to 5 percent of consumption per period.

One idea that John emphasized in his work, but which has still not been provided with a clear theoretical foundation, is that real exchange rate fluctuations should be smoothed because of a Dutch disease externality. Dutch disease may justify undervaluing the real exchange rate (although a better policy would be to subsidize the tradable goods sector), but it does not clearly justify smoothing the real exchange rate in the boom-bust cycle. Ricardo J. Caballero and Guido Lorenzoni (2009) present a model of Dutch disease in which the real exchange rate should be smoothed, but the mechanism in their paper involves a financial friction.

Another question that I encourage my graduate students to work on is how reserve accumulation works. Policymakers believe that reserve accumulation is a powerful tool to resist currency appreciation and maintain a trade surplus, and there is some evidence that this is true (Gagnon 2012). However, modern models with rational expectations imply that in the absence of friction, reserve accumulation should have no effect because of Barro-Ricardian equivalence. We know of several reasons why Barro-Ricardian equivalence might not hold, but we do not really know which ones are the most relevant in the real world. Is it because of external or domestic financial frictions? Is it because of agents' limited rationality? It would seem important to have a better sense of the underlying reason in order to design the appropriate policies, and in particular the weight that they should put on capital controls versus reserve accumulation.

The research reviewed so far has focused on small open economies and so has little to say about the international spillovers and strategic interactions related to capital account policies. An important area for further research is the theoretical case for pursuing international coordination of capital account

---

8. In a recent related paper, Emmanuel Farhi and Ivàn Werning (2012) study capital controls in the context of a dynamic optimizing model with nominal stickiness.

policies of the type advocated in Jeanne, Subramanian, and Williamson (2012). The nascent literature on this question does not provide clear-cut conclusions (Jeanne 2012). First, there is a theoretical presumption that international cooperation is desirable for capital account policies for the same reason that it is desirable in the area of international trade. At an abstract level, capital controls are taxes on intertemporal trade between countries, and there is no reason to believe that they should be less of a collective concern than taxes on intratemporal trade (i.e., tariffs). Even when capital account restrictions are justified by a domestic externality, they have an impact on the rest of the world that needs to be taken into account. For example, Kristin Forbes et al. (2012) find that capital controls in Brazil caused investors to increase the share of their portfolios allocated to other Latin American countries, possibly shifting vulnerabilities from one country to another.

Unlike for trade policies, for which the welfare benefits of international cooperation have been studied in a large literature, there has been relatively little research on the international coordination of capital account policies. Recent exceptions are Arnaud Costinot, Guido Lorenzoni, and Iv àn Werning (2011) and Anton Korinek (2011b), who reach different conclusions.

Both papers point out that international cooperation is warranted if countries are large enough to influence their intertemporal terms of trade (the world real interest rate). However, in the two-country model of Costinot, Lorenzoni, and Werning (2011), the country that borrows can raise its welfare relative to the laissez-faire level by imposing a tax on capital inflows, and in this way lower the interest rate that it must pay to the lending country. Conversely, the lending country will want to impose a tax on capital outflows in order to raise the world interest rate. The Nash equilibrium of this game leads to a Pareto inefficient "capital war" in which both countries see their welfare decreased. This is essentially the transposition to intertemporal trade of the classical "optimal tariff" argument for free trade.

Korinek (2011b), on the other hand, shows that international coopera-tion is less justified if countries are small and use capital account restrictions to redress domestic externalities. The Nash equilibrium in this case may look like a capital war and lead to a decrease in the world real interest rate, but it is Pareto efficient. The reason is that there is no true international externality: the spillovers that countries impose on each other are mediated through a price (the real interest rate) in a perfectly competitive market (the global capital market), so that the first welfare theorem applies to the decentralized equilib-rium between countries.

These papers make significant inroads, but important questions remain to be explored. In particular, it would be interesting to better understand how capital account policies interact in a Keynesian model of the global economy with insufficient global demand. Presumably, international cooperation might be justified to prevent a Nash equilibrium in which countries use capital account policies to implement beggar-thy-neighbor depreciations that boost domestic employment at the expense of foreign employment.

Finally, one way in which the world has changed since John Williamson's early writings on capital flow management is the increasing international integration of banking. The international repercussions of the collapse of Lehman Brothers in 2008 were not, for certain emerging-market countries such as Korea, like anything we had seen before. Korean banks are integrated into the global banking system, and fund themselves in the dollar wholesale funding market—a source of funding that suddenly dried up in the fall of 2008. This episode and others raise important questions about the way liquidity and lending of last resort can be effectively provided to the global banking system in a crisis, questions that have been discussed in the postcrisis G-20 debates about global financial safety nets. Banking is unique, and there may be a need to reconsider, as a separate topic, the gains and costs of international banking integration.[9]

References

Bianchi, Javier. 2011. Overborrowing and Systemic Externalities in the Business Cycle. *American Economic Review* 101, no. 7: 3400–420.

Blanchard, Olivier. 2011. What I Learnt in Rio: Discussing Ways to Manage Capital Flows. *IMF Direct* (June 3). Available at http://blog-imfdirect.imf.org/2011/06/03/what-i-learnt-in-rio-manage-capital-flows (accessed on July 31, 2012).

Caballero, Ricardo J., and Guido Lorenzoni. 2009. Persistent Appreciations and Overshooting: A Normative Analysis. MIT Department of Economics. Photocopy.

Cline, William. 2010. *Financial Globalization, Economic Growth, and the Crisis of 2007–09*. Washington: Peterson Institute for International Economics.

Costinot, Arnaud, Guido Lorenzoni, and Ivàn Werning. 2011. *A Theory of Capital Controls as Dynamic Terms-of-Trade Manipulation*. NBER Working Paper 17680. Cambridge, MA: National Bureau of Economic Research.

Dornbusch, Rudiger. 1998. Capital Controls: An Idea Whose Time Is Past. In *Should the IMF Pursue Capital-Account Convertibility?* Princeton Essays in International Finance 207: 20–28. Princeton, NJ: Princeton University Press.

Eichengreen, Barry, and Ricardo Hausmann. 2003. The Road to Redemption. In *Other People's Money: Debt Denomination and Financial Instability in Emerging-Market Economies*, ed. Barry Eichengreen and Ricardo Hausmann. Chicago: University of Chicago Press.

Farhi, Emmanuel, and Ivàn Werning. 2012. Dealing with the Trilemma: Optimal Capital Controls with Fixed Exchange Rates. MIT Department of Economics. Photocopy.

Forbes, Kristin, Marcel Fratzscher, Thomas Kotska, and Roland Straub. 2012. *Bubble Thy Neighbor: Portfolio Effects and Externalities from Capital Controls*. NBER Working Paper 18052. Cambridge, MA: National Bureau of Economic Research.

Gagnon, Joseph. 2012. *Global Imbalances and Foreign Asset Expansion by Developing Economy Central Banks*. Working Paper 12-5. Washington: Peterson Institute for International Economics.

IMF (International Monetary Fund). 2011. *Recent Experiences in Managing Capital Inflows—Cross-Cutting Themes and Possible Policy Framework*. Policy Paper. Washington: International Monetary Fund. Available at www.imf.org/external/np/pp/eng/2011/021411a.pdf (accessed on July 31, 2012).

---

9. See Shin (2012) for evidence and theory on how global banking contributed to credit easing in the United States up to 2007 and may thus have been a key factor behind the global financial crisis.

Jeanne, Olivier. 2012. Capital Flow Management. *American Economic Review, Papers and Proceedings* 102, no. 3: 203–06.

Jeanne, Olivier, Arvind Subramanian, and John Williamson. 2012. *Who Needs to Open the Capital Account?* Washington: Peterson Institute for International Economics.

Korinek, Anton. 2010. Regulating Capital Flows to Emerging Markets: An Externality View. University of Maryland. Photocopy.

Korinek, Anton. 2011a. The New Economics of Prudential Capital Controls. *IMF Economic Review* 59, no. 3: 523–61.

Korinek, Anton. 2011b. Capital Controls and Currency Wars. University of Maryland. Photocopy.

Krueger, Anne. 2001. International Financial Architecture for 2002: A New Approach to Sovereign Debt Restructuring. Presentation at the National Economists' Club, American Enterprise Institute, Washington, November 26. Available at www.imf.org/external/np/speeches/2001/112601.htm (accessed on July 31, 2012).

Obstfeld, Maurice. 2012. Does the Current Account Still Matter? In *American Economic Review, Papers and Proceedings* (forthcoming).

Ocampo, José Antonio. 2003. Capital Account and Countercyclical Prudential Regulation in Developing Countries. In *From Capital Surges to Drought: Seeking Stability for Emerging Economies*, ed. Ricardo Ffrench-Davis and Stephany Griffith-Jones. Basingstoke, UK: Palgrave Macmillan.

Ostry, Jonathan D., Atish Ghosh, Karl Habermeier, Marcos Chamon, Mahvash Qureshi, and Dennis Reinhardt. 2010. *Capital Inflows: The Role of Controls.* IMF Staff Position Note 10/04. Washington: International Monetary Fund.

Ostry, Jonathan D., Atish R. Ghosh, Karl Habermeier, Luc Laeven, Marcos Chamon, Mahvash S. Qureshi, and Annamaria Kokenyne. 2011. *Managing Capital Inflows: What Tools to Use?* IMF Staff Discussion Note 11/06. Washington: International Monetary Fund.

Rodrik, Dani, and Arvind Subramanian. 2009. Why Did Financial Globalization Disappoint? *IMF Staff Papers* 56, no. 1: 112–38.

Schmitt-Grohé, Stephanie, and Martín Uribe. 2012. Prudential Policy for Peggers. Columbia University. Photocopy.

Shin, Hyun Song. 2012. Global Banking Glut and Loan Risk Premium. *IMF Economic Review* 60, no. 2: 155–92.

Summers, Lawrence H. 2000. International Financial Crises: Causes, Prevention, and Cures. *American Economic Review, Papers and Proceedings* 90, no. 2: 1–16.

Williamson, John. 1965. *The Crawling Peg.* Princeton Essays in International Finance 50. Princeton, NJ: Princeton University Press.

Williamson, John. 1990. What Washington Means by Policy Reform. In *Latin American Adjustment: How Much Has Happened?* ed. John Williamson. Washington: Institute for International Economics.

Williamson, John. 1991. On Liberalizing the Capital Account. In *Finance and the International Economy* 5, ed. R. O'Brien. Oxford: Oxford University Press.

Williamson, John. 1992. Acerca de la liberalización de la cuenta de capitales [On Liberalizing the Capital Account]. *Estudios de Economia* 19, no. 2: 185–97. (Spanish translation of Williamson 1991.)

Williamson, John. 1995. El manejo de los flujos de entrada de capitales [The Management of Capital Inflows]. *Pensamiento Iberoamericano* 27: 197–218. English translation available on the Peterson Institute for International Economics website, www.piie.com/publications/papers/paper.cfm?ResearchID=277 (accessed on July 31, 2012).

Williamson, John. 1998. Whither Financial Liberalization? Keynote speech at the Second Annual Indian Derivatives Conference, Mumbai, India, November 13.

Williamson, John. 1999. Implications of the East Asian Crisis for Debt Management. In *External Debt Management: Issues, Lessons and Preventive Measures*, ed. A. Vasudevan. Bombay: Reserve Bank of India.

Williamson, John. 2000. *Exchange Rate Regimes for Emerging Markets: Reviving the Intermediate Option*. Policy Analyses in International Economics 60. Washington: Institute for International Economics.

Williamson, John. 2003. Proposals for Curbing the Boom-Bust Cycle in the Supply of Capital to Emerging Markets. In *From Capital Surges to Drought: Seeking Stability for Emerging Economies*, ed. Ricardo Ffrench-Davis and Stephany Griffith-Jones. Basingstoke, UK: Palgrave Macmillan.

Williamson, John. 2005. *Curbing the Boom-Bust Cycle: Stabilizing Capital Flows to Emerging Markets*. Policy Analyses in International Economics 75. Washington: Institute for International Economics.

Williamson, John. 2008. A Short History of the Washington Consensus. In *The Washington Consensus Reconsidered: Towards a New Global Governance*, ed. Narcis Serra and Joseph E. Stiglitz. New York: Oxford University Press.

III

REGIONS

9

India and the Global Crisis

SHANKAR ACHARYA

Although John Williamson and I have never actually worked together on a book or paper, our paths have crossed often over the last four decades and we have been friends, though usually separated by geography. Despite the physical distance between us, we did (and still do) share a close affinity on several key economic policy issues that have been the subject of Williamson's voluminous research. For instance, I have long maintained that his original list of "Washington Consensus" policies was a reasonable guidepost for sensible economic policies that developing countries needed to pursue in the 1980s and 1990s to spur economic development and improve macroeconomic stability. Second, my reading of Williamson's writings on exchange rate policy is that, especially for developing countries, he sees the merit of intermediate exchange rate regimes, as distinct from the polar extremes of a "hard fix" or "full flexibility." Here too I am on his side. Third, Williamson has always advocated a cautious path toward capital account convertibility for developing countries moving away from extensive restrictions on cross-border currency transactions. Once again, I agree. Because of these shared views, and the most important reason of a long friendship, it is a special pleasure to contribute to a volume in John Williamson's honor.

This chapter focuses on the policy responses by the Indian government and central bank, the Reserve Bank of India (RBI), to the global financial crisis and the ensuing Great Recession, and it assesses the macroeconomic outcomes

Shankar Acharya is honorary professor at the Indian Council for Research on International Economic Relations, non-executive chairman of Kotak Mahindra Bank, member of the Indian government's National Security Advisory Board, and member of the Reserve Bank's Advisory Committee on Monetary Policy. He was chief economic advisor to the Government of India from 1993 to 2001. He thanks Devesh Kapur for comments on this chapter.

that have followed since 2008. It begins by briefly outlining the macroeconomic developments in India since the major economic reforms of the early 1990s, with a special focus on the five years immediately preceding the crisis, that is, from 2003–04 to 2007–08.[1] It also sketches the debate on financial sector reforms and global financial integration that were going on in the mid-noughties. The chapter then turns to the initial impact of the crisis on India, highlighting the economy's apparent resilience and outlining the reasons for this resilience in terms of ongoing economic developments and fiscal, monetary, and exchange rate policies adopted in response to the crisis. The chapter emphasizes the significant slowdown in economic growth since early 2011, the decline in savings and investment, continuing inflation, and growing external and fiscal imbalances, and it identifies the key reasons for this weakening of macroeconomic performance. The final section outlines the macro and sectoral policy challenges that have to be overcome to reignite and sustain rapid and inclusive economic development.

The Indian Context[2]

After growing at less than 4 percent annually for the three decades between 1950 and 1980, India's economic expansion accelerated modestly to 5.5 percent during the 1980s. But this acceleration proved unsustainable given the complex, rigid, and often perverse controls on foreign trade, industry, and finance; the continued emphasis on inefficient public enterprises in key sectors (such as energy and transport); growing fiscal deficits; the increasing recourse to short-term external commercial borrowing; and an overvalued exchange rate (Joshi and Little 1996, Acharya 2006, Panagariya 2008).

Matters came to a head in 1991 when, following the oil price spike during the short-lived Kuwait-Iraq war of that year, India experienced a full-blown balance of payments crisis. Foreign exchange reserves plummeted despite stringent import controls, industrial output fell, inflation soared, and economic growth collapsed to 1.4 percent in 1991–92. The crisis spawned far-reaching reforms, spearheaded by the freshly appointed technocratic finance minister, Manmohan Singh, with the strong backing of Prime Minister Narasimha Rao of the newly elected Congress government. Between 1991 and 1994, India virtually abolished industrial licensing, devalued the exchange rate and then made it market-determined, eliminated import controls on capital and intermediate goods, ushered in a phased reduction of high customs duties, substantially liberalized access to foreign direct investment and portfolio investment, radically reformed the stock market, opened public sector preserves such as airlines and telecommunications to private providers, launched tax reforms

---

1. The Indian fiscal year runs from April 1 to March 31, so one-year periods cited in this chapter span portions of two calendar years.

2. For some recent accounts of India's economic policies and performance, see Acharya and Mohan (2010), Acharya (2012), and Panagariya (2008).

along with significant reforms of the domestic financial sector, and initiated disinvestment in public enterprises (Ahluwalia 2002, Acharya 2002).

The initial burst of economic reforms swiftly revived confidence and economic performance. Investment, savings, industrial output, and exports rose sharply and foreign inflows burgeoned, reducing current account deficits, swelling reserves, and transforming the external debt profile. Above all, growth took off in all major sectors. Overall GDP growth bounced back to 5.4 percent in 1992–93 and climbed steadily to a peak of 8 percent in 1996–97, with the three years from 1994–95 to 1996–97 averaging above 7 percent (figure 9.1). Real fixed investment rose by nearly 40 percent between 1993–94 and 1995–96, led by a more than 50 percent increase in industrial investment.[3]

Contrary to some external perceptions, India's economic growth did not continue to rise steadily in subsequent years. In fact, during the six years from 1996–97 to 2002–03, average economic growth dropped to a lackluster 5.2 percent. Several factors contributed to this marked deceleration. First, two successive and short-lived coalition governments between 1996 and 1998 heightened uncertainty and stalled economic reforms. Second, the Thai financial crisis in July 1997 raised the curtain on the Asian crisis, which dominated the international economic arena for the next two years and damped the region's dynamism for much longer. Third, implementation in 1997 of the excessively generous Fifth Pay Commission recommendations for government employees, coupled with income tax cuts, kicked off a period of rising fiscal deficits that increased real interest rates and crowded out private investment. Fourth, India was unlucky to suffer from several subnormal monsoons, which reduced average growth in agriculture to below 2 percent. Finally, India's nuclear tests in May 1998 triggered temporary and limited economic sanctions, which damped capital inflows and hurt the investment climate.[4]

For most of this low-growth period between 1997–98 and 2002–03, India was governed by a coalition, the National Democratic Alliance (NDA), with the Bharatiya Janata Party as the dominant partner and A. B. Vajpayee as prime minister. The NDA won power in the spring of 1998 and ruled until the spring of 2004. But it would be simplistic to attribute the growth performance to the government at the time, even if that is the typical electoral presumption. In fact, after a rocky start, the NDA government pushed through a broad range of significant economic reforms. These included a sustained reduction in import duties; removal of import restrictions on consumer goods; the New Telecom Policy of 1999 that triggered the astonishing boom in mobile telephony since then; reduction of administered interest rates on some government saving instruments, which had tended to bias the prevailing interest rates upward; a shift to a single modal rate for the central government's complex structure

---

3. See Acharya (2002) for a detailed account of India's macroeconomic developments during the 1990s.

4. Surjit Bhalla (2010) attributes much of the growth slowdown during this period to monetary tightening by the RBI.

Figure 9.1   Growth of India's GDP (at factor cost), 1991–92 to 2011–12

percent

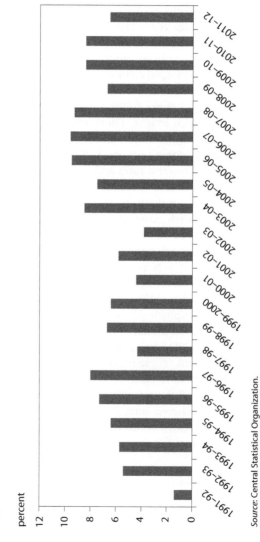

Source: Central Statistical Organization.

Table 9.1 India: Precrisis macroeconomic indicators (percent)

Indicator	2002–03	2003–04	2004–05	2005–06
Economic growth (GDP, percent per year)	3.8	8.5	7.5	9.5
Inflation (GDP deflator, percent per year)	4.0	3.7	5.9	4.6
Current account balance (percent of GDP)	1.2	2.3	–0.4	–1.2
Combined fiscal deficit (percent of GDP)	9.6	8.5	7.2	6.5
Gross domestic investment (percent of GDP)	25.2	27.6	32.8	34.7
Gross fixed investment (percent of GDP)	23.8	25.0	28.7	30.3

	2006–07	2007–08	Average (2003–04 to 2007–08)	Average (1992–93 to 1996–97)
Economic growth (GDP, percent per year)	9.6	9.3	8.9	6.6
Inflation (GDP deflator, percent per year)	7.0	6.6	5.6	9.1
Current account balance (percent of GDP)	–1.0	–1.3	–0.3	–1.1
Combined fiscal deficit (percent of GDP)	5.4	4.1	6.3	7.1
Gross domestic investment (percent of GDP)	35.7	38.1	33.8	24.2
Gross fixed investment (percent of GDP)	31.3	32.9	29.6	22.7

Sources: Central Statistical Organization and Reserve Bank of India.

of domestic excise duty rates; the ushering in of value-added tax principles in state sales tax systems; successful completion of several real privatizations (as distinct from disinvestment of minority stakes); opening up to private providers of life insurance and general insurance with foreign equity up to 26 percent; and the passage of a pioneering fiscal responsibility law.

However, the fruits of these reform measures were not reaped until the "golden age" from 2003–04 to 2007–08, when India's growth accelerated sharply to average 9 percent. Unfortunately for the NDA government, only the first year of this dynamic quinquennium fell within its reign, since the general elections in the spring of 2004 brought in the Congress-centered coalition—the United Progressive Alliance (UPA)—which has been in power since. Unprecedented fast growth was only the most obvious positive feature of the golden age. What was truly remarkable was that every other macroeconomic indicator looked good, especially when compared with the previous strong growth period of 1992–93 to 1996–97 (table 9.1). Inflation was lower, the current account deficit was less as a percent of GDP, as was the combined (central and state government) fiscal deficit, and the aggregate investment rate was much higher.

What were the factors that drove this remarkable improvement in India's economic growth and other macro parameters? The following interactive and mutually supportive factors can be identified:

- The unusually strong global economic expansion of 2002–07, which boosted growth across the world through greater international trade, capital flows, and technology transfer. Although India's net reliance on foreign savings remained limited, much higher gross capital flows (both ways) supported the exceptional Indian corporate boom in investment and profits.

- A remarkably successful fiscal consolidation that brought the combined fiscal deficit down from 9.6 percent of GDP in 2002–03 to 4.1 percent in 2007–08. This consolidation, built on rapid growth of tax revenues at both the central and state government levels and some restraint on expenditure, engendered a major improvement in public savings, a large increase in loanable funds for productive investment, and significantly lower real interest rates.[5]

- An unprecedented increase in the aggregate rate of investment from around 25 percent of GDP in 2002–03 to 35 percent by 2005–06 and higher thereafter. Most of this 10 percentage point increase in investment was financed by an equivalent surge in domestic savings, especially public savings and private corporate savings.

- The cumulative, productivity-enhancing effects of the economic reforms carried out from 1991 to 2003. In particular, much of the private corporate sector became competitive, mature, and confident in the new globalized environment.

- The 25 percent annual increase in India's service exports between 2001 and 2008, consisting mostly of information technology and business process outsourcing services, which increased from around $7 billion to over $40 billion during this period. Coupled with the boom in domestic telephony and financial services, the modern service sector became a significant contributor to GDP growth during these years.

- Deft management by the RBI of the foreign capital inflow surge between 2003 and 2007. Despite plenty of conventional and contrary advice from the International Monetary Fund and others, the RBI, under Governor Y. V. Reddy, did not hesitate to adopt heterodox policies of partially sterilized intervention to moderate exchange rate appreciation and build up foreign reserves, as well as other macroprudential measures, well before they became more mainstream (Acharya 2009; Reddy 2009, 2011; Mohan 2009, 2010).

In the middle of the last decade, as the global and Indian economic and financial boom proceeded, there was a lively debate in India on such issues as the pace of financial liberalization, capital account convertibility, the appropriate role for the central bank, and inflation targeting. These culminated in

---

5. For a detailed analysis of the unprecedented fiscal consolidation and improvement in domestic savings, see Acharya (2010).

two government-sponsored committee reports (Government of India 2007, 2008), one chaired by Percy Mistry and the other by Raghuram Rajan. Between them they reflected much of the prevailing Western orthodoxy and recommended, inter alia, a rapid transition to full capital account convertibility (by 2008, in the Mistry report), pruning the RBI's objectives to a single one of inflation targeting, and discouraging the RBI's intervention in the foreign exchange market.[6]

Fortunately, the RBI under Governor Reddy did not follow these recommendations. It continued with its cautious, iterative approach to capital account convertibility, an approach that Williamson (2006) had strongly favored, while recommending a 30-year horizon for full capital account convertibility for India. The RBI also maintained its multiple-objective approach, encompassing inflation, growth, and financial stability. Furthermore, up through 2008, the RBI continued to intervene in the foreign exchange market to reduce volatility and moderate excessive appreciation. The judgment of recent history certainly seems to favor the RBI's heterodox stances. Indeed, the earlier Western orthodoxy has crumbled with the global financial crisis, and those who pursued heterodox policies in the mid-noughties are now finding mainstream approval.

Finally, although the macroeconomic outcomes in the golden age from 2003–04 to 2007–08 were clearly the best achieved in any five-year period in India's history, progress on policy reforms was extremely disappointing. Barring the important and honorable exception of strong fiscal consolidation, the UPA government did not push through any significant economic reforms. Indeed, earlier reform efforts were diluted in such areas as privatization, petroleum product pricing, tax policy, and interest rate controls. This lackluster record was due to several factors, including the peculiar diarchy under which the head of the Congress party, Sonia Gandhi, wielded real political power but had no governmental responsibility, and the prime minister, Manmohan Singh, bore the administrative responsibility but had little real power over policies and cabinet constitution; the importance of the Left bloc of parliamentarians (led by the Communist Party of India, Marxist) in keeping the UPA government in power; and, perhaps, the inherently nonreformist instincts of the Congress party itself. The price for this inaction in economic reforms would be paid in later years.

Crisis and Response

The global financial crisis, rooted mostly in the United States and Europe, was several years in the making and had multiple causes, including the prolonged housing boom in the United States and some European countries along with the growing practice of subprime lending; persistent global imbalances in external finances, whether due to excess spending in the United States and

---

6. For critical assessments of these two reports, see Acharya (2009).

other deficit countries or to a "savings glut" in Asia and oil-exporting nations; an extended period of accommodative monetary policy in major industrial nations; the sustained borrowing binge in the United States and some European nations leading to unsustainably high ratios of debt to income; the proliferation of opaque financial derivatives, which spread the risk of dodgy mortgage (and other) loans throughout the financial systems of industrial countries; the failure of credit rating agencies, which assigned triple A ratings to complex debt securities of dubious quality; and an increasingly lax culture of financial regulation and supervision, which fueled the prolonged, and ultimately unsustainable, financial boom.

The house of financial cards began to topple in the winter of 2006–07, when house prices in the United States began to fall. By the summer of 2007 financial stress had spread widely, causing several mortgage banks and hedge funds to go under. By the autumn of that year major US and European banks were showing huge losses due to their exposure to mortgage-backed securities. In September 2007, the United Kingdom's Northern Rock Bank had to be bailed out by the central bank and government. In March 2008, Bear Stearns, the fifth-largest US investment bank, ceased to exist. The financial unraveling climaxed in September 2008, when the US Federal Reserve and Treasury had to orchestrate massive bailouts and buyouts of the government-sponsored mortgage finance institutions, Fannie Mae and Freddie Mac, the iconic investment bank Merrill Lynch, and the world's largest insurance company, AIG. On September 15, 2008, Lehman Brothers was allowed to topple into bankruptcy, resulting in a freezing of credit markets in industrial nations and the transmission of a sudden liquidity shock across the entire world. By then the financial crisis had already taken a significant toll on the real economy, with the Great Recession having begun in late 2007, bringing overall economic growth to a virtual halt in 2008 in industrial countries, which was to be followed by a 3.4 percent decline in national incomes in 2009 (table 9.2).

In India, all this was like distant thunder. Up until the summer of 2008, the mounting global crisis was viewed largely as a rich-country problem, with little relevance for major emerging-market nations like India, except for a sharp correction in overheated stock markets in early 2008. "Decoupling" was a favored view, as it foresaw strong, autonomous growth in developing nations despite a sharp slowdown in advanced economies. Indeed, in the spring and summer of 2008, the Indian economic policy debate was focused on a byproduct of the global economic boom of 2002–07, namely the surge in oil and other commodity prices, which sharply augmented inflation in India in the spring of 2008 and triggered a significant tightening of monetary policy. The implosion of US and European financial markets in September 2008 and the ensuing liquidity shock shattered the prevailing complacency, reversed the expansion of trade and capital inflows, and significantly slowed industrial growth. By the spring of 2009, economic growth had slowed markedly and many analysts expected it to drop further in 2009–10.

Table 9.2   Growth in India and the world, 2005–12 (percent)

Country	2005–07	2008	2009	2010	2011	2012 (projected)
World output[a]	3.8	1.6	−2.1	4.2	2.8	2.7
Advanced economies	2.8	0.2	−3.4	3.2	1.6	1.4
United States	2.6	0.0	−2.6	3.0	1.7	2.0
Euro area	2.6	0.4	−4.1	1.9	1.5	−0.3
Japan	2.1	−1.2	−6.3	4.4	−0.7	2.4
Emerging-market and developing economies	8.1	6.1	2.8	7.5	6.2	5.6
Russia	7.7	5.2	−7.8	4.3	4.3	4.0
China	12.7	9.6	9.2	10.4	9.2	8.0
India[b]	9.5	6.8	8.4	8.4	6.5	6.0
Brazil	4.4	5.2	−0.6	7.5	2.7	2.5

a. At market exchange rates.
b. For India, the years are April to March financial years, so 2008 refers to 2008–09 and so on for subsequent years.

Sources: International Monetary Fund, *World Economic Outlook* (WEO), April 2011, for data up to 2008; WEO Update (June 2011) for 2009; and WEO Update (July 2012) for 2010 onward. Data for India are from the Central Statistical Organization.

In fact, the Indian economy confounded skeptics by demonstrating remarkable resilience. Overall economic growth slowed relatively modestly to 6.7 percent in 2008–09. In contrast, in 2009, advanced economies contracted by 3.4 percent, Russia by nearly 8 percent, and Brazil by 0.6 percent. Overall growth of emerging-market and developing economies slumped to 2.8 percent from the 2005–07 average of 8.1 percent (table 9.2). China was the other notable outlier, recording an enviable 9.2 percent growth in the depths of the Great Recession. Furthermore, India's growth bounced back to 8.4 percent in each of the next two years, ensuring average growth of nearly 8 percent in the three years from 2008–09 to 2010–11.

What explains India's remarkable resilience in the face of the worst economic crisis in the world since the Great Depression of the 1930s? At least five factors seemed to be at work. First, as noted earlier, the years 2003–04 to 2007–08 had been exceptionally dynamic for India. Growth averaged nearly 9 percent, the fastest ever seen in five sequential years in India. Powered by a boom in private corporate investment, the share of total investment in the economy rose impressively and attained a peak of 38 percent by 2007–08, with fixed investment accounting for 33 percent of GDP. So when the downdraft from the global crisis came to Indian shores, it came to an economy expanding with a great deal of momentum.

Second, among the transmission channels for the pernicious effects of the global or, more accurately, North Atlantic crisis, the time bombs of toxic assets, woefully undercapitalized financial institutions, and unregulated shadow banking systems were mercifully absent. India, like China and some other countries, had followed a conservative, gradualist approach to both capital account convertibility and domestic regulation of banks and other financial intermediaries. Despite fairly strong pressures from the prevailing Western orthodoxy of unfettered cross-border capital mobility, divestment of financial regulation responsibilities by central banks, and "light touch financial regulation" practices, the RBI under Governor Reddy held firm to its heterodox approach. The happy result was that the Indian financial system had almost no exposure to the vast oceans of toxic assets in the world outside and was amply capitalized and closely supervised. No Indian bank or other significant financial intermediary failed or had to be bailed out during this period.

Third, quite fortuitously, 2008 happened to be a year of extraordinary fiscal profligacy, influenced, no doubt, by the imminence of the general election of the spring of 2009. Well before the dramatic collapse of Lehman Brothers in September 2008, spending by India's central government was running far above budget levels on account of government pay increases (resulting from the adoption of Sixth Pay Commission recommendations), petroleum, fertilizer and food subsidies, the new farm loan waiver scheme, and the National Rural Employment Guarantee (NREG) Program. Some of these, like pay increases, the farm loan waiver, and the NREG, had been underbudgeted. Others, such as fertilizer and oil subsidies, were the result of the international commodity price boom that hit the Indian economy in early 2008. With the government choosing to hold down controlled prices, explicit and implicit (through oil and fertilizer bonds) subsidies soared. The net result (together with steep post-Lehman cuts in central excise duties) was that the central government's fiscal deficit for 2008–09 went from the 2.5 percent of GDP budgeted in February 2008 to over 6 percent in the actual accounts and to an even higher 8 percent of GDP when the off-budget items like petroleum and fertilizer bonds were included. This massive fiscal overshoot more than wiped out in a single year all the hard-won fiscal consolidation achieved between 2003–04 and 2007–08. While storing up fiscal and inflationary problems for the future, it had the salutary effect of countering the deflationary shock from the global financial and economic crisis. Whether this order of fiscal stimulus (or profligacy) was really necessary remains debatable. What is clear is that the composition of the fiscal expansion, in the form mainly of higher government salaries, much larger subsidies for fuel, fertilizer, and food, and the ramping up of entitlement programs, seriously constrained the scope for subsequent fiscal retraction.

Fourth, after an initial hesitation, the RBI was quick to implement sharp reductions in short-term policy interest rates (down to 3.25 percent by April 2009 from 9 percent in September 2008) and reserve requirements, and to undertake other steps to ensure adequate liquidity at low prices. The exchange rate was also allowed to depreciate as foreign portfolio inflows reversed abruptly in search of safe havens and away from "risky" emerging-market assets. The speed of the RBI's response was creditable, especially since the new governor had taken charge a week before the Lehman debacle and had joined up with a mandate to fight commodity-price-fueled inflation, which was then high on the political agenda. It helped that the government's own fiscal policy approach was already expansionary in fact and very soon in theory and articulation as the full import of the global crisis was understood. Indeed, the government and the RBI worked closely to ramp up both monetary and fiscal stimuli to counter the deflationary effects of the global financial turbulence and the Great Recession.

Finally, the initial promising recovery in world output and trade in late 2009 and 2010 certainly helped buoy India's growth.

Postcrisis Developments

Although India's growth held up unexpectedly well until 2010–11, other dimensions of macroeconomic performance deteriorated significantly in the postcrisis period (table 9.3). Inflation, as measured by the GDP deflator, averaged nearly 9 percent in the four years after 2007–08, compared with 5.6 percent in the preceding five years. Consumer price indices showed higher, double-digit rates, especially for food products. The fiscal deficit more than doubled to 8.5 percent of GDP in 2008–09 and remained consistently above 8 percent thereafter, except for 2010–11, when the one-off sale of 3G telecom spectrum by the government reduced it temporarily to 7 percent. The current account deficit in the balance of payments, which had averaged less than one-half of a percent of GDP in the golden age, averaged over 2.5 percent of GDP in the three years from 2008–09 to 2010–11 before ballooning to an unsustainable 4.2 percent of GDP in 2011–12. Aggregate investment rates fell by about 3 percentage points from the 2007–08 peak of 38 percent of GDP. The drop in the domestic saving rate was considerably sharper. Finally, economic growth decelerated steeply throughout 2011–12 from an annualized rate of over 9 percent in the last quarter of 2010–11 to only 5.3 percent in the final quarter of 2011–12. Full-year GDP growth in 2011–12 slid to 6.5 percent, the lowest rate in nine years.

This marked worsening of macroeconomic outcomes was due to both unfavorable external factors and weak domestic policy, with most analysts according greater weight to the latter. Global recovery was encouragingly strong in 2010, with advanced economies growing at 3.2 percent, emerging-market and developing economies at 7.5 percent, and world output at above 4 percent. But the continued weakness in the housing sector and the fiscal policy deadlock in the United States almost halved that country's growth in 2011, while the deepening problems of sovereign fiscal stress and financial fragility in the euro area (especially in Greece, Portugal, Ireland, Spain, and Italy) throttled the area's recovery and tipped it into a second recession in 2012.

The initial recovery in advanced economies and the resilience of China and India led to a resurgence of global commodity prices in 2009. Even when the US and European recovery sputtered, prices of oil and some other commodi-

Table 9.3   India: Postcrisis macroeconomic indicators compared with precrisis average (percent)

Indicator	Average (2003–04 to 2007–08)	2007–08	2008–09	2009–10	2010–11	2011–12
Economic growth (GDP, percent per year)	8.9	9.3	6.7	8.4	8.4	6.5
Inflation (GDP deflator, percent per year)	5.6	6.6	8.5	8.1	10.6	8.8
Current account balance (percent of GDP)	–0.3	–1.3	–2.3	–2.8	–2.6	–4.2
Combined fiscal deficit (percent of GDP)	6.3	4.1	8.5	9.5	7.0	8.2
Gross domestic investment (percent of GDP)	33.8	38.1	34.3	36.6	35.8	35.5
Gross fixed investment (percent of GDP)	29.6	32.9	32.3	31.6	30.4	29.5

Sources: Central Statistical Organization and Reserve Bank of India.

ties (including gold) stayed high, partly because of geopolitical anxieties over the Middle East and partly due to heightened demand for nonfinancial hedges in a more uncertain world. Through 2011–12, India was able to insulate its export performance substantially through successful geographic diversification, but not enough to match the surge in the value of oil, gold, and other commodity imports, which widened the trade and current account deficits appreciably and was a major contributory factor to persistently high inflation during this period (table 9.4).

While elevated global commodity prices since 2008 have contributed significantly to India's high and persistent inflation over the last four years, other factors were also at work. These included high fiscal deficits, mismanagement of the government's food grain policies with respect to pricing, stocking, and distribution, the weak monsoon of 2009–10, the worsening supply bottlenecks in infrastructure, and, arguably, a belated and incremental exit from the easy monetary policies of the spring of 2009.

If inflation was one manifestation of macro imbalances, the marked rise in external deficits was another. As table 9.4 shows, the current account deficit in the balance of payments rose substantially during this period, to a record level of 4.2 percent of GDP by 2011–12. In part this was due to a surge in the value of commodity imports, including oil and gold, on account of both price and quantity increases. Another reason was the shift by the RBI to a somewhat hands-off approach toward intervention in the foreign exchange market, adopted under Governor Duvvuri Subbarao in the spring of 2009. As a conse-

Table 9.4 Key components of India's balance of payments (percent of GDP at current market prices)

Component	2002–03	2003–04	2004–05	2005–06	2006–07	2007–08	2008–09	2009–10	2010–11	2011–12
Trade balance (A – B)	–2.0	–2.2	–4.7	–6.2	–6.5	–7.4	–9.7	–8.7	–7.8	–10.3
A) Merchandise exports	10.3	10.7	11.8	12.6	13.6	13.4	15.2	13.4	14.8	16.8
B) Merchandise imports	12.3	13.0	16.5	18.8	20.1	20.8	25.0	22.0	22.6	27.1
Invisibles, net	3.3	4.5	4.3	5.0	5.5	6.1	7.5	5.9	5.1	6.1
Of which:										
A) Software exports	1.8	2.0	2.3	2.7	3.3	3.2	3.8	3.6	3.5	3.3
B) Private transfers	3.1	3.5	2.8	2.9	3.1	3.4	3.6	3.8	3.2	3.4
Current account balance	1.2	2.3	–0.4	–1.2	–1.0	–1.3	–2.3	–2.8	–2.6	–4.2
Net capital inflows	2.0	2.8	4.0	3.0	4.8	8.7	0.5	3.8	3.4	3.6
Of which:										
A) Foreign direct investment, net	1.0	0.7	0.8	1.1	2.4	2.8	1.6	1.7	0.5	1.2
B) Foreign portfolio investment, net	0.2	1.8	1.3	1.5	0.7	2.2	–1.1	2.4	1.9	1.0
C) External assistance, net	–0.6	–0.5	0.3	0.2	0.2	0.2	0.2	0.2	0.3	0.1
D) Commercial borrowings, net	–0.3	–0.5	0.7	0.3	1.7	1.8	0.6	0.2	0.7	0.5
Overall balance	3.2	5.1	3.6	1.8	3.8	7.4	–1.7	1.0	0.8	–0.8

Source: Reserve Bank of India.

169

quence, the rupee's real effective exchange rate underwent the sharpest-ever appreciation over the 18 months between March 2009 and September 2010, amounting to 25 percent according to the RBI's six-currency index and 15 percent by the 36-currency index (Acharya 2012). This undoubtedly exacerbated external imbalances and may also have contributed to the slowdown in industrial growth over the last two years.

The deterioration in macroeconomic policies has been only one manifestation of a more general entropy in government policymaking since 2009. Although the UPA coalition had been returned to power in the general election in the spring of 2009 with a larger majority and a stronger Congress party core, it was soon put on the defensive by several well-publicized scams and scandals, including some relating to the Commonwealth Games of 2010 and a much larger one pertaining to the allocation of 2G telecom spectrum in 2008. Others related to the allocation of government land and mining rights. Against this backdrop, the government was unable to push through any significant reforms or increase long-overdue administered prices of oil products, fertilizers, and food grains. An announcement to open up multibrand retail to foreign direct investment in late 2011 had to be withdrawn in the face of vociferous political opposition, including from some allies within the coalition. Failure to increase administered prices led to central government subsidies mounting to a record 2.5 percent of GDP in 2011–12.

The government's inability to muster the necessary support for sensible policies was also manifest in crucial sectors of infrastructure.[7] For example, in the critical area of electric power, the government in recent years had successfully encouraged substantial investment by private companies in power generation. But in the long, hot summer of 2012 much of this new generation capacity lay unutilized either because the necessary fuel linkages to gas or coal failed to materialize or because the state distribution companies lacked funds to purchase badly needed power for their networks because of massive underpricing to farmers and other users and large-scale thefts from the network. Gas was unavailable because of an unresolved dispute over pricing with a major private supplier, while in coal the unreformed public monopoly could not meet contracted obligations. The severity of India's power sector problems was vividly highlighted by the well-publicized grid collapses and blackouts in the last two days of July 2012. These infrastructure bottlenecks and growing problems with land acquisition and environmental clearances took a rising toll on investor sentiment. Confidence was undermined further by some ill-considered initiatives in the March 2012 budget to enact provisions for retroactive taxation and propose somewhat one-sided rules against tax evasion.

At first glance, the official national accounts data seem to indicate continued strength in investment, since the aggregate investment rate was still

---

7. Gajendra Haldea (2010) provides a useful survey of key issues in India's infrastructure sectors.

quite high at 35 percent of GDP in 2011–12. But there are some important caveats. First, some of this reflected increases in excess public food stocks and augmentation of private gold holdings, neither of which contribute directly to output. By the second half of 2011–12, the ratio of gross fixed investment to GDP had fallen to 28 percent of GDP from the 2007–08 peak of 33 percent. Second, the mounting reports of stalled projects in industry and infrastructure (especially after the sudden tightening of environmental regulations in 2010) suggest that the expenditure-based national investment estimates may be a weak guide to the ambient investment climate. Third, the collapse of manufacturing growth to only 2.5 percent in 2011–12 is certainly consistent with rapid worsening of the investment climate.

By the summer of 2012, India's economic growth had fallen below 6 percent, the investment climate had soured, industrial expansion had ground to a halt, inflation was still stubbornly high as was the fiscal deficit, infrastructure was in considerable disarray, external finances had become more vulnerable, agriculture and rural incomes were stressed by a weak monsoon, and the government's political space to undertake necessary corrective actions still appeared highly constrained.

Challenges Ahead

Short-Term Priorities

The immediate challenge facing Indian policymakers is to halt and reverse the sharp deterioration in economic performance since early 2011 that threatens to snowball into a full-fledged crisis. Three objectives must guide the package of policy correctives: reduce both domestic and external macro imbalances, improve the investment climate, and resurrect economic reforms. The prescriptions are well known: substantive reversal of the tax policy misadventures of the March 2012 budget; significant increases in administered petroleum product prices, especially diesel; revival of proposals for foreign direct investment in multibrand retail and aviation; legislative progress on pension and insurance bills; fast tracking of the long-gestating plans for an integrated national goods and services tax; coordinated efforts to resolve the bottlenecks holding up major infrastructure projects; and a slowdown in the ongoing juggernaut of weakly designed and implemented entitlement programs in employment, education, and food security.

Taken together, these measures should help contain the fiscal deficit and increase public savings, reduce the current account deficit and ease its financing, impart clear signals of forward movement on long-stalled reforms, and bring about a significant improvement in the investment climate. Whether the current politics permits the implementation of such a package is an open question. If it does not, then it is hard to see how the slide toward economic crisis can be arrested.

Medium-Term Challenges

In August 2011, the Planning Commission approved a growth target of 9 percent for the Twelfth Plan period beginning in April 2012. Against the then-prevailing backdrop of mounting global economic problems and clear signs of an economic slowdown and political weakness in India, this seemed to be optimistic, at best, and unrealistic, at worst. Since then, the continued deterioration in domestic economic policies and performance and the onset of a double-dip recession in Europe has rendered such a target even more remote. Growth targets aside, the key development challenges for the medium term are fairly clear. They are briefly outlined below.[8]

Employment and Human Resource Development

With a 500-million-plus labor force expanding by 12 million to 13 million people each year, the potential of India's "demographic dividend" is often invoked.[9] But for that potential to be fulfilled there has to be much faster creation of decent job opportunities and much greater "skilling" of the labor force. As it stands, the vast majority of the labor force has a low level of skills and little education. According to official data, a paltry 6 percent of the country's labor force was employed in decent organized sector jobs in 2008, with over half of these in the public sector, including government (Government of India 2011). The remainder—the overwhelming majority—toiled in informal, ill-paid, and insecure jobs. Clearly, the critical priority is to increase good job opportunities through strong labor-intensive growth and improve the skill levels of the massive labor pool.

The expansion of job opportunities for low-skilled labor has to come from both high growth of output, especially in manufacturing, and removal of impediments and disincentives to employment. This includes reforming India's unusually restrictive labor laws, which today protect a tiny minority in secure jobs at the cost of erecting massive disincentives for new employment.[10] Until government musters the political will to do this, the outlook for decent jobs for India's "youth bulge" will remain bleak. Indeed, the so-called demographic dividend could become a huge economic, social, and political nightmare.

At the same time, India has to do a great deal more to improve the quality of its numerically immense human resources. This requires major reforms in the provision of education and health, especially at primary and

---

8. This section draws on Acharya (2012). See also Ahluwalia (2011).

9. For an early, skeptical analysis of India's demographic dividend, see my article, "Can India Grow without *Bharat?*" in *Business Standard*, November 25, 2003.

10. See OECD (2007) for an illuminating comparison of India's labor laws with those of other countries.

secondary levels.[11] At present, in many states, much of the public school and health systems are dysfunctional, with schools without teachers and health clinics without medicines or nurses. The current emphasis on an entitlement approach (such as through the Right to Education Act) may not get far without systematic measures to improve efficiency, accountability, and probity in the public education and health care systems. Within health care, there has to be far greater emphasis on upgrading public health and other preventive measures relative to curative approaches to better health.

Agriculture

Although agriculture accounts for only about 15 percent of national output, over half of India's labor force still works in the sector. Therefore, faster growth of this sector is crucial to alleviate poverty, contain inflation, ensure food security, and expand the market for manufactures and services. Successive five-year plans have aimed at sustaining 4 percent growth but have always fallen short. However, the example of certain states such as Gujarat, where agriculture grew at 8 percent over the past decade, indicates that acceleration of agricultural growth is feasible. It requires sustained programs of water conservation and management, systematic improvement of extension services, an overhaul of rural electricity provision, strong support for nonfood crops and livestock, upgraded road networks, and reforming marketing laws and systems.[12] As in the case of education and health, the major responsibility lies with state governments.

Energy Development and Conservation

Rapid growth of the economy requires sustained expansion of energy supply and use. The medium-term outlook on international prices of oil, gas, and coal indicates a strong probability of continued high prices, though the major developments of shale oil and gas in North America in recent years may moderate this outlook. This means that India will have to rely on rapid development of its own resources of coal, oil, and gas. For this to happen, and to encourage the necessary conservation, user prices of oil and gas products have to be aligned with prevailing international prices. This entails hard policy actions such as implementing the 2010 decision to decontrol diesel prices and bring about a phased reduction of the large subsidies on kerosene and liquefied petroleum gas. It also requires greater opening of the coal industry to private sector development, subject to appropriate regulation for environmental and safety issues. With high energy prices, massive subsidies for electricity and exceptionally high transmission and distribution losses cannot continue without seriously

---

11. See Ahluwalia (2010) for a good discussion of the issues involved in the state of Punjab.

12. Ashok Gulati (2010) provides a good recent survey of agricultural issues and priorities.

jeopardizing the financial and operational viability of the system. The subsidies will need to be phased down.

India must also pursue efficient approaches to energy conservation and development of nuclear, solar, and nonconventional sources. There is much scope for energy conservation by setting standards for buildings and appliances. Big savings in energy use can be achieved through a shift to a higher proportion of freight transportation by railways rather than roads. This entails an overhaul of railway pricing that would reduce fares for freight and raise those for passengers.

Land, Water, and Natural Resources

Land and natural resources (including spectrum) have been at the center of recent scams and scandals that have rocked Indian politics and economics. At the heart of the problems have been archaic laws, excessive discretion available to governments to allocate these scarce resources, and lack of transparency and accountability. Corruption and crony capitalism have flourished, giving economic reforms a bad name when in fact it is the lack of reforms that is the main problem in these areas. Clearly it is important to modernize relevant laws and regulations, insist on competitive bidding processes in making allocations, pay due heed to environmental considerations, and strive for as much transparency and accountability as is feasible. These desiderata are important whether the allocations refer to mining rights, land, or telecommunications spectrum. It is important to move quickly with the necessary reforms, as land and natural resources are essential ingredients for the country's industrial and urban development.

Equally important for the nation's development is water, and there is less of it each passing year in relation to need. The great bulk of water use is still in agriculture. Much can be gained through various conservation measures such as watershed development, check dams, groundwater recharge schemes, and new irrigation techniques. Conservation can also be enhanced through pricing, wherever feasible and appropriate. Like any other scarce resource, water use should be priced whenever possible. This is especially true in growing urban localities where water charges have stagnated for many years. Aside from supporting conservation, this will help raise the resources to build and maintain new water supply systems.

The Urbanization Challenge

In 20 years, the proportion of India's population dwelling in cities and towns is expected to rise from 30 to 40 percent, implying an additional 230 million to 250 million urban residents (Ahluwalia 2011). This creates huge challenges for expanding urban infrastructure, including the "hardware" of roads, mass transit, electricity, water, and sanitation, and the "software" of schools, medical facilities, policing, workplaces, and recreation facilities. Financing, building, and maintaining these expensive facilities will require high-quality planning, execution, and, above all, governance. The last is perhaps the least developed in India, where urban governments have typically been weak and subordinate to state governments. In their own long-term interest, states will have to cede significantly more financial and governance authority to urban bodies. These, in turn, will need far more skilled personnel to manage complex urban systems. But it will all be necessary for India to enhance its competitiveness in manufacturing and services in the global economy.

This brief summary has given a glimpse of the daunting challenges ahead. If India is to resume growth at 7 to 8 percent growth over the decade ahead, these and other challenges will have to be met. Otherwise, we may have to reconcile ourselves to slower economic progress. The politics of achieving the necessary policy reforms do not appear favorable at this juncture.

References

Acharya, Shankar. 2002. Macroeconomic Management in the Nineties. *Economic and Political Weekly* 37, no. 16: 1515–38.

Acharya, Shankar. 2006. *Essays on Macroeconomic Policy and Growth in India.* New Delhi: Oxford University Press.

Acharya, Shankar. 2009. *India and Global Crisis.* New Delhi: Academic Foundation.

Acharya, Shankar. 2010. Macroeconomic Performance and Policies, 2000–8. In *India's Economy: Performance and Challenges,* ed. Shankar Acharya and Rakesh Mohan. New Delhi: Oxford University Press.

Acharya, Shankar. 2012. *India after the Global Crisis.* New Delhi: Orient BlackSwan.

Acharya, Shankar, and Rakesh Mohan, ed. 2010. *India's Economy: Performance and Challenges.* New Delhi: Oxford University Press.

Ahluwalia, Isher Judge. 2010. Social Sector Development: A Perspective from Punjab. In *India's Economy: Performance and Challenges,* ed. Shankar Acharya and Rakesh Mohan. New Delhi: Oxford University Press.

Ahluwalia, Montek S. 2002. Economic Reforms in India since 1991: Has Gradualism Worked? *Journal of Economic Perspectives* 16, no. 3: 67–88.

Ahluwalia, Montek S. 2011. Prospects and Policy Challenges in the Twelfth Plan. *Economic and Political Weekly* 46, no. 21: 88–105.

Bhalla, Surjit S. 2010. Indian Economic Growth, 1950–2008: Facts and Beliefs, Puzzles and Policies. In *India's Economy: Performance and Challenges,* ed. Shankar Acharya and Rakesh Mohan. New Delhi: Oxford University Press.

Government of India. 2007. *Report of the High Powered Expert Committee on Making Mumbai an International Financial Centre.* New Delhi: Ministry of Finance.

Government of India. 2008. *A Hundred Small Steps: Report of the Committee on Financial Sector Reforms.* New Delhi: Planning Commission.

Government of India. 2011. *Economic Survey 2010-11.* New Delhi: Ministry of Finance.

Gulati, Ashok. 2010. Accelerating Agricultural Growth: Moving from Farming to Value Chains. In *India's Economy: Performance and Challenges,* ed. Shankar Acharya and Rakesh Mohan. New Delhi: Oxford University Press.

Haldea, Gajendra. 2010. Infrastructure at a Crossroads. In *India's Economy: Performance and Challenges,* ed. Shankar Acharya and Rakesh Mohan. New Delhi: Oxford University Press.

Joshi, Vijay, and I. M. D. Little. 1996. *India's Economic Reforms 1991–2001.* New Delhi: Oxford University Press.

Mohan, Rakesh. 2009. *Monetary Policy in a Globalized Economy: A Practitioner's View.* New Delhi: Oxford University Press.

Mohan, Rakesh. 2010. India's Financial Sector and Monetary Policy Reforms: Fostering Growth while Containing Risk. In *India's Economy: Performance and Challenges,* ed. Shankar Acharya and Rakesh Mohan. New Delhi: Oxford University Press.

OECD (Organization for Economic Cooperation and Development). 2007. *Economic Survey: India, 2007.* Paris and New Delhi (Indian edition): Academic Foundation.

Panagariya, Arvind. 2008. *India: The Emerging Giant.* New York: Oxford University Press.

Reddy, Y. V. 2009. *India and Global Financial Crisis: Managing Money and Finance.* New Delhi: Orient BlackSwan.

Reddy, Y. V. 2011. *Global Crisis, Recession and Uneven Recovery.* New Delhi: Orient BlackSwan.

Williamson, John. 2006. Why Capital Account Convertibility in India Is Premature. *Economic and Political Weekly* 41, no. 19: 1848–50.

10

Latin America

JOSÉ ANTONIO OCAMPO

John Williamson's contributions to economics and economic policymaking are outstanding in at least two major and interlinked fields of study: analysis of the international monetary system and macroeconomic analysis. In the latter field, his analysis is particularly notable on exchange rate regimes and capital account regulations. His work on these two macroeconomic issues has been full of rich references to several Latin American experiences, a region that has been on his radar throughout his professional life. His specific contributions to Latin American debates are intrinsically linked to his drafting of the now classic "Decalogue" of the Washington Consensus (Williamson 1990), as well as his later review of Latin America's reforms and how to improve their results in the edited volume with Pedro-Pablo Kuczynski, *After the Washington Consensus: Restarting Growth and Reform in Latin America* (Kuczynski and Williamson 2003).

This chapter reviews some of the debates on the structural reforms and macroeconomic dynamics of Latin America, with a specific reference to Williamson's contributions to those debates. It first looks back at the initial Decalogue and how much it was implemented in Latin America, then examines the relevance for the region of Williamson's contributions to the analysis of exchange rates and capital account regulations, and finally the success and frustrations with market reforms in Latin America.[1]

José Antonio Ocampo is professor at the School of International and Public Affairs and member of the Committee on Global Thought at Columbia University. He was undersecretary general of the United Nations for economic and social affairs, executive secretary of the Economic Commission for Latin America and the Caribbean, and minister of finance of Colombia.

1. The discussion of the Latin American experience with market reforms borrows from Bértola and Ocampo (2012, chapter 5).

The Washington Consensus

John Williamson coined the term "Washington Consensus" in 1989 for a project for the Institute for International Economics. The Decalogue that he then drafted was neither his own agenda nor what he regarded as the neoliberal doctrine. In the first case, he aimed at setting out "what would be regarded in Washington as constituting a desirable set of economic policy reforms" (Williamson 1990, 7). In the second case, he did not include the strict neoliberal agenda, which he understood as the mix of monetarism, supply-side economics, and minimal government, none of which were part of any "consensus," even in Washington circles (Williamson 2008). Furthermore, although his own ideas were broadly in line with the Decalogue, which he conceived as a mix of "prudent macroeconomic policies, outward orientation, and free-market capitalism" (Williamson 1990, 18), he adopted rather nuanced views on several of the issues involved. Be that as it may, the term became the center of a fierce ideological debate, with critics of market reforms identifying it with market fundamentalism. To use the term of Nancy Birdsall, Augusto de la Torre, and Felipe Valencia Caicedo (2011), the consensus became a "damaged brand," which was certainly not Williamson's fault.

Half of the Decalogue was on what Williamson called "prudent macroeconomic policies": fiscal discipline and public sector spending priorities (particularly health, education, and infrastructure), and the need for tax reform, market-determined and positive real interest rates, and competitive and relatively stable real exchange rates. In the first of these areas, Williamson's view was that "a balanced budget (or at least a nonincreasing debt-to-GNP ratio) should be a minimal medium-run norm, but that short-run deficits and surpluses around that norm should be welcomed insofar as they contribute to macroeconomic stabilization," a view that, as he pointed out, was considered at the time to be too Keynesian in Washington circles to be part of any consensus (Williamson 1990, 9). In relation to interest rate policies, his view was that "interest rates should be positive but moderate, so as to promote productive investment and avoid the threat of an explosion in government debt" (Williamson 1990, 13), even hinting at the desirability of some state regulation in certain cases. He would add later that he should have made a stronger case for prudential regulation as an essential part of domestic financial liberalization. In the area of exchange rates, he showed his clear preference for intermediate exchange rate regimes. He would later regard this as wishful thinking, as he put it, as the dominant views in Washington were already leaning toward the perception that only extreme exchange rate regimes (either total flexibility or hard pegs) were desirable (Williamson 2008).

The second component of the consensus was outward orientation, which was embodied in trade policies aimed at expanding exports (particularly nontraditional exports) and import liberalization, and opening the doors for foreign direct investment. In the second area, consistent with his views on macroeconomic management, Williamson explicitly excluded capital account liberalization, a view that he would later recognize as also being his own preference rather than the dominant Washington perspective, which was moving into fuller capital account convertibility at the time. In the case of trade policy, his policy recommendations were more mainstream, but again with several caveats: acceptance of "substantial but strictly temporary protection" for infant industries, and "a moderate general tariff (in the range of 10 percent to 20 percent, with little dispersion)...as a mechanism to provide a bias toward diversifying the industrial base without threatening serious costs" (Williamson 1990, 15). Based on his evaluation of what he considered the successful European trade liberalization of the 1950s, he also expressed his preference for a "speed of liberalization [that] should vary endogenously, depending on how much the state of the balance of payments can tolerate" (Williamson 1990, 15).

The last component, free market capitalism, was embodied in the last three elements of the policy package: privatization, deregulation, and protection of property rights. Only in the first of these did Williamson express explicit caveats, particularly his perception that there are cases of public utilities (e.g., water) and services (public transportation) that should continue to be provided by the government.

Interestingly, Williamson explicitly excluded equity concerns, which only showed up in his Decalogue as public sector spending priorities. He would later assert that the reason for such an omission was not his own views but the fact that "I could not convince myself that the Washington of 1989 (or 2004, for that matter) agreed that equity was of any consequence" (Williamson 2008, 23, footnote 8). The issue would figure prominently in his post–Washington Consensus proposals. Given the enormous inequalities in Latin America, Williamson endorsed policies that would enhance equity, even at the cost of some loss in efficiency, specifically in terms of direct taxes, property taxes, elimination of tax loopholes, and better tax collection. Along with that he endorsed policies aimed at asset accumulation by the poor such as education, titling, land reform, and microcredit programs (Williamson 2003, 2008). He would also come to recognize his disregard for institutional issues in the original Decalogue.

Latin America and the Washington Consensus

Considering that the Decalogue was, after all, aimed at the Latin American governments, to what extent did they adopt the reforms? Reform indices estimated by Eduardo Lora (2001), indicate that the reforms were rapid and widespread between the mid-1980s and the mid-1990s. There were, however, significant differences in the liberalization process across the region.

Barbara Stallings and Wilson Peres (2000) divided eight Latin American countries they analyzed into two groups according to the strength and velocity of the reform process. The "aggressive" reformers (Argentina, Bolivia, Chile, and Peru) introduced rapid and fairly comprehensive reforms within a very short period of time, in fact generally as part of major macroeconomic adjustment processes (that of Chile in the mid-1970s). The "cautious" countries (Brazil, Costa Rica, Colombia, and Mexico) introduced reforms much more gradually and at differing speeds in different areas. Most of the Latin American countries probably fall into the second group.

For those elements of the Decalogue that can be measured, the most widespread reforms took place in trade and finance. There was also a high level of convergence in terms of fiscal discipline and tax structures. However, in both areas there were distinct ingredients introduced by Latin American politics, particularly regional trade integration, a significant expansion of social spending, and opposition to privatizations in several countries (as well as opposition to labor market reforms, an issue not addressed in this chapter).

In the area of fiscal discipline, the task had actually started in earnest in the 1980s, when governments undertook massive reductions in the public sector—the equivalent on average to slightly over 5 percentage points of GDP throughout the decade, or over one-fourth of central government expenditures. Since 1990, however, central government spending has started rising again (figure 10.1, graph A), reaching in recent years average levels comparable with those prior to the debt crisis. This is a reflection of increased social spending, which has risen by about 6 percentage points of GDP over the last two decades. This persistent and widespread trend can be understood as the result of democratization.

Rising spending since the 1990s was matched by rising revenues, so as to maintain moderate fiscal imbalances (between 1 and 3 percent on average; see figure 10.1, graph B). This was achieved mainly by raising value-added taxes, but direct tax revenues also started to increase over the past decade. In any case, comparisons with Organization for Economic Cooperation and Development countries show that Latin America's tax structures are still biased toward indirect taxes and nontax natural resource revenues. Starting in the late 1990s, there was also the spread of explicit fiscal targets of various types (e.g., targets for the primary surplus, and balanced budgets or caps on increases in public spending) as part of broader packages of fiscal responsibility rules, which included norms for regional or local fiscal authorities in federal or strongly decentralized systems. Chile was the only country that adopted a countercyclical fiscal rule at the time (Williamson's clear preference), a practice that has been followed more recently by Colombia. All of this can be read as being consistent with the first three elements of the Decalogue.

These reforms were accompanied by the elimination of most foreign exchange controls and by the liberalization of domestic financial markets. With a few exceptions, the first did not follow Williamson's recommendation to be cautious with capital account liberalization. Action in the domestic financial sector included the liberalization of interest rates, elimination of most forms of directed credit, and reduction and simplification of bank reserve requirements. Financial liberalization generally unfolded with a glaring lack of prudential regulation, and thus led to frequent domestic financial crises. In fact, two-thirds of the countries of the region (12 of 18, excluding Cuba)

Figure 10.1 Central government finances, 1990–2010 (percent of GDP, simple averages)

a. Revenues and primary spending

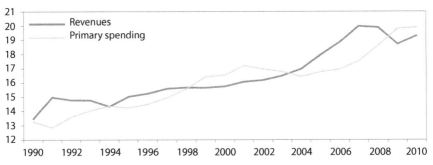

b. Central government balance

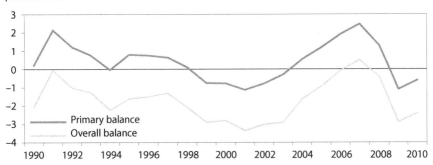

Note: Figure excludes Brazil and Dominican Republic until 1996.

Source: Author's estimates based on data from the UN Economic Commission for Latin America and the Caribbean (ECLAC).

endured national financial crises in the 1990s or early 2000s (Laeven and Valencia 2008). Prudential regulation and supervision were generally strengthened after these collapses.

With regard to the second component of the Decalogue, outward orientation, Latin America had already evolved prior to the debt crisis from a strict import-substitution model to a mixed model that combined export promotion (including a layer of export subsidies on the interventionist trade structures typical of the past) and regional integration (Bértola and Ocampo 2012, chapter 4). This process started earlier in the smaller economies, but most midsize and large economies went in the same direction starting in the mid-1960s when a Latin American invention, the crawling peg (in the line of Williamson's intermediate exchange rate regime), was introduced by several countries. The result was a turnaround of the downward trend in the export coefficient and the beginning of diversification of the export basket, both of which clearly predated market reforms. This was mixed in the 1970s with a rationalization of the tariff and nontariff structure, which nonetheless remained complex, with the exception of Chile.

The generalized reform process that took off in the mid-1980s led to a sharp reduction in the level and dispersion of tariffs, the virtual elimination of quantitative import restrictions, and the reduction of export subsidies. These reforms were undertaken rapidly (over one to three years). All Latin American countries also became members of the World Trade Organization when it was created in 1993. With very few exceptions (notably Mexico's oil industry), steps were also taken to open up the economies to foreign direct investment.

There were also two elements in this process, however, that violated the orthodox call for nondiscriminatory trade liberalization. The first again had political origins: regional integration. The landmarks were the creation of the Southern Common Market (Mercosur) in 1991 and the simultaneous revitalization of the Andean Community and the Central American Common Market. The second, which was led by Mexico and Chile, was the subscription of a myriad of free trade agreements that ushered in a "neo-orthodox" approach to trade liberalization by signing free trade treaties with industrialized countries as well. The first such accord, the North American Free Trade Agreement, was signed in 1993, but many were added in later years and they included an increasing number of Latin American countries.

In the third area of the Washington consensus policies, free markets, several countries privatized a wide array of state-owned enterprises and opened up public utilities to private investment. However, in Costa Rica and Uruguay, there was open and successful opposition to privatization, and in many other countries various enterprises, especially public utilities and oil and mining firms, remained in state hands. In the financial sector, many development banks and state-run first-tier banks survived as well. Even Chile, the country that championed these reforms early on, held on to its state-owned copper and oil enterprises, as well as its development bank and a government-run first-tier bank. In fact, only three countries took a truly radical approach to privatization: Argentina, Bolivia, and Peru. Deregulation included eliminating price controls, reducing red tape, and lowering entry barriers. There was recognition of the need to adopt regulatory schemes for privatized public utilities and stronger antitrust legislation. However, this new regulatory agenda was put into practice at a slow and irregular pace.

The Decalogue has thus been broadly followed by Latin American countries. However, there were significant variations in the strength and speed of reforms, along with several ingredients introduced by democratic politics. Needless to say, the diversity in approaches became even greater in the early years of the 21st century, largely because of the victory of leftist political movements opposed to market reforms. The positions they most had in common were rejection of free trade treaties with industrial countries and support for regional integration. Again, however, diversity was also the rule among the left-wing governments, an issue that cannot be explored here.[2] Washington itself also became more nuanced, as reflected in Kuczynski and Williamson (2003) and Birdsall, de la Torre, and Valencia Caicedo (2011), among others. There have been all along proposals for an alternative agenda, notably by the United Nations Economic Commission for Latin America and the Caribbean.[3]

Macroeconomic Policy: Exchange Rate Regimes and Capital Account Management

There is probably no area where Latin America owes more to John Williamson than in his proposals for macroeconomic policy management. His work on this topic is dominated by what can be regarded as his two well-grounded obsessions: how to avoid exchange rate misalignment and how to mitigate the effects of boom-bust cycles in external financing. Decisions about these policies have serious implications for the design of the international monetary system, which, in his view, should include both a system of reference exchange rates (Williamson 1983, 2007) and some form of capital account regulations for emerging economies (Jeanne, Subramanian, and Williamson 2012). In relation to economic policy in emerging economies, Williamson has advocated consistently throughout his professional life for both intermediate exchange rate regimes (Williamson 2000) and capital account regulations (Williamson 2005), a term that I prefer to that of capital controls. Needless to say, exchange rate misalignment and boom-bust cycles in external financing have left a legacy of crises and poor macroeconomic performance in Latin America.

These proposals are, of course, part of a broader conception of how to manage stabilization (countercyclical) policies in open economies, and particularly how to make them crisis-proof. The full set of Williamson's recommended policies—as spelled out, for example, in Williamson (2003, 2008)—includes countercyclical fiscal policies; hard budget constraints for subnational governments; countercyclical monetary policies; intermediate exchange rate regimes focused on maintaining competitive real exchange rates; accumulation of foreign exchange reserves or stabilization funds when exports are strong; prudential regulation and supervision; minimization of domestic use of the dollar; and explicit policies aimed at curbing foreign currency indebtedness, such as a widespread use of domestic financing by governments, regulation of bank borrowing and lending in foreign exchange to avoid currency mismatches in domestic portfolios, and prudential capital account regulations.

Interestingly, while Williamson correctly recognized that this package was not mainstream Washington thinking, and that exchange rate competitiveness and capital account regulations should not have figured in his initial

---

2. See, in this regard, Levitsky and Roberts (2011).

3. Among the several reports from this institution, see ECLAC (2000).

Decalogue, his views very much align with those of economists who have been characterized as Latin American "neo-structuralists." These include Ricardo Ffrench-Davis (2006), Roberto Frenkel (2008) and myself (Ocampo 2003; Ocampo, Rada, and Taylor 2009). In turn, his skepticism about capital account liberalization, well argued in Williamson (2005) and Jeanne, Subramanian, and Williamson (2012) among many of his writings, is now part of a broad-based trend in economic thinking.[4] His views of financial markets as subject to boom-bust dynamics follows an even larger tradition, which includes the pioneering work by Charles Kindleberger (Kindleberger and Aliber 2005) and the most recent account by Carmen Reinhart and Kenneth Rogoff (2009). A recent diagnosis by the IMF (2011, chapter 4) indicates that the volatility of capital flows has increased over time and is more pronounced for emerging than for advanced economies, that bank lending is more volatile (followed by portfolio debt flows), and that, interestingly, foreign direct investment vola-tility has increased and is now similar to that for portfolio debt flows.

Williamson's views on the exchange rate system are intrinsically tied to his perception that a competitive exchange rate is essential for growth in open economies to encourage dynamic export growth and diversification, and to avoid balance of payments crises. In Williamson (1990, 14), he asserted: "In the case of a developing country, the real exchange rate needs to be suffi-ciently competitive to promote a rate of export growth that will allow the economy to grow at the maximum rate permitted by its supply-side potential, while keeping the current account deficit to a size that can be financed on a sustainable basis." He went immediately on to argue that the *stability* of the real exchange rate around the competitive level was equally important, particu-larly to guarantee an adequate response of nontraditional exports: "Growth of nontraditional exports is dependent not just on a competitive exchange rate at a particular point in time, but also on private-sector confidence that the rate will remain sufficiently competitive in the future to justify investment in potential export industries…. Thus, it is important to assess the stability of the real exchange rate as well as its level" (Williamson 1990, 14).

Although Williamson's proposals have always emphasized the need for competitive real exchange rates—or "fundamental equilibrium exchange rates," as he called them in Williamson (1983)—he has held a sort of asym-metric view on this issue that shows a stronger obsession with overvaluation generated by excessive capital inflows. In his 2008 paper, he thus pointed out that "overvalued exchange rates are worse than undervalued rates, but a rate that is neither overvalued nor undervalued is better still" (Williamson 2008, 17, footnote 3). In any case, in his view, undervaluation should be equally avoided, both for domestic reasons (it can have domestic inflationary effects and can limit investment, as domestic savings will have to be partly used to finance the current account surplus) and because it contributes to global imbalances

---

4. See, for example, the contributions to Ocampo and Stiglitz (2008).

if practiced by large economies—a point that is of course forcefully made in Jeanne, Subramanian, and Williamson (2012). This distances Williamson from the authors that see undervaluation as a policy instrument, in a sense as a substitute for industrial policy (see below).

Competitive exchange rates can only be guaranteed by active policy decisions, which are best guaranteed in intermediate exchange rate regimes. Williamson (2000) provides a full critique of the doctrine of polar exchange rate regimes as well as Williamson's defense of intermediate regimes. He argues that even hard pegs are subject to the risks of overvaluation and speculative pressures typical of fixed exchange rate regimes in general. But he equally argues that totally flexible exchange rates are not a good solution either, as "markets displayed at best only a weak tendency to pull exchange rates back to any plausible medium-term equilibrium rate" (Williamson 2000, 6). Hence, his case for intermediate regimes "is motivated not by an irrational fear of floating, but by legitimate concerns that floating will generate misalignments" (Williamson 2000, 63).

The typology of intermediate regimes includes crawling pegs, crawling bands or target zones, reference rates, and (somewhat against Williamson's preference) managed floating. He agrees that none of these regimes is free from misalignment and speculative pressures. The first risk arises if authorities try to use the crawl as a nominal anchor for the price level. The second arises because interventions may attract further inflows and speculative movements that may generate self-fulfilling expectations. To avoid these problems, Williamson suggests several alternatives, including reference rates and soft margins, that imply no short-run commitment to intervene, and monitoring bands that would only call for interventions beyond a certain deviation from what is believed to be the equilibrium rate. In any case, the essential point is to provide markets with information as to what authorities believe is an equilibrium rate. If confirmed by specific policy actions (market interventions but also monetary or fiscal policies) aimed at not deviating substantially from that equilibrium rate, such information can actually generate stabilizing speculation. Williamson's lack of or lukewarm support for managed floating is based on the view that this regime does not provide such information to market agents and, since it lacks well-defined rules, is not a transparent form of intervention either.

Williamson's defense of capital account regulations is closely tied to his views both that international capital markets are subject to boom-bust cycles, and that booms may lead to substantial exchange rate misalignment. In his 1990 paper, he argued that, aside from liberalization of foreign direct investment, "there is relatively little support for the notion that liberalization of international capital flows is a priority objective for a country that should be a capital importer and ought to be retaining its own savings for domestic investment" (Williamson 1990, 14). Although he accepted in later writings that this view was not a source of consensus in Washington circles, he held to his views

Table 10.1   GDP growth: Dynamics and volatility

Period	Average growth (percent)	Standard deviation (percent)	Coefficient of variation
Weighted average			
1950–1980	5.5	1.7	0.31
1990–2011	3.4	2.4	0.71
Simple average			
1950–1980	5.0	1.1	0.21
1990–2011	4.0	2.0	0.51

Note: Data exclude Cuba and Haiti.

Source: Author's estimates based on GDP data from the UN Economic Commission for Latin America and the Caribbean (ECLAC).

and continued to expound upon them, particularly in Williamson (2005) and Jeanne, Subramanian, and Williamson (2012).[5]

Latin America's experience has always figured in Williamson's work on boom-bust cycles, exchange rate regimes, and capital account regulations. This includes, early on, his contributions to one of the most lucid collections on the financing boom that led to the Latin American debt crisis, the volume edited by Ricardo Ffrench-Davis (1983). In Williamson's later writings, some regional policy practices figure prominently, particularly the experience of several Latin American countries with crawling pegs and later with crawling bands, as well as the prudential capital account regulations (unremunerated reserve requirements) put in place by Chile in 1991 and Colombia in 1993.

To what extent can we say that Latin America followed the policies recommended by John Williamson? No doubt, the region shows significant achievements in macroeconomic policies over the past quarter century. They include the aforementioned advances in fiscal discipline as well as significant reductions in inflation rates, with single-digit inflation having become the rule in the region since 2001 (with two major exceptions, Argentina and Venezuela). However, these advances have not been matched by equivalent progress in reducing Latin America's traditional vulnerability to external shocks from both boom-bust cycles in external financing and commodity price cycles. Thus, if we compare the recent decades to 1950–80, Latin America has experienced since 1990 much sharper business cycles (table 10.1). Furthermore, macroeconomic policy has continued to be procyclical in a number of ways. In particular, although fiscal balances tend to vary in a countercyclical way, tending to fall during booms and increase during crises (figure 10.1, graph B), government spending has continued to be procyclical through the recent business cycle in

---

5. As some of the proposals to manage financial instability are dealt with in other parts of this volume—particularly prudential capital account regulations and GDP-linked bonds—I will not deal with them here.

a large number of countries (IDB 2008, IMF 2009, Ocampo 2012). Thus, the countercyclical pattern of the overall deficit is more a reflection of the procyclical behavior of government revenues (both taxes and revenues from natural resources). As indicated, Chile is the only country that has followed for some time a countercyclical fiscal rule.

Credit, and particularly private credit, has also continued to exhibit strong procyclical patterns, largely associated with external financing cycles. Monetary policy continued to be relatively procyclical in most countries during the 2004–08 boom as, with the exception of Colombia, interest rate hikes came rather late in the process, that is, only when the food price shock hit in 2008. This may be associated with biases introduced by focusing primarily on inflation, as exchange rate appreciation during booms helps achieve low inflation rates despite booming domestic demand, with the current account of the balance of payments deteriorating to absorb excess domestic demand. There were, nonetheless, major achievements in countercyclical monetary policy during the recent crisis, when countries were able to avoid the initial increase in interest rates that was characteristic of previous crises (García and Marfán 2011). Also, and quite aside from orthodox recommendations, countercyclical credit policies during the recent crisis included the active use of public sector banks to increase domestic lending.

Three policies were essential to increase the room to maneuver for countercyclical monetary policies during the recent crisis, all of which vindicate Williamson's views. The first was the decrease in external borrowing and an increase in foreign exchange reserves relative to GDP during the 2004–08 boom, both of which led to a sharp reduction in the external debt net of reserves (figure 10.2). The second was the broader use of domestic bond markets to finance governments and increasingly, though less so, the corporate sector. This, together with foreign exchange reserve accumulation, led to the improvement in external balance sheets, which was the single major advance in terms of macroeconomic policy during the boom years. Third, thanks to the reinforcement of prudential regulation following past crises, the 2008–09 recession was the first in recent decades that was not accompanied by any domestic financial crisis.

From this perspective, however, there are two remarkable failures in macroeconomic policy in the region. The first is that, despite more active interventions in foreign exchange markets, real exchange rates have tended to be very volatile in countries using more flexible exchange rate regimes, a fact that frequently leads to overvaluation at the end of external financing booms. This reflects the strong tendency of several countries to appreciate the exchange rate during booms and depreciate it during crises. This is seen in figure 10.3, which shows the instability of the monthly real exchange rate over 2004–11 in Latin American countries classified according to the IMF's "de facto" exchange rate regime, with countries with more exchange rate flexibility on top and those with dollarized regimes at the bottom. In any case, none of the economies in the first group have followed a clean flexible exchange rate policy but rather a managed floating policy that mixes variables of exchange rate flexibility and

Figure 10.2   External debt as percent of GDP at 2000 exchange rates, 1998–2011

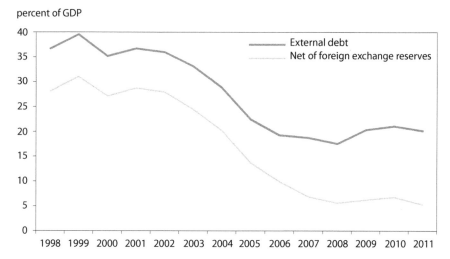

percent of GDP

Source: Author's estimates based on data from the UN Economic Commission for Latin America and the Caribbean (ECLAC).

active foreign exchange interventions and, more generally, reserve management (and in the case of Chile, fiscal stabilization funds).

Only one country, Peru, stands out in the first group in terms of its capacity to reduce exchange rate volatility. It heavily intervenes in the foreign exchange market and regulates the dollar assets and liabilities of its domestic financial system in a comprehensive countercyclical way. In contrast, the two countries using prudential capital account regulations, Colombia at the end of the previous boom and Brazil in recent years, are among the countries with the most unstable real exchange rates. In fact, Brazil, together with Venezuela, which uses an old-fashioned exchange rate system (multiple exchange rates and strong exchange controls), are the countries with the most unstable real exchange rate. The high volatility of real exchange rates in the first group is perhaps a demonstration of Williamson's view that managed floating is not the best intermediate regime, as it does not provide adequate information to markets to encourage stabilizing speculation.

The second failure is the incapacity to smooth aggregate demand management, as reflected in the strong tendency of the current account of the balance of payments to deteriorate during booms. This was hidden during both the 2004–08 and 2010–11 upswings by booming terms of trade. As figure 10.4 indicates, when the effects of terms of trade are netted out, there was a sharp deterioration of the current account to deficits that since 2008 have been significantly higher than prior to the 1997–98 crisis. This shows that Latin America has essentially spent its booming terms of trade and, indeed, in 2008 started to overspend its exceptional commodity revenues.

Figure 10.3   Coefficient of variation of the real exchange rate, 2004–11

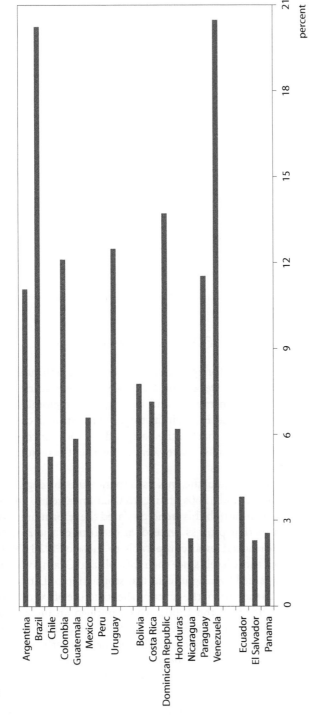

Note: Countries are classified according to the International Monetary Fund's "de facto" exchange rate regime, with countries with more exchange rate flexibility on top and those with dollarized regimes at the bottom.

Source: Author's estimates based on monthly series of the real exchange rate from the UN Economic Commission for Latin America and the Caribbean (ECLAC).

Figure 10.4 Current account balance with and without adjustment for terms of trade, 1997–2011 (terms of trade of 2003 = 1)

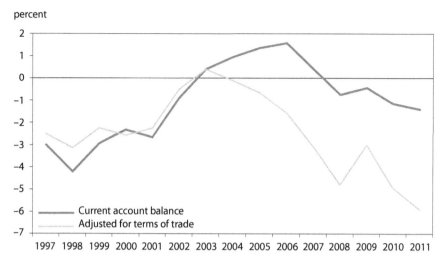

percent

Source: Author's estimates based on data from the UN Economic Commission for Latin America and the Caribbean (ECLAC).

The Light and Shadow of Outward Orientation

In many ways, the trade and foreign direct investment liberalization components of John Williamson's Decalogue have been success stories in Latin America. Exports have grown rapidly and the region's economies are more open today than at any time in their history. Transnational corporations have a much greater presence than in the past, and the more successful Latin American firms (the "translatinas") have expanded within the region and some have become world-class players.

At the aggregate level, the coefficients used to measure the degree of openness began to climb in the mid-1960s, thanks to what I referred to above as the mixed model. However, although this trend predated the reform process, it was certainly accelerated by that process. Indeed, at the turn of the 21st century, the export coefficient reached levels comparable to those of 1928–29, and has consistently surpassed those levels since then (Bértola and Ocampo 2012, figure 4.2). This was accompanied by a significant transformation of Latin America's export structure. Up to the turn of the century, the structure of exports followed the trend that had held since the 1960s, which implied an increasing share of manufacturing exports and a reduction in the share of natural resources and natural-resource-based manufactures. Since then, just the opposite has occurred: a "re-commoditization" of the region's export structure.

This process has followed different paths in different parts of the region, generating two basic patterns of specialization that broadly follow a regional "North-South" division. The northern pattern, typical of Mexico and Central

America, is one of diversification toward exports of manufactures with a large component of imported inputs (in its most extreme form, *maquila*) that are primarily destined for the US market. The southern pattern, typical of South America, is made up of a combination of extraregional exports of commodities and natural-resource-based manufactures and a diversified range of goods that are traded within the region. Intraregional trade has thus made a significant contribution to the growth of exports of manufactures but has exhibited strong procyclical patterns, particularly in South America.

The recent re-commoditization of the export structure is closely associated with growing trade with China. These trade flows show significant imbalances: Latin America exports to the Asian giant a limited set of commodities (oil, soybeans, copper, iron ore and scrap iron, and pulp) and imports an increasing array of manufactures. Demand from China is also one of the major sources of the commodity price boom that has benefited the region since 2004 (with a brief interruption in 2008–09), particularly South America.

Foreign direct investment also rose sharply in the 1990s and peaked at the end of that decade. Although inflows remained high (2.8 percent of Latin America's GDP in 2004–08 versus 3.3 percent of GDP in 1997–2003), mounting outflows in the form of profit remittances and rising foreign direct investment outflows by the translatinas have cut deeply into the net transfer of resources generated by foreign direct investment (0.1 percent of GDP in 2004–08 versus 2.2 percent in 1997–2003). The nature of foreign direct investment flows has been closely interlinked with those of trade. So, the northern pattern of specialization has attracted transnational corporations that are active players in internationally integrated production networks, whereas in South America, investment has been concentrated in services and natural resources.

However, contrary to the expectations of reformers, the relative success of Latin America in terms of increasing exports and foreign direct investment has not been reflected in rapid GDP or productivity growth. Table 10.1 compares average GDP growth rates in 1990–2011 with the average for 1950–80. The results are striking. Even when we take into account the 2004–08 boom and the rapid recovery after the recent global financial crisis, growth has not only been slower by more than 2 percentage points but, as already pointed out, has also been more volatile. The comparison is less striking if we refer to per capita GDP. In this case, however, the rising demographic dependency ratio tended to depress that indicator in 1950–80, whereas the "demographic dividend" (the decline of such a ratio) buoyed per capita GDP growth during the reform period.

The most telling disappointment is productivity growth. A comparison of trends in labor productivity (GDP per worker) shows a much poorer performance during the period of reforms compared to 1950–80 (0.6 percent in 1990–2010 versus 2.7 percent in 1950–80), except for Chile, the Dominican Republic, and Uruguay—though in the latter case with poor performance in both periods (Bértola and Ocampo 2012, figure 5.10). This is also what total factor productivity trends show. For example, an IDB (2010) study indicates that, after climbing until the mid-1970s, total productivity fell sharply during the debt crisis, and its growth was sluggish or even slightly negative between 1990 and 2005 (the last year for which the study provides estimates).

The reasons for the poor performance of economic and productivity growth during the reform period continue to be subject to debates. An essential feature that has characterized this process is the large asymmetry between the productivity gains achieved by successful firms and sectors, on the one hand, and overall productivity trends, on the other. The poor performance of the latter should be understood, therefore, as a reflection of an increasing underutilization of production resources, particularly labor. So while productivity rose in leading firms and sectors, no doubt supported by growing integration into the world economy, the large or even growing share of informal labor dragged down overall productivity trends. The idea that an increase in productivity in internationalized sectors would spread to the rest of the economy and boost economic growth has therefore not been borne out.

To overcome the shortcomings in terms of growth and equity that have characterized market reforms, Kuczynski and Williamson (2003) proposed a comprehensive agenda made up of four major elements: (1) further crisis-proofing, along the lines mentioned in the previous section; (2) completion of first-generation reforms, particularly with more flexible labor markets to expand formal employment, and enhanced access to markets of developed countries; (3) second-generation reforms to create the institutional infrastructure of a market economy to provide public goods, build national innovation systems, and develop deeper financial sectors that operate in local currency (but, as explicitly stated, *not* industrial policies); and (4) reforms to improve income distribution and accelerate social development.

One of the most controversial issues in this policy diagnosis is whether poor growth and productivity during the reform period are associated with structural trade and production patterns and, therefore, if active productive sector policies are necessary to overcome them. In this regard, Williamson's view is that the basic reason for poor growth was macroeconomic rather than structural in character, and was related therefore to the issues discussed in the previous section. In his own words: "The results have not been comparably encouraging in...Latin America. But the blame for this seems to lie in the misguided macroeconomic policies—like allowing exchange rates to become overvalued and making no attempt to stabilize the cycle—that accompanied the microeconomic reforms, rather than in the latter themselves" (Williamson 2008, 26).

Notwithstanding the agreement on the role played by short-term macroeconomic policies in enhancing volatile growth, other schools of thought have emphasized the problems generated by Latin America's patterns of specialization in inducing poor growth and productivity performance. Thus, if Williamson and Latin American neo-structuralists stand in the same camp on short-term macroeconomics, they stand in opposite camps in the interpretation of frustrations with growth. The associated problems include premature de-industrialization, as the shares of manufacturing production and employment started to fall at lower levels of per capita GDP than those typical of patterns that have been previously experienced by industrialized countries (Bértola and Ocampo 2012, figure 4.4). To this one could add the fact that the region tended to increase its share in world markets in sectors that have tended to reduce their weight in world trade, in sharp contrast to the patterns of East Asia (Palma 2011), and in activities that offer fewer opportunities for diversification and for making improvements in product quality (Hausmann 2011). To use Ricardo Hausmann's terminology, the region tended to specialize in a part of the "product space" that offers fewer opportunities for technological change.

The region's manufacturing sectors also lagged behind the world technological frontier, and this was true not only of labor-intensive and engineering-intensive sectors but even of natural-resource-intensive sectors. Moreover, the technological gap has been widening, in relation not only to the more diversified industrialized and dynamic Asian economies, but also to the more developed natural-resource-intensive economies. This is reflected in a lower share of engineering-intensive industries, meager resources directed toward research and development, and a near absence of patenting of technological innovations in relation to all these groups of economies (ECLAC 2007, Cimoli and Porcile 2011).

These alternative interpretations are part of a broader debate on the relationship between growth and economic structure. One significant part of this debate relates to the clues to the success of East Asia. In this regard, Williamson (2003, 2008) stands on the side of those who consider that selective industrial policies were not the clue to the success of East Asia, and he quotes Marcus Noland and Howard Pack (2003) to support this view. This is in contrast to the views of Alice Amsden (1989) and Robert Wade (2003), among others, who emphasize the interventionist nature of East Asian policies and their focus on structural change and technological upgrading of exports as critical factors behind their success.

In broader terms, the structuralist interpretations of the success stories in the developing world have emphasized the capacity of a given development strategy to facilitate the technological upgrading of exports and domestic production generally (Ocampo, Rada, and Taylor 2009). In this line of thought, Ricardo Hausmann, Jason Hwang, and Dani Rodrik (2007) have argued that the "quality" of exports—which could be understood as their technological content—is the factor that has been associated with faster economic growth in developing countries, not trade openness per se. Therefore, active policies focused on increasing the technological content of production may be a necessary ingredient in a successful export-led strategy. It is probably better to argue today for broader production sector policies, as they may involve not only industrial sectors but also the technological upgrading of natural resource production and the development of modern services, particularly those with high technological and human capital content.

The mainstream view in relation to this issue is that there is no role for industrial policies. Williamson belongs to a more nuanced camp, where there is a positive view of "horizontal" production sector policies—that is, those that have no sectorial bias and are thus "neutral" in their sectorial effects. The view is particularly positive toward those policies aimed at building national innovation systems to diffuse technological innovation, fund and create tax incentives for research and development, and encourage venture capital and industrial clusters (Williamson 2003, 2008). As noted above, even in his 1990 paper, Williamson favored gradual import liberalization, a moderate tariff, and infant industry protection. But this nuanced view that he still holds remains opposed to selective (or "vertical") policies, as they involve picking winners, a rather risky strategy and one that creates opportunities for rent seeking.

The basic argument against "neutral" policies is that different sectors have different capacities to induce technological change and growth. These policies do involve risks of failure, but such risks are often at the center of success stories of individual private sector firms, which must constantly search for opportunities for new activities in order to grow. Furthermore, developing such new activities is a learning process in which winners are in a sense created rather than chosen a priori. In this view, the new activities that are promoted depend on domestic capacities, must be carried out in close partnership with the private sector, and should have technological upgrading as the central criterion for selection. In any case, active production sector strategies do have additional institutional requirements, and involve risk of rent seeking that must be avoided. Because of these special institutional requirements, some economists, such as Dani Rodrik (2008), visualize exchange rate undervaluation as a substitute for industrial policies, as it also generates a bias in favor of tradable sectors. However, it is an imperfect substitute, as it is not a selective strategy and, if practiced by large economies, generates global imbalances. As already mentioned, Williamson is also against undervaluation as a development strategy.

This remains, therefore, an open debate. In any case, Latin America's actions in this area have remained limited. Since the turn of the century there has been a partial return to more active production sector policies, but it was not until the 2008 launch of Brazil's production development policy that it can be said that there was a return to an ambitious production sector development strategy. In the rest of the countries, policies in this area remain limited. The incentives the countries provide to businesses are weak and complex, and they are a far cry from the protectionist measures and other incentives provided during the previous phase of development. So even in this area it can be argued that the Decalogue still rules in Latin America.

References

Amsden, Alice H. 1989. *Asia's Next Giant: South Korea and Late Industrialization.* New York: Oxford University Press.

Bértola, Luis, and José Antonio Ocampo. 2012. *The Economic Development of Latin America since Independence.* New York: Oxford University Press.

Birdsall, Nancy, Augusto de la Torre, and Felipe Valencia Caicedo. 2011. The Washington Consensus: Assessing a "Damaged Brand." In *The Oxford Handbook of Latin American Economics,* ed. José Antonio Ocampo and Jaime Ros. Oxford: Oxford University Press.

Cimoli, Mario, and Gabriel Porcile. 2011. Learning, Technological Capabilities and Structural Dynamics. In *The Oxford Handbook of Latin American Economics,* ed. José Antonio Ocampo and Jaime Ros. Oxford: Oxford University Press.

ECLAC (United Nations Economic Commission for Latin America and the Caribbean). 2000. *Equity, Development and Citizenship.* Santiago.

ECLAC (United Nations Economic Commission for Latin America and the Caribbean). 2007. *Progreso técnico y cambio estructural en América Latina.* Santiago: ECLAC and the International Development Research Centre.

Ffrench-Davis, Ricardo, ed. 1983. *Las relaciones financieras externas: Su efecto sobre la economía latinoamericana.* Mexico City: Fondo de Cultura Económica.

Ffrench-Davis, Ricardo, ed. 2006. *Reforming Latin America's Economies after Market Fundamentalism.* Houndmills, UK: Palgrave Macmillan.

Frenkel, Roberto. 2008. The Competitive Real Exchange Rate Regime, Inflation and Monetary Policy. *CEPAL Review* 96 (December): 191–201.

García, Pablo, and Manuel Marfán. 2011. Monetary Policy in Latin America: Performance under Crisis and the Challenges of Exuberance. In *The Oxford Handbook of Latin American Economics,* ed. José Antonio Ocampo and Jaime Ros. New York: Oxford University Press.

Hausmann, Ricardo. 2011. Structural Transformation and Economic Growth in Latin America. In *The Oxford Handbook of Latin American Economics,* ed. José Antonio Ocampo and Jaime Ros. Oxford: Oxford University Press.

Hausmann, Ricardo, Jason Hwang, and Dani Rodrik. 2007. What You Export Matters. *Journal of Economic Growth* 12, no. 1: 1–25.

Jeanne, Olivier, Arvind Subramanian, and John Williamson. 2012. *Who Needs to Open the Capital Account?* Washington: Peterson Institute for International Economics.

IDB (Inter-American Development Bank). 2008. *All That Glitters May Not Be Gold: Assessing Latin America's Recent Macroeconomic Performance.* Washington.

IDB (Inter-American Development Bank). 2010. *The Age of Productivity: Transforming Economies from the Bottom Up.* New York: Palgrave Macmillan.

IMF (International Monetary Fund). 2009. *Regional Economic Outlook: Western Hemisphere: Crisis Averted—What Is Next?* (October). Washington.

IMF (International Monetary Fund). 2011. *World Economic Outlook* (April). Washington.

Kindleberger, Charles P., and Robert Z. Aliber. 2005. *Manias, Panics, and Crashes: A History of Financial Crises.* Somerset, NJ: John Wiley & Sons.

Kuczynski, Pedro-Pablo, and John Williamson, ed. 2003. *After the Washington Consensus: Restarting Growth and Reform in Latin America.* Washington: Institute for International Economics.

Laeven, Luc, and Fabian Valencia. 2008. *Systemic Banking Crises: A New Database.* IMF Working Paper 08/224. Washington: International Monetary Fund.

Levitsky, Steven, and Kenneth M. Roberts, ed. 2011. *The Resurgence of the Latin American Left.* Baltimore: Johns Hopkins University Press.

Lora, Eduardo. 2001. *Structural Reforms in Latin America: What Has Been Reformed and How to Measure It.* IDB Research Department Working Paper 466. Washington: Inter-American Development Bank.

Noland, Marcus, and Howard Pack. 2003. *Industrial Policy in an Era of Globalization: Lessons from Asia.* Washington: Institute for International Economics.

Ocampo, José Antonio. 2003. Capital Account and Countercyclical Prudential Regulation in Developing Countries. In *From Capital Surges to Drought: Seeking Stability for Emerging Markets,* ed. Ricardo Ffrench-Davis and Stephany Griffith-Jones. London: Palgrave Macmillan.

Ocampo, José Antonio. 2012. How Well Has Latin America Fared during the Global Financial Crisis? In *The Global Economic Crisis in Latin America: Impact and Responses,* ed. Michael Cohen. New York: Routledge.

Ocampo, José Antonio, and Joseph E. Stiglitz, ed. 2008. *Capital Market Liberalization and Development.* New York: Oxford University Press.

Ocampo, José Antonio, Codrina Rada, and Lance Taylor. 2009. *Growth and Policy in Developing Countries: A Structuralist Approach.* New York: Columbia University Press.

Palma, Gabriel. 2011. Why Has Productivity Growth Stagnated in Latin America since the Neo-Liberal Reforms? In *The Oxford Handbook of Latin American Economics,* ed. José Antonio Ocampo and Jaime Ros. Oxford: Oxford University Press.

Reinhart, Carmen M., and Kenneth Rogoff. 2009. *This Time Is Different: Eight Centuries of Financial Folly.* Princeton, NJ: Princeton University Press.

Rodrik, Dani. 2008. The Real Exchange Rate and Economic Growth. *Brookings Papers on Economic Activity* 2 (Fall): 365–412.

Stallings, Barbara, and Wilson Peres. 2000. *Growth, Employment and Equity: The Impact of Economic Reforms in Latin America and the Caribbean.* Washington: Brookings Institution Press.

Wade, Robert. 2003. *Governing the Market,* 2nd edition. Princeton, NJ: Princeton University Press.

Williamson, John. 1983 (revised in 1985). *The Exchange Rate System.* Policy Analyses in International Economics 5. Washington: Institute for International Economics.

Williamson, John. 1990. What Washington Means by Policy Reform. In *Latin American Adjustment: How Much Has Happened?* ed. John Williamson. Washington: Institute for International Economics.

Williamson, John. 2000. *Exchange Rate Regimes for Emerging Economies: Reviving the Intermediate Option.* Policy Analyses in International Economics 60. Washington: Institute for International Economics.

Williamson, John. 2003. Overview: An Agenda for Restarting Growth and Reform. In *After the Washington Consensus: Restarting Growth and Reform in Latin America,* ed. Pedro-Pablo Kuczynski and John Williamson. Washington: Institute for International Economics.

Williamson, John. 2005. *Curbing the Boom-Bust Cycle: Stabilizing Capital Flows to Emerging Economies.* Policy Analyses in International Economics 75. Washington: Institute for International Economics.

Williamson, John. 2007. *Reference Rates and the International Monetary System.* Policy Analyses in International Economics 82. Washington: Peterson Institute for International Economics.

Williamson, John. 2008. A Short History of the Washington Consensus. In *The Washington Consensus Reconsidered: Towards a New Global Governance,* ed. Narcis Serra and Joseph E. Stiglitz. New York: Oxford University Press.

IV

CONCLUSION

11

On Designing Economic Policy

JOHN WILLIAMSON

Not long ago, many economists thought that we had tamed the business cycle. We were in the era of the Great Moderation. All that changed in a hurry as the West found itself facing the Great Recession—the most severe financial crisis in over half a century, followed by the European sovereign debt crisis. Those who boasted that nowadays the International Monetary Fund (IMF) only lent to emerging-market and developing countries had to eat their words, as programs were put in place for Iceland, Greece, Ireland, and Portugal. No one is yet sure that Italy and Spain will emerge from the crisis without having to go to the IMF as well.

One does not get into a crisis if economic policy in the preceding years is reasonably adequate; and one does not overcome a crisis unless economic policy makes a big, and usually rather unpleasant, change. In both cases economic policy is critical. This is not true everywhere: For example, the (supply-side) rate of growth is (according to some of us) determined far more by sociological and technological factors than by economic policy. But economic policy plays a critical role in preventing the buildup of dangerous imbalances and in correcting them when they do emerge.

The design of economic policy has been one of my major interests over the years—indeed, it was probably what attracted me to economics in the first place. Initially, while an undergraduate, my principal interest was in politics per se. I remember being delighted at the discovery of Keynesian economics, and the belief that there are nice straightforward rules that can be applied by

John Williamson, senior fellow at the Peterson Institute for International Economics, has been associated with the Institute since 1981. He is indebted to participants in the preliminary conference on this volume, and in particular to C. Randall Henning and Simon Johnson, for their perceptive comments on a previous draft. He also expresses thanks to Howard Rosen and Sweder van Wijnbergen for helpful reactions.

anyone with basic training. At graduate school I clearly veered toward a more technocratic approach (and yielded for a while to a feeling that I would love to lend my name to some abstruse theorem with no conceivable policy implication). I do not think my attitudes changed greatly during my first five years of teaching, but my entry into the UK Treasury in 1968 had profound consequences. I quickly came to believe that my comparative advantage lay in understanding a sufficient range of models to be able to authoritatively decide which one was appropriately applied to a particular problem, which is still surely an eminently technocratic approach. There my attitude stayed through most of my career, though perhaps with increasing admiration for those economists who rose to the challenge of undertaking the political responsibility of designing economic policy. But it was only with the transition, and the associated conference that I designed and ran for the Institute for International Economics, that I confessed to the world my admiration for those whom (following Jorge Dominguez) I called "technopols" (Williamson 1994). A technopol is defined as an economist who is given the political responsibility to design economic policy. Let me emphasize that my admiration for those economists who are prepared to accept this challenge does not amount to blanket endorsement of their performance in office; many have been called, few chosen.

It was in reading Anders Åslund's (2011) discussion of the inadequacy of European policy during the European sovereign debt crisis that I realized that I wanted to draw an important distinction that is not commonly recognized. This distinction is between the economic policies that are called for in normal times and those needed to confront a crisis. Prior to the 2008 crisis, the West had enjoyed a long period largely free of crises[1] (except in other countries), and extrapolated this without seeming to worry that remaining that way depended on economic policy continuing to meet certain minimal standards. When a crisis nonetheless broke out, an initial common reaction was the assertion that crises are inherent to the system and will inevitably recur. Such a view strikes me as lacking in theoretical foundation. But once a crisis has broken out, addressing it requires completely different policies from those needed to prevent one from breaking out. The genie cannot be put back in the bottle by declaring, or even implementing, anticrisis policies.

I devote the next section of this chapter to what I describe as "normal" policies. It is not possible to characterize the policies needed to confront a crisis in the same way, for these will inevitably differ depending on the nature of the crisis. But it is possible, as Åslund (2011) showed graphically, to advance some useful propositions. In the final section I discuss certain policies that might help democratic polities sustain the sound economic policies that will prevent crises from developing.

---

1. There were of course several instances during this period that were labeled "crises"—the end of Bretton Woods, the oil crisis, the inflation crisis, the dollar crisis, not to mention umpteen sterling crises—but clearly they did not threaten the continuity of the regime.

Policies in Normal Times

Although it often did not feel like it at the time, the West enjoyed a long period of what in retrospect can be seen as relatively normal times from a period following the Second World War (dated most clearly in Germany, with the Ludwig Erhard reforms, or at the latest by the early 1950s) until the global financial crisis went nuclear in September 2008.

The period started with Keynesianism in the ascendancy, and until the early 1970s its influence progressively increased. This was the period when Paul Samuelson's neoclassical synthesis—which said that neoclassical economics was microeconomically relevant if, but only if, the authorities kept the economy at full employment using Keynesian tools—reigned supreme.[2] But just as US President Richard Nixon declared that "We are all Keynesians now," the challenge of monetarism, which had been propagated vigorously by Milton Friedman over many years, came to dominate the economics profession, and the policy truce sought by the neoclassical synthesis was no more. Since then the American economics profession has been divided into what Paul Krugman has dubbed "freshwater economists"—whose intellectual headquarters are Chicago and Minnesota and who believe that departures from full employment are unimportant—and "saltwater economists" based on the two coasts of the United States who are prepared to use Keynesian analysis when a demand shock pushes the economy from full employment.

In designing economic policy it is necessary to have a theoretical base, and I am clearly a saltwater economist. That is, I believe that demand shocks occur, and can be important. Policy should therefore seek to maintain demand close to full capacity, interpreted as a level that will not generate a significant rate of inflation. This is known in the literature as pursuing internal balance. The two instruments traditionally used to influence aggregate demand are fiscal and monetary policy. Fiscal policy can be discretionary (as it tends to be in the United States) or automatic (relying on built-in stabilizers as in Europe). The latter seems to me preferable, not only to prevent pointless repeated political battles but also to ensure that policy is timely. The principal purposes of basing monetary policy on stabilizing the expected rate of inflation at a low rate two or so years in the future (based on the British model) are that (1) there is a built-in anticyclical thrust (making it unnecessary to add output targeting), and (2) there is a constant need for policymakers to reexamine their views of the nonaccelerating inflation rate of unemployment, so that they are unlikely to end up sleepwalking into high inflation as happened in the early 1970s.

---

2. Admittedly, I seem to have a very different concept of the neoclassical synthesis from that put forth by Hyman Minsky (2008). He identified the neoclassical synthesis with Don Patinkin and his book (1956), which I think of as presenting the neoclassical model. No wonder he argued that the neoclassical synthesis was all neoclassical and no synthesis. But that is not true of the version that I here attribute to Paul Samuelson.

Three issues arise. The first is what to adopt as the neutral fiscal benchmark from which the built-in stabilizers will tend to depart when a positive or negative demand shock occurs. In principle I am conventional in saying that the fiscally neutral outcome should be a budget deficit intended to keep the ratio of public debt to output (D/Y) constant when the latter is at or below a target. But I am probably less conventional in that I would choose to focus on net rather than gross debt, and I would place this target at zero. That is, when a country is in a cyclically normal situation, its ideal would be to borrow only insofar as real assets with an at-least equivalent value are to be created in the public sector. The reason for focusing on net rather than gross debt is that this permits stepping up expenditures on infrastructure during a cyclical recession, just when infrastructure can be produced for the least social cost and offers the greatest social benefit in terms of providing real jobs when they are most needed. The reason for adopting a target of zero is that this is consistent with intergenerational equity: One does not pass on a part of the burden to succeeding generations. Equally, the present generation is not denied the benefits of adequate investments in public infrastructure because of shibboleths of inherited debt. Attaining this target is not to be treated as a high-priority objective any more than attaining price stability in a high-inflation country was in 1990. However, countries like Chile and Colombia did ultimately achieve something close to stable prices, even though this was not treated as a high-priority policy objective.

The second issue concerns the design of the built-in stabilizers. What proportion of a change in demand should the stabilizers aim to replace? Given that "fiscal policy" is really a bundle of instruments, can we say anything useful about which fiscal instruments should be used? Ceteris paribus, the greater the proportion of demand replaced the better, but ceteris is not always paribus, and incentive effects presumably come into play at some stage. (For example, think of the implications for the labor market if unemployment compensation were 100 percent of wages.) But one would worry if a very low proportion of demand were to be replaced. Fifty percent is a nice round number that is high enough to generate a strong stabilizing feedback, so it will be adopted as a target, meaning that one would ask whether the built-in stabilizers could be strengthened if what seems sensible on allocative grounds did not achieve that figure. Some expenditure items, like unemployment insurance, behave countercyclically, and many others—like health in a country with a national health service—are unaffected by short-run tax receipts. The German experience in terms of its rapid and impressive recovery from the Great Recession suggests the virtue of paying from public funds a part of the wages of those not fired who agree to work one or two days less than normal. But one is unlikely to approach 50 percent without a contribution from tax revenue. The important principle suggested by the newer theories of the consumption function is that one needs to bring an intertemporal substitution effect into play if one wishes to have much impact on the spending of all but the most impoverished in a high-income society. This means varying value-added, sales, or (if they existed) consumption taxes, rather than income or corporate taxes. Unfortunately no one has yet devised a formula under which such changes would be automatic rather than discretionary, so in practice built-in stabilizers depend largely on variations in spending, with some minor contribution from income tax.

The third issue is whether we have not been taught by the global financial crisis that inflation targeting is too simple, a conclusion that appears to have been endorsed by the IMF (see Blanchard 2011). We certainly learned that telling the central bank to think only of targeting inflation was an error; if there was one thing we learned from the European crisis, it is that knowing that a central bank stands behind the money supply is the best assurance that a sovereign debt crisis in the domestic currency will not occur.[3] I nevertheless remain convinced that monetary policy should focus on stabilizing inflation at a low level. The need seems to me to be not to deflect the central bank from concern with this target, but to recognize that it needs also to address additional needs in a way that will not jeopardize its ability to attain the target of low inflation. One need is that already cited: The knowledge that a central bank can ultimately be relied on to buy a country's sovereign debt does not conflict with the anti-inflationary objective, because there is no danger of inflation developing in the sort of situation where a central bank might have to implement this commitment. Another case can be envisaged: tightening regulations to head off or limit an asset price boom. Regulations and monetary policy constitute two distinct instruments. While tightening regulations can be expected to diminish demand, there is no doubt that its comparative advantage lies in curbing asset prices. If one is to tell a central bank to care for the financial sector as well as manage inflation, then one needs to give it a second instrument. I envisage the central bank as having the two instruments of interest rates and regulation in order to pursue the two objectives of low inflation and the avoidance of financial crises. This provides an answer to the supposed conundrum as to whether one should have raised interest rates in 2006 to head off the housing price boom: It would not have been necessary if the central bank instead had imposed (or raised) a minimum down payment requirement on houses. And if that had curbed demand too much, the Federal Reserve could have cut interest rates. Of course, this does assume that the Fed would have recognized that there was a boom in housing; the ability to recognize booms as such would be a prime condition sought in Fed chairmen.

If one could guarantee that a polity would address these three issues, I do not believe that one would have to face crises arising from excessive domestic indebtedness, of the sort with which we have become so familiar. But in the macroeconomics that I was taught there was a second condition that a country should pursue, which was called external balance. Since the advent of floating exchange rates in 1973, it has become customary to disregard this objective in the belief that a crisis of excessive external indebtedness is impossible in

---

3. See chapter 4 by Paul De Grauwe and Yuemei Ji in this volume.

a country with a floating currency because if it were to be threatened, the exchange rate would depreciate and thus take care of external considerations. This seems to some of us too sanguine. When countries (admittedly, usually with nonfloating currencies) overdevalue as a result of having to go to the IMF, the return of confidence is typically far from instantaneous. It seems all too likely that if the United States continues to pursue a laissez-faire policy toward the dollar (often called one of "benign neglect"), then the dollar will continue on its errant path, with the result of increasing external indebtedness, until no acceptable depreciation of the dollar is capable of restoring US prospects. A part of the process will, once again, be a crisis.

Does avoidance of the threat of an external crisis involve abandoning internal balance? I doubt that one can give a categorical assurance that this will never be part of the price; many countries, primarily but not exclusively (think of Iceland) those with more-or-less fixed exchange rates, have seen temporary violations of internal balance as part of the price of restoring external balance. Nevertheless, one could show a reasonable concern with keeping a competitive exchange rate without threatening internal balance. To begin with, the US Treasury Secretary could respond in an adult manner to questions about the dollar. Instead of averring constant fealty to a strong dollar, he could say that he wants to see the dollar near a reasonable estimate of its long-run equilibrium, like a real effective exchange rate between 3 and 4 percent weaker than in April 2012 (Cline and Williamson 2012). While the interest shown by foreign exchange market traders in US actions suggests that this would not be as ineffective as floaters are prone to suggest, one would surely need to back it up by a willingness to (1) intervene when the dollar becomes greatly misvalued, potentially at the cost of diverting monetary policy from the path that would be preferred on internal grounds, and (2) charge taxes on the entry of (or, alternatively, on the yield of) foreign-owned money.

So much for the policies that are desirable in normal times. Their essence is the challenge posed to central bankers many years ago by William McChesny Martin to be prepared to remove the punchbowl just as the party gets going. Politicians are unlikely to accept such advice with rapture, which brings us to the problem of how to fortify their willingness to act on advice that they will not welcome. The last section of this chapter discusses how that might be accomplished.

Policies in Abnormal Times

Abnormal times in my experience involve countries entering the transition and countries stricken by debt crises. It may be that countries in other highly abnormal situations, like those emerging from war, would behave completely differently. But I would be surprised if that were the case. I like to imagine that I am advancing propositions that are generally true for countries in abnormal times.

One thing that cannot be assumed is that after a crisis a country will have a similar potential growth rate to that when it entered. One can think of cases where potential growth was accelerated (most transition countries), reduced (many countries with debt crises, perhaps on account of a major resource switch from investment to the balance of payments), and largely unaffected by the crisis. The likely impact on medium-term growth is one of the issues that the reformers need to think about.

In the article referred to earlier in this chapter, Åslund (2011) argues that there are 12 rules for countries in crisis. He based some of his assertions on the evidence provided in a book of mine (Williamson 1994). His rules are outlined below.

1. It is essential to recognize that a crisis has erupted and that the old economic order has to change in a fundamental way.

One of the issues we debated in 1994 is whether a crisis is essential for getting major reforms approved. I argued that it was not, on the basis that our (unscientific) sample of 10 major reformers—Australia starting in 1983, Chile starting in the mid-1970s, Colombia during 1990–91, Indonesia starting in 1983, Mexico starting in 1988, New Zealand starting in 1984, Poland in 1990, Portugal starting in 1986, Spain starting in 1975, and Turkey starting in 1980—contained two examples of countries that had undertaken major reforms without facing an existential crisis (Colombia and Indonesia). It is difficult to deny that the reforms in those two countries, while needed and worthwhile, were less fundamental than those in New Zealand or Poland. A sufficiently great statesman—the best example may be Deng Xiaoping in China in 1978—may manage to sell a reform program that is not dictated by immediate circumstances. It is true that China was coming out of the Cultural Revolution in 1978, a revolution that had laid the country low. But the simplest solution would have been to avoid further changes and allow a gradual recovery. Or else there could have been a temptation to demand immediate changes everywhere, a classic "big bang." Deng in fact chose to initiate a process of gradual reform, which ended up transforming Chinese society into what some of us regard as a pretty capitalist model. Gradual reform without a crisis, where there is a statesman with the power and foresight to make it happen, may well be the best of all worlds. The odds, of course, are against such transformations as that which occurred in China. Just look at the squabbling over the US budget deficit for a contemporary example. Be that as it may, fundamental reforms are certainly aided by the belief that there is not an alternative, which has at times been assiduously cultivated even when it was extremely questionable.

2. A crisis almost always requires new leadership. Old leaders, even if they were adept at running a country in normal times, seldom are up to the task of facing the very different challenges of extraordinary times.

Deng Xiaoping is a classic example of the proposition that new leaders are required to confront a new situation of extreme crisis. Franklin D. Roosevelt, on the other hand, is a counterexample. He was a great peacetime leader who plucked the United States from the Great Depression, and when circumstances changed he also proved himself a great leader in a time of war. But it is difficult to think of additional examples (much as one may hope that Angela Merkel will prove to be one). Åslund recognized that there may be exceptions, but as a normal rule he appears correct.

3. Crisis resolution requires new, clear principles, not the horse trading and compromises that are the stuff of conventional politics.

When a system has come to the end of the road and is engulfed by crisis, one needs leaders who can envisage what the new world is going to look like and are not constrained by the existing system.

4. Crisis leaders need to concentrate on key concerns and not get distracted by side issues.

A leader who succeeds in overcoming a crisis is one who maintains his or her focus on the key concerns and refuses to be sidetracked by secondary questions, such as being reelected.

5. Constitutions may need to be changed, laws may need to be reformed, and new institutions may need to be created, rather than taking existing constitutions and laws as unchangeable.

Constitutions and laws reflect the rules of the game of a particular system, such as those of the nation-states that compose the euro system. They may need to be changed to reflect the new world that has to be created. Reluctance to implement needed changes may prevent rapid emergence from a crisis.

6. A comprehensive, consistent, and credible program needs to be developed quickly. It should not be too large but must cover all essential policies.

A new government needs to give priority to articulating a comprehensive but comprehensible vision of the system it is aiming to create. One cannot in the nature of the issue outline the content of the plan, since this is bound to depend on the circumstances of the particular case. For example, the threatened breakup of the euro area poses quite different challenges from the transition from communism.

7. It is no use seeking consensus: Vested interests of old elites need to be destroyed, not compromised. Appeal should instead be made directly to the public. Democracy is an ally.

Åslund makes it clear in this point that he is envisaging reform being undertaken by a philosopher-king who is supported by the democratic public. He does not consider the possibility that reform will be possible only to the extent that the reformers gain the support of certain factions (maybe including elites) and that it may be necessary to bribe some of those factions. He asserts that vested interests can always be combated, not accommodated. Perhaps a weakness of the Greek program in the current crisis is that it was drawn up by the old elite, and is mindful of its interests, and has therefore offended the rest of Greece.

8. Transparency is vital.

Only the corrupt benefit from an absence of transparency.

9. International support (particularly from the IMF) is needed.

In the present era in Europe, rather than in the past in Asia, the international system is on the right side of history, and international support for a reform program should be expected and is critical. As Åslund rightly observed, the key international economic institution is the IMF.

10. An anticrisis program must be sufficiently financed.

It would seem obvious that such a program must be sufficiently financed, but this is by definition of the word "sufficient," which is relative. The substantive point is that reform cannot be had on the cheap.

11. An anticrisis program is best implemented early and decisively, during a honeymoon period of extraordinary politics when the public will accept exceptionally radical measures.

An anticrisis program will encounter resistance that can easily kill it if it is launched at a deliberate speed and if the situation is perceived as likely to continue to deteriorate in the long run. Precisely because an anticrisis program is bound to ask for significant sacrifices from large segments of the population, it is important that it be launched quickly, preferably during a government's initial "honeymoon" period. It has been argued that this is a principal reason for the success of the Latvian program (Blanchard 2012). There were cases among the 10 countries cited earlier in which reforms were widely spaced out rather than concentrated at the start of an administration, but such tools as blaming unpopular steps on a predecessor government (a familiar political trick) are unavailable to those who fail to take advantage of the honeymoon.

12. Successful reforms need to concentrate on reducing expenditures rather than raising revenue, but austerity must be perceived as reasonably equitable.

I would not dispute that austerity must be perceived to be reasonably equitable, but promulgating as a general rule that expenditure cuts need to predominate over tax increases in restoring fiscal discipline strikes me as an illegitimate generalization. That is doubtless fair enough when discussing Europe, but there are many developing countries where the tax revenue collected by the central government is in single digits,[4] whereas increasing public expenditure, including that on development, is urgent. One would not want to see spending cut further in those situations, and an increase in tax receipts is needed to promote development spending. The United States is also a low-tax country where revenue increases will have to play a major role when (and if) fiscal discipline is restored.

---

4. According to the World Bank's *World Development Indicators*, http://data.worldbank.org/data-catalog/world-development-indicators (accessed on August 1, 2012).

Just what reforms will need to be adopted to counter a particular crisis cannot be foreseen without specifying the nature of what triggered that crisis. But these rules of how to behave when a crisis develops appear to be robust. The failure to observe them during the Great Recession and the consequential European sovereign debt crisis may help to explain why the world is still in crisis five years after the problems started. On the other hand, the rules do raise the possibility of a crisis being insoluble. It is assumed that the public will give sufficient power to a philosopher-king, maybe only temporarily, to enable resolution of the issue at hand. But there is no guarantee that this will always be possible. Disasters happen.

Perpetuating Normality

It was argued above that the reason crises arise is political reluctance to interfere with good times. Central bankers are paid to remove the punchbowl just when the party has got going, but there is not much point in their self-sacrifice if every other agent in society seeks perpetuation of the good times even when they are unsustainable. One needs to cultivate a general hostility to excessive expenditure and greed, and certainly not cultivate them.[5]

Perhaps a main reason why the public does not always seem ready to tighten its belt is because people do not get the information they need. It would take quite a superman to convince people to change their ways if they think that they could be eating cake instead of saving and sacrificing. If there is no authoritative voice calling for self-discipline, there may not be very much of it on display. Thus there is a need to strengthen and make more reliable the sources calling for self-discipline when that is in fact what is needed, and to penalize the natural political temptation to interpret all facts as supporting one's political position. Such counterchecks are already done in the United States on the political front, where those standing for election have to withstand the scrutiny of Factcheck.org (run by the Annenberg Foundation), Politifact.com (*Tampa Bay Times*), and Fact Checker (*Washington Post*). All three analyze political statements with a view to determining their truth. But the need is to go beyond identifying individual untrue statements to establishing reasonable grounds for believing that some promises are inconsistent, including inconsistency with a viable future.

One approach to tempering the good times is to prescribe fiscal rules that countries resolve ex ante to obey. The problem with this is that unless one is content to make deficits cyclically destabilizing, it is necessary to make exceptions for cyclically induced deficits, at which point the rules may cease to be sufficiently clear cut to act as an effective discipline. One example of the ex ante approach is the European Union's Growth and Stability Pact. It remains to be

---

5. I am thinking of promises of $2.50 gasoline, tax cuts, and balanced budgets (to be financed by unspecified cuts in discretionary expenditure), all on display during the Republican primary elections of 2012.

seen, however, whether the newly revised version of the pact has a happier fate than the first version, which was eviscerated by Germany and France as soon as it threatened to become inconvenient to them.

A frequent reaction to this problem has been to create so-called fiscal councils, which are normally financed by, but independent of, government and charged with providing macroeconomic advice on fiscal issues (and sometimes also providing microeconomic costing of individual programs). For example, this role is fulfilled by the Congressional Budget Office (CBO) in the United States, the Parliamentary Budget Office in Canada, the Council of Economic Experts in Germany, the Central Planning Bureau (CPB) in the Netherlands, and (since 2010) the Office of Budget Responsibility in the United Kingdom.[6] These councils may report directly to government or parliament, but the hope is that they will also influence public opinion and temper the deficit bias that has been prevalent in many countries in recent years.

The public is surely better informed in countries that have them because of the activities of fiscal councils. And in some cases (e.g., the Netherlands) they appear to have been an effective force in restraining the growth of government debt. But it is clear that they are not a panacea for avoiding a deficit bias. For example, no one could dismiss the CBO as doing its job ineffectively or in a biased way, and yet the long-term position of the United States appears as difficult as any.

In addition to fiscal councils in the public sector, a number of nongovernmental organizations (NGOs) are now active in providing the public with information on the public finances, often reflecting a feeling of desperation at the deteriorating public situation. The United States has the Center for Budget Priorities and Policies (an all-service think tank); the Tax Policy Center (a joint initiative of Brookings and the Urban Institute, devoted as its name implies to analysis of the revenue side of the budget); the Committee for a Responsible Federal Budget (mainly interested in reducing public debt); and the Bipartisan Policy Center (distinguished by its wide terms of reference and bipartisan nature, which in a fractured political system like that in the United States implies that the great breadth is accompanied by little depth). Britain has the Institute of Fiscal Studies (IFS).

Two countries have institutions responsible for analyzing the programs of political parties as presented at election time. In the Netherlands this service is performed by the same CPB (whose official English title is the Netherlands Bureau for Economic Policy Analysis) that also acts as the fiscal council. In

---

6. Additional fiscal councils are mentioned on the excellent website on this subject maintained by Simon Wren-Lewis of Oxford University, www.economics.ox.ac.uk/members/simon.wren-lewis/fc/fiscal_councils.htm (accessed on August 1, 2012). They include the Public Debt Committee of Austria, the Federal Planning Committee (in association with the High Council of Finance) in Belgium, the Economic Council in Denmark, the Irish Fiscal Advisory Council, the Portuguese Public Finance Council, the National Assembly Budget Office in Korea, and the Swedish Fiscal Council. This list includes only existing fiscal councils and not those being planned (or the one in Hungary that was dismissed because it refused to kowtow to the government).

the other country that has an "election watchdog," the United Kingdom, the service is instead performed by an NGO, IFS.

The CPB has been analyzing the effects of political parties' declared programs on a range of variables, including aggregate demand, employment, and government finances, since 1986.[7] This is now a regular part of the election cycle in the Netherlands, in which CPB (in association with the Netherlands Environmental Assessment Agency) offers its analysis, according to the best-accepted scientific methods, of the implications of any party program that is voluntarily submitted to it. It considers the impact on government finances, both during the following four-year government term and on a long-term basis, measured in principle in 2040. It also examines the income (demand) and employment effects at the end of the forthcoming government term and, where possible, the effects on accessibility; climate and energy; agriculture, rural areas, and the environment; education and innovation; the housing market; and the health care sector. The results are published in advance of each election in *Keuzes in Kaart* (translated from the Dutch as *Charted Choices*). In the most recent Dutch general election in 2010 the programs of all nine major parties were submitted for analysis.

CPB is organized as a part of the government—actually, as part of the Ministry of Economic Affairs, Agriculture, and Innovation. It is nevertheless guaranteed full independence, and is apparently trusted by the populace to act completely independently, despite the fact that in another role it prepares the macroeconomic forecasts on which the government relies. CPB declines to speculate: If it concludes that there is an insufficient agreed-upon scientific basis to give an authoritative judgment, it says so, and leaves politicians and the electorate to make their choice on other grounds. And while the CPB estimates the effects of the proposals that the political parties submit to it, it does not check that these are the same as those on which they campaign. The CPB has commented caustically (on its website) that it does not analyze promises of all gain and no pain—for example, of proposals to increase civil service efficiency (which it regards as free lunches)—since if these were really available they would have been implemented long ago.[8]

CPB's judgments are reputed to play a major role in Dutch election campaigns. The public does not read CPB's report, but the report serves as the basis for much press comment, which is widely read. The benefits of such an arrangement are clear enough: It enables those casting their votes to be much

---

7. A very helpful paper on the several roles played by CPB, including that of election watchdog, is contained in Bos and Teulings (2012). The English-language version of CPB's own website is www.cpb.nl/en.

8. The CPB website also describes how a contractual reduction of civil service wages of 4.2 percent led to a rise of discretionary wage payments of 3.4 percent (2.6 percent more than the private sector), so it similarly disregarded proposals for a public service pay lag. But perhaps such proposals should be analyzed rather than rejected a priori: Public sector wages may at times lead, as a result of which generalized public pay restraint may be exactly what is needed.

better informed about what they are voting for, it helps parties avoid unintended consequences, and it avoids factual questions muddying the waters in the postelection negotiations about the inevitable coalition government.

But some of the asserted costs are also potentially important: that CPB biases the debate in favor of the type of proposal that contributes to medium-run demand and employment (because this is what CPB's model measures best) and against expenditures that have the effect of prolonging longevity, on education, and the environment (whose benefits are not measured by the main model, while the costs are). CPB replies that it has developed supplementary models to measure these benefits and presents a tradeoff in *Keuzes in Kaart*. The counter response is that because this is not comparable to the main analysis it tends to be ignored in the public debate, and therefore biases the parties against such expenditures.

The other country that subjects political proposals to systematic analysis designed to expose inconsistencies is the United Kingdom. Since 1997, the nonpartisan and independent IFS has published a series of preelection Briefing Notes comparing the proposals of various parties on specific subjects.[9]

There are stark differences between what the IFS does and the older CPB approach: the IFS analysis is undertaken in a series of Briefing Notes on particular subjects rather than in one comprehensive document; each note quantifies what it considers quantifiable on the basis of the models available, drawing where possible on other IFS work, but the analysis is presented in verbal form; and the inputs are not ground to a form that will enable them to enter into the main model. I tend to prefer this approach, which is less model-dependent than that of CPB, but I have the impression that at least to date the IFS has made much less impression on the British public than CPB has upon the Dutch public. Perhaps this is due to the fact that the Dutch initiative has been running longer, or perhaps it reflects the fact that the Dutch assessment is performed not by an NGO but rather by a part of government—surprisingly to a foreigner, a part of government that seems to be widely trusted to be neutral, perhaps a vestige of the distinguished pedigree of CPB's founder, Jan Tinbergen. In the most recent election in the United Kingdom in 2010, no party displayed a willingness to discuss how they proposed to make the economies that were widely recognized to be necessary, but at least they avoided making grandiose and expensive promises, which might be taken as a modest mark of success.

Is there any other mechanism that might bring home to the public the need for intertemporal consistency? Consider the possibility of enhancing the status of "election watchdogs" (and establishing them where they do not presently exist). What we are interested in is basically deploying economic expertise, so the election watchdogs need to include economists, however unpopular economists may be at the moment. I see three problems with this proposal:

9. A summary of the 2010 Briefing Notes is available on the IFS website at www.ifs.org.uk/publications/4850 (accessed on August 1, 2012).

(1) how to achieve a useful measure of professional agreement among economists, (2) how to have their prognostications taken seriously by the electorate, and (3) how to get the politicians to accept them.

The first challenge would seem to demand a dual approach. One element would be to restrict the questions that are posed to the watchdog to those that have an answer that demands purely economic expertise. For example, rather than ask the watchdog to draw up a proposal for resolving the budget deficit (which inevitably involves weighing tax increases against expenditure cuts and deciding who is to pay for austerity), one should pose questions about particular proposals being advanced by parties (or candidates). Does a given slate of proposals resolve the deficit problem (defined as stabilizing the debt-to-GDP ratio at a specified level)? How much is left to be resolved in the future? These are factual questions, though inevitably surrounded by a margin of uncertainty.

The other element of the dual approach concerns the question of how the panel of economists to whom the question is referred should be selected. Clearly one wants economists whose predominant loyalty is to truth rather than to a party, and who would not allow their professional integrity to be compromised by concern for a party. Getting such a panel seems to me to demand a two-pronged approach. First, a pool needs to be established with that criterion in mind, as judged by all the relevant parties (say, those that received at least 5 percent of the vote in the previous election). Would there be a danger of a party vetoing every potential candidate except those that toe its particular line? It seems impossible to rule out this possibility, but the reputational cost of such a tactic would presumably be great. Second, assuming that there is a pool from which to draw, I would envisage the relevant parties appointing candidates from the pool, perhaps seven or nine in all, with appointment power proportional to votes in the preceding election (subject to a minimum of one for any party polling 5 percent of the vote).

The second challenge to establishing election watchdogs would be to convince the public to take the panel's prognostications seriously. One problem seems inescapable: Economists are not in very good repute with the public at the moment for the rather compelling reason that they have performed their job poorly in the recent past. Very few economists saw the weaknesses in the financial sector and the absurdities of housing finance in advance; we assumed (wrongly, as it turned out) that the financial sector knew what it was doing. Yet since it is economic expertise that is relevant, there seems no alternative but to seek economists, even if one might hope to leaven them with some acquainted with other disciplines as well. It is perhaps likely that, at least initially, the panel would have to labor long and hard out of the limelight and finally publish a report that would be reported only in the serious press (rather like the IFS). The hope is that it would attract increasing attention as it matured, and one day a panel might even be invited by a television company to deliberate in public. This proposal is advanced in the belief that there are many electors who are tired of half-truths but who are aware that they lack the ability to discern what is true and what is not. The object of the proposal is to help them decide, and in the process ensure that the future is no longer in danger of being sacrificed by the democratic mechanism.

The proposal still requires that the politicians consent to the establishment of such election watchdogs. Of course, politicians do not have a monopoly over ventures such as the IFS Briefing Notes, but they would necessarily have the ability to veto the establishment of an election watchdog on the lines here suggested, since their naming of nominees to the panel who are acceptable to their political opponents and of appointees from the panel to the watchdog are integral parts of the proposal. While such a degree of bipartisanship may be natural in many countries, it is not clear that it is in all of them.

Failure of the proposal for this reason would be a shame, but one can still hope that circumstances will change. Its success, on the other hand, could mark a step toward implementing the types of measures that promote intertemporal consistency and thus perpetuate normality.

References

Åslund, Anders. 2011. The Failed Political Economy of the Euro Crisis. RealTime Economic Issues Watch, November 18. Washington: Peterson Institute for International Economics. Available at www.piie.com/blogs/realtime/?p=2515 (accessed on August 2, 2012).

Blanchard, Olivier. 2011. The Future of Macroeconomic Policy: Nine Tentative Conclusions. *IMF Direct* (March 13). Available at http://blog-imfdirect.imf.org/2011/03/13/future-of-macro-economic-policy.

Blanchard, Olivier. 2012. Lessons from Latvia. *IMF Direct* (June 11). http://blog-imfdirect.imf.org/2012/06/11/lessons-from-latvia (accessed on August 1, 2012).

Bos, Frits, and Coen Teulings. 2012. *The World's Oldest Fiscal Watchdog: CPB's Analyses Foster Consensus on Economic Policy.* CPB Discussion Paper 207 (March 21). Available at http://ssrn.com/abstract=2026815. [Forthcoming in *Restoring Public Debt Sustainability: The Role of Independent Fiscal Institutions,* 2012, ed. G. Kopits, Oxford University Press.]

Cline, William R., and John Williamson. 2012. *Estimates of Fundamental Equilibrium Exchange Rates, May 2012.* Policy Briefs in International Economics 12-14. Washington: Peterson Institute for International Economics.

Klein, Naomi. 2007. *The Shock Doctrine: The Rise of Disaster Capitalism.* New York: Metropolitan Books.

Minsky, Hyman. 2008. *Stabilizing an Unstable Economy.* New York: McGraw Hill.

Patinkin, Don. 1956. *Money, Interest, and Prices.* Evanston, IL: Row, Peterson and Co.

Williamson, John, ed. 1994. *The Political Economy of Policy Reform.* Washington: Institute for International Economics.

Selected Publications of John Williamson

Exchange Rates

Books

1965. *The Crawling Peg*. Princeton Essays in International Finance 50. Princeton, NJ: Princeton University Press.

1971. *The Choice of a Pivot for Parities*. Princeton Essays in International Finance 90. Princeton, NJ: Princeton University Press.

1981. *Exchange Rate Rules: The Theory, Performance and Prospects of the Crawling Peg* (editor). London and New York: Macmillan and Saint Martin's Press.

1985. *The Exchange Rate System*. Policy Analyses in International Economics 5. Washington: Institute for International Economics. (Original edition 1983, Cambridge, MA: MIT Press for the Institute for International Economics).

1994. *Estimating Equilibrium Exchange Rates* (editor). Washington: Institute for International Economics.

1995. *What Role for Currency Boards?* Policy Analyses in International Economics 40. Washington: Institute for International Economics.

1996. *The Crawling Band as an Exchange Rate Regime: Lessons from Chile, Colombia, and Israel*. Washington: Institute for International Economics.

2000. *Exchange Rate Regimes for Emerging Markets: Reviving the Intermediate Option*. Policy Analyses in International Economics 60. Washington: Institute for International Economics.

2003. *Dollar Overvaluation and the World Economy* (coedited with C. Fred Bergsten). Special Report 16. Washington: Institute for International Economics.

2004. *Dollar Adjustment: How Far? Against What?* (coedited with C. Fred Bergsten). Special Report 17. Washington: Institute for International Economics.

2007. *Reference Rates and the International Monetary System.* Policy Analyses in International Economics 82. Washington: Peterson Institute for International Economics.

Chapters in Books

1976. Generalized Floating and the Reserve Needs of Developing Countries. In *The Developing Nations and the International Monetary System*, ed. D. Leipziger. Washington: US Agency for International Development.

1979. The Failure of Global Fixity. In *The Emerging European Monetary System*, ed. R. Triffin. Brussels: National Bank of Belgium.

1983. Exchange Rates and Trade Policy (with C. Fred Bergsten). In *Trade Policy in the 1980s*, ed. William R. Cline. Washington: Institute for International Economics.

1987. A FEER for the Canadian Dollar. Appendix in *The United States and Canada: The Quest for Free Trade,* by Paul Wonnacott. Policy Analyses in International Economics 16. Washington: Institute for International Economics.

1988. Roundtable on Exchange Rate Policy (with Stanley W. Black and Dale Henderson). In *Misalignment of Exchange Rates.* Cambridge, MA: National Bureau of Economic Research.

1989. The Stabilizing Properties of Target Zones (with Marcus Miller and Paul Weller). In *Macroeconomics Policies in an Interdependent World*, ed. R. C. Bryant et al. Washington: Brookings Institution.

1990. Target Zones and Monetary Stability. In *International and European Monetary System*, ed. E. M. Claassen. New York: Praeger.

1991. Advice on the Choice of an Exchange Rate Policy. In *Exchange Rate Policies in Developing and Post Socialist Countries*, ed. E. M. Claassen. San Francisco, CA: ICS Press.

1991. Convertibility. In *The Transition to a Market Economy*, ed. P. Marer and S. Zecchini. Paris: Organization for Economic Cooperation and Development.

1999. The Case for a Common Basket Peg for East Asian Currencies. In *Exchange Rate Policies in Emerging Asian Countries*, ed. S. Collignon, J. Pisani-Ferry, and Y. C. Park. Routledge Studies on the Growth Economies of Asia. London and New York: Routledge.

1999. Foreword. In *Exchange Rate Misalignments: Concepts and Measurement for Developing Countries*, ed. L. E. Hinkle and P. J. Montiel. Washington: Oxford University Press for the World Bank.

2001. Exchange Rate Policy in Latin America: The Costs of the Conventional Wisdom. In *New Challenges of Crisis Prevention: Addressing Economic Imbalances in the North and Boom-Bust Cycles in the South*, ed. J. J. Teunissen. The Hague: FONDAD.

2001. The Case for a Basket, Band and Crawl (BBC) Regime for East Asia. In *Future Directions for Monetary Policies in East Asia*, RBA Annual Conference Volume, ed. David Gruen and John Simon. Sydney: Reserve Bank of Australia.

2008. Do Development Considerations Matter for Exchange Rate Policy? In *Current Account and External Financing*, volume 12, ed. Kevin Cowan, Sebastián Edwards, and Rodrigo O. Valdés. Santiago: Central Bank of Chile.

Articles

1982. A Survey of the Literature on the Optimal Peg. *Journal of Development Economics* 11, no. 1 (August): 39–61.

1985. On the Optimal Currency Peg for Developing Countries: Reply. *Journal of Development Economics* 18, nos. 2-3 (August): 561–62.

1986. Target Zones and the Management of the Dollar. *Brookings Papers on Economic Activity* 17, no. 1: 165–74. Washington: Economic Studies Program, Brookings Institution.

1987. Exchange Rate Management: The Role of Target Zones. *American Economic Review* 77, no. 2 (May): 200–204.

1987. Exchange Rate Flexibility, Target Zones, and Policy Coordination. *World Development* 15, no. 12 (December): 1437–43.

1987. On Evaluating and Extending the Target Zone Proposal (with Hali J. Edison and Marcus H. Miller). *Journal of Policy Modeling* 9, no. 1: 199–224.

1987. The Search for a New Exchange Rate Regime. *Science*, July 31.

1989. The Case for Roughly Stabilizing the Real Value of the Dollar. *American Economic Review* 79, no. 2, Papers and Proceedings of the Hundred and First Annual Meeting of the American Economic Association (May): 41–45.

1991. FEERs and the ERM. *National Institute Economic Review* 137 (August): 45–50.

1993. Exchange Rate Management. *Economic Journal* 103, no. 416 (January): 188–97.

1997. Exchange Rate Policy and Development Strategy. *Journal of African Economies* 6, no. 3: 17–36.

1998. Crawling Bands or Monitoring Bands: How to Manage Exchange Rates in a World of Capital Mobility. *International Finance* 1, no. 1 (October): 59–79.

2002. The Evolution of Thought on Intermediate Exchange Rate Regimes. *The Annals of the American Academy of Political and Social Science* 579 (January): 73–86.

2004. The Dollar/Euro Exchange Rate. *Économie Internationale*, no. 100, issue 4: 51–60.

2006. A Worldwide System of Reference Rates. *International Economics and Economic Policy* 3, no. 3 (December): 341–52.

2007. The Case for an Intermediate Exchange Rate Regime. *Singapore Economic Review* 52, no. 03: 295–307.

2009. Exchange Rate Economics. *Open Economies Review* 20, no. 1 (February): 123–46.

Policy Papers and Working Papers

Estimation of Equilibrium Exchange Rates

2008. *New Estimates of Fundamental Equilibrium Exchange Rates* (with William R. Cline). Policy Briefs in International Economics 08-7. Washington: Peterson Institute for International Economics.

2009. *2009 Estimates of Fundamental Equilibrium Exchange Rates* (with William R. Cline). Policy Briefs in International Economics 09-10. Washington: Peterson Institute for International Economics.

2010. *Estimates of Fundamental Equilibrium Exchange Rates, May 2010* (with William R. Cline). Policy Briefs in International Economics 10-15. Washington: Peterson Institute for International Economics.

2011. *Estimates of Fundamental Equilibrium Exchange Rates, May 2011* (with William R. Cline). Policy Briefs in International Economics 11-5. Washington: Peterson Institute for International Economics.

Exchange Rate Policy and Regimes

1975. The Future Exchange Rate Regime. *Banca Nazionale del Lavoro Quarterly Review*, no. 113 (June): 127–44.

1989. *The Stabilizing Properties of Target Zones* (with M. Miller and P. Weller). The Warwick Economics Research Paper Series (TWERPS) 318. Coventry: Department of Economics, University of Warwick.

1990. Currency Convertibility in Eastern Europe (with C. Fred Bergsten). *Proceedings*: 35–49. Federal Reserve Bank of Kansas City.

1991. *Advice on the Choice of an Exchange-Rate Policy.* United Nations World Employment Programme Paper 3. San Francisco, CA: International Center for Economic Growth.

1999. *Crawling Bands or Monitoring Bands: How to Manage Exchange Rates in a World of Capital Mobility.* Policy Briefs in International Economics 99-3. Washington: Institute for International Economics

2005. *A Currency Basket for East Asia, Not Just China.* Policy Briefs in International Economics 05-1. Washington: Institute for International Economics.

2006. *Choosing Monetary Arrangements for the 21st Century: Problems of a Small Economy.* Policy Briefs in International Economics 06-8. Washington: Peterson Institute for International Economics.

2008. *Exchange Rate Economics.* Working Paper 08-3. Washington: Peterson Institute for International Economics.

2008. *A Worldwide System of Reference Rates.* Working Paper 130. Vienna: Oesterreichische Nationalbank.

International Monetary System and Its Reform

Books

1977. *The Failure of World Monetary Reform, 1971–74.* Sunbury-on-Thames, Middlesex: Nelson & Sons.

1985. *Economy of International Money: In Search of a New Order.* London: Royal Institute of International Affairs.

1987. *Political Economy and International Money: Selected Essays of John Williamson,* ed. Chris Milner. Brighton: Wheatsheaf.

1993. *The G-7's Joint-and-Several Blunder* (with B. A. Aghion). Princeton Studies in International Economics 189. Princeton, NJ: Princeton University Press.

Chapters in Books

1975. The International Financial System. In *Higher Oil Prices and the World Economy,* ed. E. R. Freid and C. L. Schultze. Washington: Brookings Institution.

1976. Generalized Floating and the Reserve Needs of Developing Countries. In *The Developing Nations and the International Monetary System,* ed. D. Leipziger. Washington: US Agency for International Development.

1976. The Benefits and Costs of an International Monetary Nonsystem. In *Reflections on Jamaica,* ed. Edward M. Bernstein et al. Princeton Essays in International Finance 115. Princeton: Princeton University Press.

1977. Transferência de Recursos e o Sistema Monetário Internacional [Resource Transfer and the International Monetary System]. In *Estudos sobre Desenvolvimento Econômico* [*Studies on Economic Development*]. Rio de Janeiro: BNDES.

1978. Machlup on International Monetary Reform. In *Breadth and Depth in Economics: Fritz Machlup—The Man and His Ideas*, ed. J. S. Dreyer. Lexington, MA: Lexington Books.

1982. The Failure of World Monetary Reform: A Reassessment. In *The International Monetary System Under Flexible Exchange Rates: Global, Regional, and National*, ed. R. N. Cooper et al. Cambridge, MA: Ballinger.

1982. The Growth of Official Reserves and the Issue of World Monetary Control. In *The International Monetary System: A Time of Turbulence*, ed. J. S. Dreyer, G. Haberler, and T. D. Willett. Washington: American Enterprise Institute.

1983. International Monetary Reform: An Agenda for the 1980s. In *Towards a New Bretton Woods*. London: Commonwealth Secretariat.

1983. Keynes and the International Economic Order. In *Keynes and the Modern World*, ed. G. D. N. Worswick and J. S. Trevithick. Cambridge University Press.

1984. International Liquidity: Are the Supply and Composition Appropriate? In *The International Monetary System: Forty Years After Bretton Woods*. Boston, MA: Federal Reserve Bank of Boston.

1987. Bancor and the Developing Countries: How Much Difference Would It Have Made? In *Keynes and Economic Development*, ed. A. P. Thirlwall. London: Macmillan.

1990. The "Blueprint" Proposals for International Monetary Reform. In *Lloyd's Bank Annual Review*, ed. C. Johnson. London.

1992. International Monetary Reform and the Prospects for Economic Development. In *Fragile Finance: Rethinking the International Monetary System,* ed. J. J. Teunissen. The Hague: FONDAD.

1994. Managing the Monetary System (with C. Randall Henning). In *Managing the World Economy: Fifty Years after Bretton Woods*, ed. P. B. Kenen. Washington: Institute for International Economics.

1994. The Rise and Fall of the Concept of International Liquidity. In *The International Monetary System*, ed. P. B. Kenen, F. Papadia, and F. Saccomanni. Cambridge University Press.

2006. Revamping the International Monetary System. In *Reforming the IMF for the 21st Century*, ed. Edwin M. Truman. Washington: Institute for International Economics.

Articles

1963. Liquidity and the Multiple Key Currency Proposal. *American Economic Review* 53, no. 3 (June): 427–33.

1973. Surveys in Applied Economics: International Liquidity. *Economic Journal* 83, no. 331 (September): 685–746.

1974. The Financial Implications of Reserve Supply Arrangements. *IMF Staff Papers* 21, no. 3 (November): 563–82.

1975. International Monetary Issues and the Developing Countries: A Comment. *World Development* 3, no. 9 (September): 639–40.

1976. Exchange-Rate Flexibility and Reserve Use. *Scandinavian Journal of Economics* 78, no. 2: 327–39.

1980. Economic Theory and International Monetary Fund Policies. *Carnegie-Rochester Conference Series on Public Policy* 13, no. 1 (January): 255–78.

1985. On the System in Bretton Woods. *American Economic Review* 75, no. 2 (May): 74–79.

1988. The International Monetary System: An Analysis of Alternative Regimes (with Marcus Miller). *European Economic Review* 32, no. 5 (June): 1031–48.

1992. On Designing an International Monetary System. *Journal of Post Keynesian Economics* 15, no. 2 (Winter): 181–92.

1994. The Theory Behind the Blueprint. *British Review of Economic Issues* 16 (June): 1–22.

2004. The Future of the Global Financial System. *Journal of Post Keynesian Economics* 26, no. 4 (October): 607–11.

2010. Introduction: Is the Era of the Dollar Over? *Journal of Globalization and Development* 1, no. 2: 9.

2010. The Future of the Reserve System. *Journal of Globalization and Development* 1, no. 2: 15.

Policy Papers and Working Papers

1979. *World Stagflation and International Monetary Arrangements*. Textos para discussão 5. Rio de Janeiro, Brazil: Department of Economics PUC-Rio.

1984. Can the Economy Be Managed? Lecture delivered to the Liberal Summer School, Matlock, England.

1988. *The International Monetary System: An Analysis of Alternative Regimes* (with Marcus Miller). CEPR Discussion Papers 266. London: Centre for Economic Policy Research.

1998. Globalization: The Concept, Causes, and Consequences. Keynote address to the Congress of the Sri Lankan Association for the Advancement of Science, Colombo, Sri Lanka, December 15.

2009. *Why SDRs Could Rival the Dollar*. Policy Briefs in International Economics 09-20. Washington: Peterson Institute for International Economics.

2009. *Understanding Special Drawing Rights (SDRs)*. Policy Briefs in International Economics 09-11. Washington: Peterson Institute for International Economics.

2010. *Currency Wars?* (with William R. Cline). Policy Briefs in International Economics 10-26. Washington: Peterson Institute for International Economics.

Bretton Woods Institutions and International Coordination

Books

1982. *The Lending Policies of the International Monetary Fund*. Policy Analyses in International Economics 1. Washington: Institute for International Economics.

1983. *IMF Conditionality* (editor). Washington: Institute for International Economics.

1987. *Targets and Indicators: A Blueprint for the International Coordination of Economic Policy* (with Marcus H. Miller). Policy Analyses in International Economics 22. Washington: Institute for International Economics.

2002. *Delivering on Debt Relief: From IMF Gold to a New Aid Architecture* (with Nancy Birdsall). Washington: Institute for International Economics and Center for Global Development.

Chapters in Books

1977. SDRs: The Link. In *The New International Economic Order: The North-South Debate*, ed. J. N. Bhagwati. Cambridge, MA: MIT Press.

1982. The Economics of IMF Conditionality. In *For Good or Evil: Economic Theory and North-South Negotiations,* ed. G. K. Helleiner. Buffalo and Oslo: University of Toronto Press and Universitetsforlaget.

1991. Whither Macroeconomic Policy Coordination? In *Evolution of the International and Regional Monetary System*, ed. A. Steinherr and Daniel Weiserbs. London: Macmillan.

1995. On the Modalities of Macroeconomic Policy Coordination. In *The UN and the Bretton Woods Institutions: New Challenges for the Twenty-First Century*, ed. M. ul Haq, R. Jolly, P. Streeten, and K. Haq. London: Macmillan.

2000. The Role of the IMF: A Guide to the Reports. In *Developing Countries and the Global Financial System*, ed. S. Griffith-Jones and A. Bhattacharya. London: Commonwealth Secretariat. (Also published as Policy Briefs in International Economics 00-5, Institute for International Economics, Washington.)

Articles

1980. Economic Theory and International Monetary Fund Policies. *Carnegie-Rochester Conference Series on Public Policy* 13, no. 1 (January): 255–78.

1983. On Seeking to Improve IMF Conditionality. *American Economic Review* 73, no. 2 (May): 354–58.

1985. On the System in Bretton Woods. *American Economic Review* 75, no. 2 (May): 74–79.

1995. Reform of the International Financial Institutions. *Canadian Foreign Policy Journal* 3, no.1 (Spring): 15–22.

Policy Papers and Working Papers

1972. SDRs, Interest, and the Aid Link. *Banca Nazionale del Lavoro Quarterly Review*, no. 100 (June): 199–205.

1982. Global Macroeconomic Strategy. Annex to *Promoting World Recovery: A Statement on Global Economic Policy*, by Twenty-Six Economists (December). Washington: Institute for International Economics.

1998. A New Facility for the IMF? *Macroeconomics* 9809013, EconWPA.

Capital Flows, Debt, and Crises

Books

1966. *How to Stop Stop-Go*. London: Liberal Publication Department for New Orbits Group.

1985. *Financial Intermediation Beyond the Debt Crisis* (with Donald R. Lessard). Policy Analyses in International Economics 12. Washington: Institute for International Economics.

1987. *Capital Flight: The Problem and Policy Responses* (with Donald R. Lessard). Policy Analyses in International Economics 23. Washington: Institute for International Economics.

1987. *Capital Flight and Third World Debt* (with Donald R. Lessard). Washington: Institute for International Economics.

1988. *Voluntary Approaches to Debt Relief.* Policy Analyses in International Economics 25 (revised 1989). Washington: Institute for International Economics

1998. *A Survey of Financial Liberalization* (with Molly Mahar). Princeton Essays in International Finance 211. Princeton, NJ: Princeton University Press.

2005. *Curbing the Boom-Bust Cycle: Stabilizing Capital Flows to Emerging Markets.* Policy Analyses in International Economics 75. Washington: Institute for International Economics.

Chapters in Books

1971. On the Normative Theory of Balance-of-Payments Adjustment. In *Monetary Theory and Monetary Policy in the 1970s*, ed. G. Clayton et al. Oxford University Press.

1978. The Balance of Payments. In *Demand Management*, ed. M. Posner. London: Heineman.

1982. The Why and How of Funding LDC Debt. In *Development Financing: A Framework for International Financial Co-operation*, ed. Salah Al-Shaikhly. London and Boulder, CO: Francis Pinter and Westview Press.

1984. The Outlook for Development Finance After the Debt Crisis. In *Crisis of the 80s*, ed. K. Haq. Islamabad: North South Roundtable.

1984. The External Environment and the Adjustment Process. In *Adjustment with Growth: A Search for an Equitable Solution*, ed. K. Haq and C. Massad. Islamabad: North South Roundtable.

1991. On Liberalizing the Capital Account. In *Finance and the International Economy* 5, ed. R. O'Brien. Oxford: Oxford University Press.

1994. Issues Posed by Portfolio Investment in Developing Countries. In *Investing in Emerging Markets*, ed. M. J. Howell. London: Euromoney Publications in association with the World Bank.

1997. Pension Funds, Capital Controls, and Macroeconomic Stability (with Helmut Reisen). In *The Economics of Pensions: Principles, Policies, and International Experience*, ed. S. Valdes-Prieto. Cambridge, UK: Cambridge University Press.

1998. Current Account Targets (with Molly Mahar). Appendix in *Real Exchange Rates for the Year 2000*, ed. S. Wren-Lewis and R. Driver. Washington: Institute for International Economics.

1999. Implications of the East Asian Crisis for Debt Management. In *External Debt Management: Issues, Lessons and Preventive Measures*, ed. A. Vasudevan. Bombay: Reserve Bank of India.

Articles

1973. Another Case of Profitable Destabilizing Speculation. *Journal of International Economics* 3, no. 1 (February): 77–83.

1973. Payments Objectives and Economic Welfare. *IMF Staff Papers* 20, no. 3 (November): 573–90.

1984. Is There an External Constraint? *National Institute Economic Review,* no. 109 (August): 73–77.

1984. The Debt Crisis in Perspective. *Journal of International Affairs* 38, no. 1 (Summer): 21–25.

1986. The Outlook for Debt Relief or Repudiation in Latin America. *Oxford Review of Economic Policy* 2, no. 1 (Spring): 1–6.

1991. The Debt Crisis: Lessons of the 1980s. *Asian Development Review* 9, no. 2: 1–13.

1992. Acerca de la liberalización de la cuenta de capitales [On Liberalizing the Capital Account]. *Estudios de Economia* 19, no. 2 (December): 185–97. University of Chile, Department of Economics.

1997. Prospects for Avoiding Crises with Liberalized Capital Flows. *Estudios de Economia* 24, no. 2: 287–95 (December). University of Chile, Department of Economics.

2001. Issues Regarding the Composition of Capital Flows. *Development Policy Review* 19, no.1 (March): 11–29.

2004. The Years of Emerging Market Crises: A Review of Feldstein. *Journal of Economic Literature* 42, no. 3 (September): 822–37.

Policy Papers and Working Papers

1985. Four Lessons of the Debt Crisis. *Development and South-South Cooperation* 1, no.1 (December): 24–33.

1999. *Whether and When to Liberalize Capital Account and Financial Services.* Working Paper ERAD 99-03. Geneva: World Trade Organization, Economic Research and Analysis Division.

2002. *Proposals for Curbing the Boom-Bust Cycle in the Supply of Capital to Emerging Markets.* WIDER Discussion Paper 2002/3. United Nations University–World Institute for Development Economic Research (UNU-WIDER).

2007. *Global Imbalances: Time for Action* (with Alan Ahearne, William R. Cline, Kyung Tae Lee, Yung Chul Park, and Jean Pisani-Ferry). Policy Briefs in International Economics 07-4. Washington: Peterson Institute for International Economics. (Also published as Bruegel Policy Brief 2007/02.)

2011. *Getting Surplus Countries to Adjust*. Policy Briefs in International Economics 11-1. Washington: Peterson Institute for International Economics.

Country and Regional Studies

Books

1972. *European Monetary Integration* (with G. Magnifico). London: Federal Trust.

1980. *The Financing Procedures of British Foreign Trade* (with S. Carse and G. E. Wood). Cambridge, UK: Cambridge University Press.

1983. *Prospects for Adjustment in Argentina, Brazil and Mexico: Responding to the Debt Crisis* (editor). Special Report 2. Washington: Institute for International Economics.

1985. *Inflation and Indexation: Argentina, Brazil, and Israel* (editor). Special Report 3. Washington: Institute for International Economics.

1986. *African Debt and Financing* (coedited with Carol Lancaster). Special Report 5. Washington: Institute for International Economics.

1987. *Adjusting to Success: Balance of Payments Policy in the East Asian NICs* (with Bela Balassa). Washington: Institute for International Economics (revised May 1990).

1990. *The Progress of Policy Reform in Latin America*. Policy Analyses in International Economics 28. Washington: Institute for International Economics.

1990. *Latin American Adjustment: How Much Has Happened?* (editor). Washington: Institute for International Economics.

1991. *The Economic Opening of Eastern Europe*. Washington: Institute for International Economics.

1991. *From Soviet disUnion to Eastern Economic Community?* (with Oleh Havrylyshyn). Washington: Institute for International Economics.

1991. *Currency Convertibility in Eastern Europe* (editor). Washington: Institute for International Economics.

1992. *Trade and Payments after Soviet Disintegration*. Washington: Institute for International Economics.

1993. *Economic Consequences of Soviet Disintegration* (editor). Washington: Institute for International Economics.

1999. *Economic Reform: Content, Progress, Prospects*. New Delhi: Indian Council for Research on International Economic Relations.

Chapters in Books

1971. Trade and Economic Growth. In *The Economics of Europe*, ed. J. Pinder. London: Charles Knight.

1975. The Implications of European Monetary Integration for the Peripheral Areas. In *Economic Sovereignty and Regional Policy*, ed. J. Vaizey. London: Gil and Macmillan Ltd.

1982. On the Concepts, Objectives, and Modalities of Monetary Integration. In *Arab Monetary Integration: Issues and Prerequisites*, ed. K. El-Din Haseeb and S. Makdisi. London: Croom Helm.

1989. The Global Economic Environment and Prospects for Recovery in Latin America. In *Debt, Adjustment, and Recovery: Latin America's Prospects for Growth and Development*, ed. S. Edwards and F. Larrain. Oxford: Basil Blackwell.

1991. Current Issues in Transition Economics. In *International Financial Policy: Essays in Honor of Jacques J. Polak*, ed. Jacob Frenkel and Morris Goldstein. Washington: International Monetary Fund.

1992. External Implications of EMU. In *Economic Convergence and Monetary Union in Europe*, ed. R. Barrell. London: Sage Publications.

1993. Why Did Output Fall in Eastern Europe? In *The Political Economy of the Transition Process in Eastern Europe*, ed. L. Somogyi. Aldershot, UK, and Brookfield, USA: Edward Elgar.

1995. Output Decline in Eastern Europe—Summing Up the Debate. In *Output Decline in Eastern Europe: Unavoidable, External Influence, or Homemade?* ed. R. Holzman, J. Gacs, and G. Winckler. London: Kluwer Academic Publishers.

1995. Policy Reform in Latin America in the 1980s. In *Structural Adjustment: Retrospect and Prospect*, ed. D. Schydlowsky. Westport, CT: Praeger.

1997. Mexican Policy Toward Foreign Borrowing. In *Coming Together? Mexico-US Relations*, ed. B. P. Bosworth, S. M. Collins, and N. C. Lustig. Washington: Brookings Institution.

Articles

1966. Profit, Growth, and Sales Maximization. *Economica* 33, no. 129 (February): 1–16.

1976. The British Inflation: Indigenous or Imported? (with G. E. Wood). *American Economic Review* 66, no. 4 (September): 520–31.

1983. A Comparison of Macroeconomic Strategies in South America. *Development Policy Review* 1, no. 1: 22–33.

Policy Papers and Working Papers

1991. Soviet Monetary Disintegration, European Monetary Integration: Is Someone Making a Mistake? *International Economic Outlook* (December).

1991. *Britain's Role in EMU: A Positive Approach*. Open Forum Series of Pamphlets of the (British) Liberal Democrats. Dorchester: Liberal Democrat Publications.

1992. *The Eastern Transition to a Market Economy: A Global Perspective*. Centre for Economic Performance Occasional Paper 2. London: London School of Economics and Political Science.

1998. Pakistan and the World Economy. *Pakistan Development Review* 37, no. 4: 181–201.

1999. *Implications of the East Asian Crisis for Debt Management*. CSGR Hot Topics: Research on Current Issues 05. Coventry: Centre for the Study of Globalisation and Regionalisation (CSGR), University of Warwick.

2002. *Is Brazil Next?* Policy Briefs in International Economics 02-7. Washington: Institute for International Economics.

2010. *Exchange Rate Policy in Brazil*. Working Paper 10-16. Washington: Peterson Institute for International Economics.

Macroeconomics

Books

1983. *The Open Economy and the World Economy: A Textbook in International Economics*. New York: Basic Books.

1988. *World Economic Problems* (coedited with Kimberly Ann Elliott). Washington: Institute for International Economics.

1991. *The World Economy: A Textbook in International Economics* (with Chris Milner; revised 1983 edition). Brighton: Harvester Wheatsheaf.

Chapters in Books

1985. The Theorists and the Real World. In *The Political Economy of International Money: In Search of a New Order*, ed. Loukas Tsoukalis. London: Sage Publications for the Royal Institute of International Affairs.

1989. The Problem of Indexation. In *Incomes Policies*, ed. V. L. Urquidi. London: Macmillan.

1995. Structural Policies in an Era of High Unemployment. In *The Future of the World Economy*, J. V. Moller, rapporteur. Washington: Aspen Institute.

Articles

1962. Patinkin on Unemployment Disequilibrium (with J. G. Cross). *Journal of Political Economy* 70, no. 1 (February): 76–81.

1967. Consumption Taxes and Compensatory Finance (with A. T. Peacock). *Economic Journal* (March): 27–45.

1967. The Price-Price Spiral. *Bulletin of Economic Research* 19, no. 1 (May): 3–14.

1970. A Simple Neo-Keynesian Growth Model. *Review of Economic Studies* 37, no. 2 (April): 57–71.

1971. The Impact of Customs Unions on Trade in Manufactures (with A. T. Bottrill). *Oxford Economic Papers* 23, no. 3 (November): 323–51.

1974. Friedman on the Theory of Economic Adjustment (with N. Rau). *Journal of Economic Studies* 1, no. 2 (December): 77–87.

1980. A Teoria da Indexação Consistente [The Theory of Consistent Indexation] (with F. L. Lopes). *Estudos Econômicos* 10, no. 3.

1994. The Analysis of Inflation Stabilization. *Journal of International and Comparative Economics* 3, no. 1: 65–72.

Political Economy and the Washington Consensus

Books

1994. *The Political Economy of Policy Reform* (editor). Washington: Institute for International Economics.

2003. *After the Washington Consensus: Restarting Growth and Reform in Latin America* (coedited with Pedro-Pablo Kuczynski). Washington: Institute for International Economics.

Chapters in Books

1990. What Washington Means by Policy Reform. In *Latin American Adjustment: How Much Has Happened?* ed. John Williamson. Washington: Institute for International Economics

1996. Lowest Common Denominator or Neoliberal Manifesto? The Polemics of the Washington Consensus. In *Challenging the Orthodoxies*, ed. R. M. Auty and J. Toye. London: Macmillan.

1997. The Washington Consensus Revisited. In *Economic and Social Development into the XXI Century*, ed. Louis Emmerij. Washington: Johns Hopkins University Press.

2008. A Short History of the Washington Consensus. In *The Washington Consensus Reconsidered: Towards a New Global Governance*, ed. Narcis Serra and Joseph E. Stiglitz. New York: Oxford University Press.

Articles

1982. On the Characterization of Good Economic Policy: Is There a Consensus? *World Development* 10, no. 9 (September): 695–700.

1993. Democracy and the "Washington Consensus." *World Development* 21, no. 8 (August): 1329–36.

2000. What Should the World Bank Think about the Washington Consensus? *World Bank Research Observer* 15, no. 2 (August): 251–64.

2004. The Strange History of the Washington Consensus. *Journal of Post Keynesian Economics* 27, no. 2 (December): 195–206.

2007. Shock Therapy and the Washington Consensus: A Comment. *Comparative Economic Studies* 49, no. 11 (March): 59–60.

2008. Letter: The Spence Commission and the Washington Consensus. *The Economists' Voice* 5, no. 4: 4.

About the Contributors

Shankar Acharya is honorary professor at the Indian Council for Research on International Economic Relations, non-executive chairman of Kotak Mahindra Bank, member of the Indian government's National Security Advisory Board, and member of the Reserve Bank's Advisory Committee on Monetary Policy. He was chief economic adviser to the Government of India (1993–2001) when many of India's major economic reforms were implemented, member of the Prime Minister's Economic Advisory Council (2001–03), and member of the Securities and Exchange Board of India. Earlier, he served in the World Bank, where he led the World Development Report team for 1979 and was research adviser to the Bank (1979–82). His published work focuses mainly on economic development, macroeconomic policy, international economics, and public finance. His five recent books are *Essays on Macroeconomic Policy and Growth in India* (2006), *Can India Grow without* Bharat? (2007), *India and Global Crisis* (2009), *India's Economy: Performance and Challenges*, edited with Rakesh Mohan (2010), and *India after the Global Crisis* (2012). He serves on the governing boards of a number of companies, national research organizations, and charitable bodies; writes regularly in the *Business Standard* newspaper; and is a consultant to international organizations. He holds a BA in politics, philosophy, and economics from Oxford University and a PhD in economics from Harvard University.

C. Fred Bergsten has been director of the Peterson Institute for International Economics since its creation in 1981. On January 1, 2013, he will step down as director and become president emeritus and senior fellow. He was assistant secretary for international affairs at the US Treasury (1977–81); assistant for international economic affairs to Henry Kissinger at the National Security Council (1969–71); and senior fellow at the Brookings Institution

(1972–76), the Carnegie Endowment for International Peace (1981), and the Council on Foreign Relations (1967–68). Bergsten is a member of the President's Advisory Committee on Trade Policy and Negotiations (ACTPN) and the Advisory Committee to the Export Import Bank and co-chairman of the Private Sector Advisory Group to the United States–India Trade Policy Forum. He chaired the "Shadow G-7" during 2000–05 and was chairman of the Eminent Persons Group of the Asia Pacific Economic Cooperation (APEC) forum (1993–95) and the Competitiveness Policy Council created by Congress (1991–95). He was the most widely quoted think tank economist in the world during 1997–2005. Bergsten ranked 37 in the top 50 "Who Really Moves the Markets?" (*Fidelity Investment's Worth*) and was named "one of the 10 people who can change your life" (*USA Today*). He is the author, coauthor, or editor of 40 books on a wide range of international economic issues, including *The Long-Term International Economic Position of the United States* (2009), *China's Rise: Challenges and Opportunities* (2008), *China: The Balance Sheet—What the World Needs to Know Now about the Emerging Superpower* (2006), *The United States and the World Economy: Foreign Economic Policy for the Next Decade* (2005), and *Dollar Adjustment: How Far? Against What?* (2004).

Stanley Fischer has been governor of the Bank of Israel since May 2005. He was reappointed for a second term in May 2010. Prior to joining the Bank, Fischer was vice chairman of Citigroup from 2002 through 2005. He was the first deputy managing director of the International Monetary Fund, from 1994 until 2001. Before joining the IMF, he was the Killian Professor and Head of the Department of Economics at MIT. He was a member of the MIT Department of Economics from 1973 to 1994, when he left to join the IMF. From 1988 to 1990 he was vice president, development economics, and chief economist at the World Bank.

Paul De Grauwe is the John Paulson Professor at the London School of Economics. He was a member of the Belgian parliament from 1991 to 2003. He was a visiting professor at various universities in Paris, Amsterdam, Berlin, Kiel, Milan, Pennsylvania, and Michigan. He is a research fellow at the Centre for European Policy Studies in Brussels and at CESifo in Munich. He obtained his PhD from the Johns Hopkins University in 1974. He is honorary doctor of the University of Sankt Gallen (Switzerland), the University of Turku (Finland), and the University of Genoa.

Stephany Griffith-Jones is the financial markets director of the Initiative for Policy Dialogue at Columbia University in New York and associate fellow at the Overseas Development Institute. She specializes in international finance and development, with emphasis on reform of the international financial system, specifically in relation to financial regulation, global governance, and international capital flows. Previously, she was professorial fellow at the Institute of Development Studies at Sussex University. She was deputy director of international finance at the Commonwealth Secretariat and worked at the United Nations Department of Economic and Social Affairs and at the United Nations Economic Commission for Latin America and the Caribbean. She started her career in 1970 at the Central Bank of Chile. She has served as senior consultant to governments in Eastern Europe and Latin America and to many international agencies, including the World Bank, the Inter-American Development Bank, the European Commission, UNICEF, UNDP, and UCTAD. She has published over 20 books and written many scholarly and journalistic articles.

C. Randall Henning, visiting fellow, has been associated with the Peterson Institute for International Economics since 1986. He is professor of international economic relations at American University's School of International Service and specializes in global economic governance, international and comparative political economy, and regional integration. His research focuses on the European debt crisis, regional cooperation in East Asia, relations between regional and multilateral financial institutions, exchange rate policy and macroeconomic policy coordination. Henning is the author or coauthor of *Fiscal Federalism: US History for Architects of Europe's Fiscal Union* (2012), *Coordinating Regional and Multilateral Financial Institutions* (2011), *Accountability and Oversight of US Exchange Rate Policy* (2008), *East Asian Financial Cooperation* (2002), *Transatlantic Perspectives on the Euro* (2000), *Global Economic Leadership and the Group of Seven* (1996), *Currencies and Politics in the United States, Germany, and Japan* (1994), among other publications, and coeditor of *Governing the World's Money* (2002). Journals in which he has published articles include *International Organization, Review of International Political Economy, Journal of Common Market Studies,* and *The World Economy.* He has testified to several congressional committees and served as the European Community Studies Association Distinguished Scholar.

Dagmar Hertova is an economist at the Development Policy and Analysis Division of the Department of Economic and Social Affairs at the United Nations in New York. Her research is focused on poverty reduction, the Millennium Development Goals (MDG), and trade. She coauthored the 2009–2012 editions of the MDG Gap Task Force Report. She was an economic researcher at the Regional Bureau for Latin America and the Caribbean at the UNDP. She has participated in several development projects and coauthored several papers on topics related to trade integration, middle classes, regional financial institutions, and GDP-linked bonds. Hertova obtained her master's degree in economics from the London School of Economics and holds a BA in economics and contemporary European studies from the University of Sussex.

Olivier Jeanne has been senior fellow at the Peterson Institute for International Economics since 2008. He is a professor of economics at the Johns Hopkins University and has taught at the University of California Berkeley (1997) and Princeton University (2005–06). He is a research affiliate at the National Bureau of Economic Research (NBER), Cambridge, MA, and a research fellow at the

Center for Economic Policy Research, London. From 1998 to 2008 he held various positions in the Research Department of the International Monetary Fund. Jeanne is coauthor of *Who Needs to Open the Capital Account?* (2012). He has published articles in the *American Economic Review, Journal of Political Economy, Review of Economic Studies, Journal of International Economics,* and *International Finance.* He has served on the editorial boards of several journals, including the *Journal of International Economics* and *International Journal of Central Banking.*

Yuemei Ji is a researcher at LICOS, University of Leuven. She is also a visiting fellow at the Center for European Policy Studies, Brussels. She studied economics at Fudan University, Shanghai, and obtained her PhD in economics from University of Leuven in 2011.

Marcus Miller is professor of economics at Warwick University. He was educated at Oxford (PPE) and then at Yale University (PhD) with James Tobin and Don Hester as thesis supervisors, where he was in the same class as Peterson Institute Senior Fellows William R. Cline and Edwin M. Truman. Miller taught at the London School of Economics and Manchester University before moving to Warwick, where he essentially replaced John Williamson. Numerous visits to the Peterson Institute, Federal Reserve Board, International Monetary Fund, and World Bank facilitated extended collaboration with John on exchange rates. Miller publishes regularly in economic journals and has coedited several books, such as *Exchange Rate Targets and Currency Bands* with Paul Krugman. He has worked at the Bank of England, advised the Treasury Committee of the House of Commons, and served as joint director of the International Macroeconomics Programme at the Centre for Economic Policy Research, London. His current research interests include the mischievous behavior of banks in Britain and debt problems in Europe.

José Antonio Ocampo is professor, director of the Economic and Political Development Concentration in the School of International and Public Affairs, fellow of the Committee on Global Thought, and copresident of the Initiative for Policy Dialogue at Columbia University. He has occupied numerous positions at the United Nations and his native Colombia, including UN under-secretary-general for economic and social affairs, executive secretary of the UN Economic Commission for Latin America and the Caribbean (ECLAC), and minister of finance of Colombia. He has received numerous academic distinctions, including the 2008 Leontief Prize for Advancing the Frontiers of Economic Thought and the 1988 Alejandro Angel Escobar National Science Award of Colombia. He has published extensively on macroeconomic theory and policy, international financial issues, economic and social development, international trade, and Colombian and Latin American economic history. His most recent books include *The Economic Development of Latin America since Independence,* with Luis Bértola (forthcoming 2012), the *Oxford Handbook of Latin American Economics,* edited with Jaime Ros (2011), *Time for a Visible Hand: Lessons from the 2008 World Financial Crisis,* edited with Stephany Griffith-Jones and Joseph E. Stiglitz (2010), and *Growth and Policy in Developing Countries: A Structuralist Approach*, with Lance Taylor and Codrina Rada (2009). He holds a BA in economics and sociology from the University of Notre Dame and a PhD in economics from Yale University.

Avinash D. Persaud is chairman of Elara Capital Plc, chairman of PBL, chairman of Intelligence Capital Limited, and board director of Beacon Insurance and RBC Latin America & the Caribbean. He is emeritus professor, Gresham College; fellow, London Business School; and visiting fellow, CFAP, Judge Institute, Cambridge University. He was a senior executive at JP Morgan, UBS, State Street Bank & Trust, and GAM London Limited. He was a governor and member of the Council of the London School of Economics and Political Science and was the 2010 president of the British Association for the Advancement of Science (Section F). He won the Jacques de Larosière Award in Global Finance from the Institute of International Finance in 2000. Persaud was chairman of the Warwick Commission on International Financial Reform; chairman of the regulatory subcommittee of the UN High Level Task Force on Financial Reform; co-chair of OECD Emerging Market Network; member of the UK Treasury's Audit and Risk Committee; and member of the Intergovernmental Task Force on Financial Taxes.

Edwin M. Truman, senior fellow at the Peterson Institute for International Economics since 2001, served as assistant secretary of the US Treasury for International Affairs from December 1998 to January 2001 and returned as counselor to the secretary in March–May 2009. He directed the Division of International Finance of the Board of Governors of the Federal Reserve System from 1977 to 1998. From 1983 to 1998, he was one of three economists on the staff of the Federal Open Market Committee. Truman has also been a visiting economics lecturer at Amherst College and a visiting economics professor at Williams College. He has published on international monetary economics, international debt problems, economic development, and European economic integration. He is the author, coauthor, or editor of *Economic Policy Coordination Reconsidered* (forthcoming), *Sovereign Wealth Funds: Threat or Salvation?* (2010), *Reforming the IMF for the 21st Century* (2006), *A Strategy for IMF Reform* (2006), *Chasing Dirty Money: The Fight Against Money Laundering* (2004), and *Inflation Targeting in the World Economy* (2003).

Index

boom-bust cycle, 8, 111–14, 118, 124–25
  curbing (*See* capital controls)
Borensztein-Mauro securities, 128–29, 131,
    132
Brazil
  capital controls, 148, 151
  exchange rate system, 188
  production development policy, 194
  Williamson in, 3
Bretton Woods system
  collapse of, 27, 31, 34, 39, 83
    developments since, 84, 85f
  elements of, 28–31, 50
  success of, 109
BRICS, 20n
built-in stabilizers, 9, 202–203
"bull" traders, 94, 95f
Bush, George W., 110
business cycles, Latin America, 186
business-friendly environment, Washington
    Consensus agenda, 17–18

Canada, Parliamentary Budget Office, 209
capital account
  India, 163, 166
  Latin America, 178–81, 183–88
  management of (*See* capital controls)
  Williamson's work on, 2–3, 34–35, 36f–37f,
    146, 183
capital adequacy requirements, 8, 114–16,
    119–20, 166–67
capital controls
  international coordination of, 151–52
  Latin America, 183–88
  research questions, 149–52
  types of, 148–49
  Williamson's work on, 1–3, 5, 7–8, 54–55,
    108, 125, 144–46, 149, 183–86
capital flows, 143–54
  boom-bust cycle, 8, 111–14, 118, 124–25
    curbing (*See* capital controls)
  composition of, 145
  exchange rate crises and, 86
  GDP-linked securities (*See* growth-linked
    securities)
  in 1990s, 143–47, 144f
  in 2000s, 147–49
  sudden stops, 54, 78, 86, 108, 112
carry trade, 64–65
Center for Budget Priorities and Policies, 209
Central American Common Market, 182
central banks
  autonomy of, 18n
  development policy, 21

equity issues, 75
inflation target approach, 203
"light touch" regulation, 86n, 97n, 166
"chartist" forecasting rules, 92
Chile
  capital controls, 145, 147, 147n, 186
  economic reforms, 15, 21, 205
  fiscal policy, 180
  price stability, 202
  productivity growth, 191
  regional integration, 182
China
  Beijing Consensus, 22
  development policy, 21
  economic reforms in
  exchange rate flexibility, 7
  international monetary system and,
    99–101, 100t
  Latin American trade with, 191
  response to global financial crisis, 165,
    167–68
Chow test, 65–66, 69n
collective cognition, 87
Colombia
  capital controls, 186
  economic reforms in, 205
  fiscal policy, 180, 187–88
  growth-linked securities, 132
  price stability, 202
Committee for a Responsible Federal Budget,
    209
Committee of Twenty (IMF), 3, 4, 27–29
commodity prices, 167–68
corner solutions, 4
Costa Rica, 182
countercyclical charges, 114–16, 118, 120
crawling pegs, 4, 27, 83, 108, 181, 185
credit policies, in Latin America, 187
credit risk, 117–18
*Curbing the Boom-Bust Cycle: Stabilizing Capital
    Flows to Emerging Markets* (Williamson),
    147–48
currency appreciation
  capital flows and, 145–46, 150
  Indian rupee, 170
currency band, exchange rate in, 88, 88f
Currency Composition of Official Foreign
    Exchange Reserves (COFER) database,
    42, 45, 46
Currency Convertibility in Eastern Europe
    (Williamson), 2
currency markets. *See also* exchange rate
  behavioral theory of, 90–94, 101
currency risk premium, 96–97

microprudential regulation, 113–14, 121
MIST countries, 21n
model pluralism, 5
monetarism, 201
monetary policy
  inflation targets, 201–203
  monitoring rules and, 94, 95f
  Williamson's work on, 9
monetary union
  embedded in fiscal union, 79–80
  in Europe (*See* euro area)
  fragility of, 53–55
  multiple equilibria theory, 54–59
    policy implications, 69–80
    testing, 59–69
  Williamson's work on, 2, 7
money supply
  inflation target approach, 203
  target zones and, 87–88
moral hazard, 75, 79, 130
multicurrency system, stability of, 46–48
multiple equilibria theory, 54–59
  policy implications, 69–80
  testing, 59–69
multiple key currency proposal, 27
Muslim investors, 129–30

Nash equilibrium, 100, 151
natural resources, India, 174
neoclassical synthesis, 201, 201n
neoliberalism, 14, 19, 178
neostructuralist approach, 9, 184, 192
Netherlands
  Central Planning Bureau (CPB), 209–11
  fiscal councils, 9
  solvency shock, 58
neutral fiscal benchmark, 9
New Zealand, 205
Nixon, Richard, 201
noise traders, 90–92
nongovernmental organizations (NGOs), 209
nonlinear equations, government debt, 62–66
normal policies, 9, 200, 201–204
North American Free Trade Agreement, 182
Northern Rock Bank, 164

"On Liberalizing the Capital Account"
    (Williamson), 144–45
Overseas Development Council, 13

Padoa-Schioppa group, 80
Pareto inefficient "capital war," 151
Peru, 188

Peterson Institute for International
    Economics, Williamson's work for, 2n,
    3, 7, 16, 84, 146, 178, 200
Pilot External Sector Report (IMF), 5, 48
Plaza Accord, 4, 84, 110, 110n
Poland, 205
policy design
  Williamson's approach to, 9, 108, 199–213
    during crisis, 204–208
    crisis prevention, 208–13
    normality, 9, 200, 201–204
  Williamson's influence on, 3, 6
policy implications
  exchange rate system, 84
  international finance, 109–11
  monetary union fragility, 69–80
political economy
  boom-bust cycle, 114
  during crisis, 206
  fiscal councils, 209–11
  Greece, 206
  India, 159–63, 170
  international policy coordination, 109
  target zones, 99
  United States, 208, 208n
  Washington Consensus and, 21
  Williamson's work on, 6
Political Economy of Policy Reform (Williamson),
    3
Politifact.com, 208
Pontifícia Universidade Católica do Rio de
    Janeiro, 3
portfolio reallocations, 47, 48
Portugal
  bond spreads, 69
  economic reforms, 205
  solvency shock, 58
  unit labor cost, 77
positive externalities, growth-linked securities,
    140
Princeton University, 3
private sector portfolio reallocations, 47, 48
privatization, in Latin America, 182
productivity growth, 191–94
public information, 208–13
  election watchdogs, 9, 209–13

random walk perspective, 83–84, 88
rating agencies, 62
Reagan, Ronald, 15, 110
real effective exchange rate
  government debt and, 61–69, 63t–68t
  Indian rupee, 170
  Latin America, 184–85, 187–88, 188f

Milton Keynes UK
Ingram Content Group UK Ltd.
UKHW050843080124
435586UK00010BA/489

9 780881 326628